D0205825

The African Liberation Reader

Edited by Aquino de Bragança
and Immanuel Wallerstein

The Guerillas

For the Fighting Men in Southern Africa

1

. . . and I lie with my body curved to the light clay
and it lies along the length of my hip and thigh
like the yielding firmness of your warm flesh
and my body melts with a tenderness along my frame
while brittle thorn-twigs pierce the clear sky
while far-off sounds — harsh birds — blunderings —
    crackle like snapped twigs . . .
and ants scurry on the smooth curve of the clay.

2

. . . the birds wheel in their great circles in the mind
heat beats at the eyes through a curtain of sweat
the salt-tasting mouth is papered by thirst
    and other things
In time, heat and fatigue
will beat the stiff, anxious, aching neck down.

3

. . . a sense of lost opportunity like a squall of rain
marching away leaving an aching hollowness
while the big ants crawl over the torn flesh and the
black streaks of crusted blood.
Who will break through the barriers of indifferent
bone and stubborn flesh and the grey waves of
newsprint gruel?
O my friends where are the voices to plead your cause
to roar your challenge to trumpet your heroism?
to speak the words of brave resolve that you live
and die?

4

There is such a pleasure at last in handling a cool
efficient weapon most modern, highly automatic and
moving off at the ready —
wishing they could see at home — the friends, and
especially the children, and imaging the deeds of
flame and terror — terror from this weapon, terrible
and cold.

5

Chiefly, it is a job to be done, with drills to be followed
and observed, the enemy an analysable factor
or a brute so deadly that he must die first: but sometimes there comes the thought of home the angry
longing of the exile and a fierce will to smash an
evil cruel thing.

Dennis Brutus

The African Liberation Reader

Volume 2

The National Liberation Movements

Edited by Aquino de Bragança and Immanuel Wallerstein

Zed Press, 57 Caledonian Road, London N1 9DN

The African Liberation Reader was originally
published in Portuguese; first published in
English by Zed Press Ltd., 57 Caledonian
Road, London N1 9DN in 1982.

Copyright © Aquino de Braganca and
Immanuel Wallerstein

Copyedited by Beverley Brown
Proofread by Stephen Gourlay, Rosamund
    Howe , Liz Hasthorpe and Anne Gourlay
Typeset by Lyn Caldwell
Cover design Jacque Solomons
Cover photo courtesy of MAGIC
Printed by Krips Repro, Meppel, Holland

U.S. Distributor
Lawrence Hill and Co., 520 Riverside
Avenue, Westport, Conn. 06880, USA

British Library Cataloguing in Publication Data

The African liberation reader.
    Vol.2: The national liberation movements
    1. Africa, Sub-Saharan — Politics and
    government — Addresses, essays, lectures
    I. Braganca, Aquino de II.Wallerstein,
    Immanuel
    320.9'67   JQ1872
    ISBN 0-86232-068-2

The African Liberation Reader

Publisher's Note

Zed Press gratefully acknowledge a grant from the WCC Programme to Combat Racism towards the cost of typesetting this project. Zed Press also wishes to thank the Swedish International Development Authority for making possible the gift of copies of each of these 3 volumes to the liberation movements of Southern Africa.

Contents

Preface

This collection of documents was originally assembled by the editors in 1973-74 and completed just as the revolution in Portugal broke out in April 1974. This event, completed in 1975 by the independence of all the former Portuguese colonies in Africa, transformed the political situation in Southern Africa. We decided to proceed with the publication of this book in its Portuguese version, since independence in the former Portuguese colonies constituted a clear turning-point in the historical development of their national liberation movements.

We hesitated however about an English-language version. The struggle was continuing in Zimbabwe, Namibia, and South Africa. Should the story stop in 1974? If today we have decided to publish this collection as it was constructed in 1974, it is because we believe that the Portuguese Revolution and the Independence, particularly of Angola and Mozambique, constituted an historical turning-point for the national liberation movements of Zimbabwe, Namibia, and South Africa as well.

Indeed so much has happened in those three countries since 1974 that all of us are tempted to forget the historical evolution of the movements in these countries as well as the importance of the early intellectual debates within the movements and their continuing relevance today. We wish to reinvigorate this historical memory which hopefully may serve as a tool of the ongoing struggle itself. It is in this spirit that we have decided to publish today the English-language version of this collection.

Introduction

National liberation movements do not emerge one fine day out of the mind of some superman or at the instigation of some foreign power. They are born out of popular discontent. They emerge over long periods to combat oppressive conditions and express aspirations for a different kind of society. They are, in short, the agents of class and national struggle.

Neither the classes nor the nations, however, have been there forever. They, too, are creations of the modern world and, in the case of Southern Africa, they were born in the crucible of the colonial experience. To understand the national liberation movements, we must first understand the social forces they represent and the ways in which these social forces were shaped by their historical circumstances.

The capitalist world economy came into existence in Europe in the 16th Century. Its internal functioning — the endless drive for capital accumulation, the transfer of surplus from proletarian to bourgeois and from periphery to core, the cyclical pattern of alternating phases of economic expansion and stagnation — combined to make necessary the regular, albeit discontinuous, expansion of the outer boundaries of the world economy. Slowly, over several centuries, other historical systems were destroyed and incorporated into this ever-growing octopus.

The forms of incorporation into the world economy have varied both according to the strength of the political systems in place in the zones undergoing incorporation and according to the internal configuration of forces among core states within the world economy during the period of incorporation. Sometimes incorporation involved direct colonial overrule, sometimes 'informal imperialism', and sometimes first this indirect mode of conquest followed by a later phase of direct colonialism.

Incorporation has everywhere involved two major changes for the zone being incorporated. First, the production structures were reorganized so that they contributed to the overall division of labour in the world economy. Secondly, the political structures were reorganized so that they facilitated the flow of factors of production in the world economy. In the case of Southern Africa, the reorganization of production structures involved the development both of cash crops and of mining operations for export on the world market. The reorganization of political structures meant the creation of colonial states in the region, the eventual boundaries of which were a function primarily of the struggles among the various European imperial and settler forces.

It is this reorganization of production structures which created the new classes and this reorganization of political structures which created the new nations. These classes and nations are institutional consequences of the development of the capitalist world economy. They are, in fact, the principal structural outcome of its hierarchical relations. They are at one and the same time the mode of social imposition of these hierarchies and the mode of social resistance to the inequalities bred by the system.

The object of imperialist expansion is to utilize the labour-power of the peoples of the newly incorporated peripheries at rates of real remuneration as low as possible. Securing such a labour force requires the establishment of a three-part geographical division of peripheral areas: a first zone to produce the export products, within which there is initially often forced labour, later low-paid wage labour; a second zone to produce surplus food to feed the labour force of the first zone, within which there tends to be household production; a third zone to serve as a manpower reserve to produce the labour force for the first zone (and even occasionally for the second), within which there tends to be so-called subsistence production. (The three zones do not necessarily have to fall within a single colonial state.)

It is this three-zone system, with its large component of migrant labour (persons, largely men, leaving the third zone for limited periods, sometimes only once in a lifetime, and returning afterwards to that zone), which permits the super-exploitation of labour in the first (or wage labour) zone. The 'migrant' workers located in such a zone participate in extended households, and over their lifetime the costs of reproduction are disproportionately borne by the work done in non-wage sectors. Thus the employer of wage labour can in effect pay *less than* the minimum necessary wage (that is, the wage assuring the reproduction of the labour force).

It is clear, then, why the conceptual categories which evolved in the context of the core zones of the capitalist world economy — concepts such as proletarian (meaning by that a life-long industrial wage labourer living in an urban area with his whole household) and peasant (meaning a life-long agricultural worker with some kind of hereditary rights to land utilization) — do not seem to fit exactly when we look closely at the peripheral zones of the world economy. The work-force there is not divided into 'traditional' peasants owning the means of production and 'modern' proletarians who have been expropriated from the means of production. Most (or at least many) workers' households are in fact composed of *both* 'proletarians' and 'peasants', the same individuals often being both for part of their lives. It is this combination of roles which defines the relationship of these workers to the world economy and permits the particular extreme form of exploitation they encountered in the colonial era.

The pattern of the creation of the work-force, with its institutionalized interaction between rural 'home' areas and the urban (or mining or cash-crop) areas, favoured the continued recruitment to wage employment through 'family' or 'ethnic' channels, and hence the emergence in the urban and commercialized zones of an 'ethnic' consciousness (called by the colonial overlords 'tribalism'), an ethnic consciousness which was in fact very much the expression of the emerging class position of the various groups integrated into the wage work-force.

The ambiguous relationship of class and ethnic 'membership' is hence a structural reality, indeed a structural creation, of the colonial situation, of colonies located within the capitalist world economy. The initial subjective confusions of large segments of the new work-forces were reinforced deliberately by the colonial authorities with their classic divide-and-rule tactics. It is within this framework and against this definition of the situation that the movements of resistance are born. While awareness of the real inequalities of the colonial situation was central to the demands of these movements from the very beginning, the complexities of the class-ethnic structures were a hindrance to their development. These movements evolved amidst contradictory consciousnesses of class and ethnicity and incorporated these contradictions into their very structures — sometimes in the form of competing movements, more often within a single national liberation movement, and frequently in both ways (as this whole collection of documents illustrates).

The history of each individual political unit (colony) is complex and these histories vary from colony to colony. Generally speaking, however, the story of anti-colonial resistance is the story of the construction of a national liberation movement, more or less unified, more or less representative, which seeks to incarnate the class and national struggles of the majority of the work-force. These histories cannot be appreciated or analysed in isolation. The emergence of such a movement in a particular country is itself the function in part of the political evolution of the world system as a whole.

Beginning in a modest way in the 19th Century, and achieving great force in the 20th, the contradictions of the capitalist world economy have led to the rise of a network of anti-systemic movements. These movements have taken different forms, sometimes emphasizing their class character, sometimes emphasizing their national character, usually doing a bit of both. They have sought to counter the oppressions of the world system and, in their more radical versions, to destroy it.

To build an anti-systemic movement, it is necessary to mobilize popular force, and usually it is politically necessary to mobilize this force initially within the confines of particular states. This narrow geographical definition of anti-systemic movements has been at once their strength and their weakness. It has been their strength because it has forced them to remain close to the concrete grievances of the working classes — urban and rural — they have been mobilizing. It has made it possible for them to achieve political power in some preliminary way — in the case of colonies, to obtain independence. But this narrow geographical focus has also been their weakness. Their enemy, the world bourgeoisie, has seldom hesitated to combine *its* strength on an inter-state level. In the case, for example, of the former Portuguese colonies in Africa, the movements in the separate colonies faced a single colonial power, and one that was in turn widely supported by other imperial powers. Furthermore, when such anti-colonial movements have come to power, they have found that juridical state sovereignty is in part a fiction since they were still bound by the constraints of the inter-state system, the political superstructure of the capitalist world economy.

The movements have not been unaware of these contradictions which have posed dilemmas, both strategic and tactical, for their operations. This book seeks to organize in a coherent manner their reflections on the dilemmas and their perspective on the solutions they might find. These solutions are not facile ones, and it is in the quality of these reflections and the action consequent upon them that we can distinguish those movements which have been truly anti-systemic in their impact and those which have fallen by the wayside, to become open or hidden agents for the maintenance and further development of the capitalist world economy.

The hard thinking of the movements in Southern Africa has been of great consequence for the struggle in that part of the world. But it is of great consequence for movements elsewhere as well. The reinforcement of the world-wide network of movements is in fact the great task of our times, a task in process but far from completed.

1. Historic Roots

Editors' Introduction

In a text included previously, Amilcar Cabral said: 'We situate our cause in history.' This has perforce been the strategy and the thesis of all the major national liberation movements.

There were really two points the movement sought to make, individually and collectively. The first was that resistance to colonial rule has been continuous, if outwardly intermittent, from the very beginning of contact with the conquering power and throughout the period of colonial rule. Colonial rule has never been legitimate or legitimated by its victims, even if some cadres were forced or bribed into complaisance. This was fundamental to the debate about violence, which is our next theme. For if colonialism is and has been by its very nature illegitimate, then the original and ceaseless violence has been the violence of conquest and overrule.

But there was a second reason for concern with the historic roots. Though resistance had been continuous, it had nevertheless taken a new form in recent years in Portuguese and Southern Africa. For it moved from being the dispersed revolts of separate and separated groups of peasants (as well as, of course, of urban dwellers) to becoming a *national* resistance, the work of a *national* liberation movement.

For South Africa, Namibia, and Zimbabwe, we present texts of the ANC, SWAPO, and ZAPU respectively. For Angola, we present first a declaration of an early grouping of movements from the Portuguese colonies, the FRAIN, followed by two texts of the MPLA, one on the sixteenth century and one on the twentieth. We present also a text of the FNLA and of UNITA on the latter period. How each presented recent history explains much of the different perspectives of these movements. For Mozambique, we have an essay by Mondlane. We also include an appreciation by the ANC of Eduardo Mondlane after his assassination, which enlightens us about the biographical links that movements sometimes establish across territories. We give two texts of the PAIGC, one for Guinea Bissau and one for the Cape Verde Islands. A careful reading of these texts will enable the reader to understand how the PAIGC perceived the problem of creating a single modern nation out of two geographically separate areas. Finally, we present a text of the CONCP on Sao Tome e Principe, which helps us to comprehend the difficulties which the Comite de Libertacao de Sao Tome e Principe, the CLSTP, member of the CONCP, had in launching the armed struggle there.

Our Anti-Imperialist Commitment
Alfred Nzo

Excerpt from an article by Alfred Nzo, Secretary-General of the ANC (South Africa) that appeared in Sechaba *(ANC), IV, 2, February 1970.*

The foundation of the character and role of the White racist regime in South Africa in world imperialism was established the very moment that the Whites landed, settled and invaded South Africa.

From that moment to date South Africa became a vital and strategic area for European colonial powers in their hideous plots to conquer and subjugate, pillage and plunder, oppress and exploit the peoples of Africa and Asia. The involvement of South Africa in colonialism in its pre-imperialist stage is inter-linked with its present role in world imperialism and in turn the irredeemable commitment of the European imperialist powers to the White racist and fascist South African regime.

At first, the interest of the colonial powers like Portugal, Spain and Holland in the Cape was to find a sea route to the East with the aim of finding an easy and convenient way of plundering raw materials, like spices, cotton, sugar and tobacco and also to find a market for European industrial goods.

The voyages of Vasco da Gama and other navigators who found the sea route round the Cape made a dramatic change in the enrichment of the trade and industry in Europe. The trade route via the Cape ensured a continuously expanding market for European industrial goods and rapid increase of raw materials.

But even when Vasco da Gama first landed at Mossel Bay, in November/December, 1497 and was received with hospitality and kindness by our people who were herdsmen and shepherds, he looked with greedy eyes at the cattle of our people and their grazing land. He thanked their generosity by naming the area the Bay of Cows and erected a landmark which still exists, claiming that the land belonged to the King of Portugal. This was the first act of shameless robbery in South Africa. Britain, France and Holland and other powers later joined in the struggle for the supremacy of the seas and the seizure of colonies in Africa and Asia. This struggle involved primarily the dominance and control of the Cape which was the most strategic gateway to the East.

The Dutch in 1652 colonized and occupied part of South Africa known as the Cape of Good Hope; their initial purpose was to establish a half-way refreshment station for the ships of the Dutch East India Company and others which were plying their booty of plunder from the East and industrial goods from Europe. This was the beginning of the most ruthless plunder of the land, and cattle of our people the Khoisan and Khoikhoi. The Khoisan were the victims of the most barbaric genocide and were virtually exterminated. The Khoikhoi were robbed of their cattle and forced to work as slaves. This period began the robbery and enslavement of our people in the interests of European colonial commerce and colonialism. It also marked the beginning of colonial expansion of the European colonialists into the interior of South Africa.

European colonial powers did not confine themselves to the plunder of the raw materials but also began a brutal and inhuman traffic of slaves from Africa and Asia, to west European countries and other colonies. The Cape became deeply involved in this sordid international slave trade and slaves were imported and exported. The Cape became one of the important international slave markets. This accounts for its mixed population today, Malays from Batavia, Africans from Mozambique and as far as West Africa.

The slave trade crippled the social, political and economic development of Africa. It greatly impoverished the continent but accelerated the development of European capitalism. It was an important factor in the partition of Africa amongst a few European countries. South Africa, undeveloped as she was then, played an important part in this tragic, callous and criminal accumulation of wealth and capital together with European colonialists. Through slavery South African White economy also developed. Comfort, luxury and wealth were the prerogatives of the Whites; poverty, misery and suffering were the plight of the slaves. Thus was laid the foundations of a society in South Africa which closely resembled the wealthy economic advancement of the European colonialists and the appalling poverty of the colonial countries.

Very early in this history the White settlers had developed a community of interests with the European colonial powers; politically and ideologically, they were the agents of European colonial interests and shared in the piratical booty. The European powers justified their inhuman acts in Africa by claiming that the Africans were savages who had to be civilized – racialism, that abominable doctrine was also adopted by the Whites in South Africa. It has remained to this day, in its most virulent form, apartheid, as the ideology of oppression and exploitation of the non-White people. It is defended and protected overtly and covertly by South African imperialist allies.

The Dutch invaders were later followed by the British, and our country and people became the arena of conflicting interests of European colonial interests and the interests of a group of White settlers who had colonial interests in South Africa.

The Dutch settlers had adopted expansionist predatory and aggressive policies towards our people, in order to capture their land, cattle and labour. Their aggression met with fierce resistance from our people. Wars were waged for over 200 years. Wherever the Dutch or Boers went they were defeated. Had it not been for the arrival of the British the course of South African history might well have been different.

The arrival of the British forces at the beginning of the 19th century brought about radical changes in the resistance struggle of our people. The forces of colonialism and national oppression were greatly increased.

After a protracted struggle of more than 250 years our people were overwhelmed and subdued at the close of the 19th Century.

There were many reasons for this calamitous defeat, and many lessons for future leaders to learn from the grave mistakes and weaknesses which resulted from our defeat. Our people fought an enemy with superior modern weapons like guns, while our people were virtually unarmed, except for spears. In addition our people were not nationally united in the country. The colonizers fought tribes separately and at different times.

But even more fundamental was the fact that towards the middle of the 19th Century colonialism had assumed its new phase of international monopoly finance capitalism, known as imperialism. Our people fought their battles in isolation from other oppressed and exploited peoples of the continent and the world, whereas despite their conflicts and contradictions the imperialist powers were already developing as a combined international military, economic and political force, in the world.

In the 19th Century, Britain which was then a leading imperialist state stepped up her colonial expansion of Africa. With the opening of the Suez Canal, the shortest route to the East, Egypt became of great importance.

But South Africa with its strategic geographical position and favourable climate became the target of European colonialism and in particular British imperialism.

The discovery of large gold and diamond deposits towards the end of the 19th Century in South Africa was a significant land-mark in the economic and political history of the country. It ushered in the rapid development of capitalism in a country which was previously basically agricultural and pastoral.

Mining, which was basically controlled by Cecil Rhodes' De Deers Mining Company developed into a world monopoly, linked South African economy more closely with international capital and imperialism. Cecil Rhodes, the most rabid and outspoken British imperialist dreamt of the most heartless and ruthless exploitation of the land, labour power and resources of Africa. For this criminal plan, South Africa was the base and starting point, and springboard. British capital ruthlessly seized extensive territories in Africa under Cecil Rhodes' evil imperialist projects. These included what were called Northern Rhodesia and Southern Rhodesia, which are now Zambia and Zimbabwe. British monopolist capitalists captured large resources of diamond and gold fields and fertile land.

These predatory schemes resulted in one of the first imperialist wars in South Africa — the Anglo-Boer war. The British were intent on dislodging the Boers from the gold and mining areas which the Boers had through fraud and subterfuge occupied in the Cape and Transvaal. The Anglo-Boer war of 1899-1902 ended with the military defeat of the Boers. The African people were vitally interested in the war because by typical British duplicity the

British pretended that the war was not an imperialist war for British mono-poly finance interests, but one to assist the Africans to free themselves from Boer domination.

The Africans made outstanding sacrifices and rendered invaluable service to the British. They made a direct contribution to British victory in the hope that this would result in radical social, economic and political changes. They repeated these sacrifices again in the First and Second World Wars.

The reward of the Africans was the shameless and bitter betrayal of their political interests in the Vereeniging Peace Conference. Their position was worse than before the Anglo-Boer war. The British imperialists had achieved their own economic purpose and left all political power in the hands of the Boers and other Europeans to carry out as their agents the most ruthless deprivation of the land of our people, their enslavement in the growing mining industrial and agricultural complex, which has now made South Africa what it is, the most highly developed country in Africa.

The De Beers Company and about seven of the largest gold mine com-panies composed of White local bourgeoisie and the capitalists established control over mining and nearly the entire manufacturing industry in South Africa. These are the foundations which started South Africa on its capitalist and imperialist path. The rapid development of capitalism was fundamentally due to the most brutal exploitation of African cheap labour. The betrayal by the British is now being repeated in Zimbabwe for similar reasons.

Day of Commemoration
SWAPO

> *From an Editorial in* Namibia News *(SWAPO), I, 4 & 5,*
> *June-July 1968.*

26 August is a day of commemoration for our people. One of our early uprisings against the Germans took place on this date and ever since the date has been remembered. On 26 August this year it is two years since we, the people of Namibia, entered a new phase in our fight against the racist white minority by launching our armed struggle. Until then we fought by non-violent means, but this brought us nothing but increased violence and brutality from our enemy. When we saw there was no way out — the last straw was the let-down by the world community in The Hague — we took up arms.

Namibia's history contains many accounts of armed uprising against foreign invaders. For instance, from 1904 to 1907 the Germans faced contin-uous revolts which were led by the dynamic chiefs, Maherero and Witbooi. The Germans met the resistance with what they called 'a war of extermin-ation', during which they ruthlessly killed any Namibian they could find, whether soldier or civilian. When the war ended, the population in parts of our country was reduced by two-thirds. In 1917 another uprising took place, this time under the leadership of King Mandume. Mandume's men fought the Boers in the South and the Portuguese in the North. Although this revolt was crushed, we did not lose our determination to free our country from white overlordship. Today we are again engaged in an armed battle against our enemy, but this time we cannot be stopped until we have liberated Namibia from the white-settler regime.

From Fraudulent Concession to Federation

Joshua Nkomo

> *Excerpt from a statement made by Joshua Nkomo, President of ZAPU, to the UN Special Committee on Decolonization on March 19, 1962 (that is, before the Unilateral Declaration of Independence by the white settlers).*

Many representatives here have recalled the history of the colonization of Southern Rhodesia. I should like briefly to follow up some important points since 1888 because, as I have said, the whole process of oppression started when Rhodes through Rand squeezed out a fraudulent concession known as the Rand concession from King Lobengula. Three years after they had been given this document by Lobengula, the British settlers came back in 1890, in an aggressive manner, with settlers and soldiers collected from South Africa. When in 1888 the British came and said they wanted to protect our people from Portuguese colonialism, of course they had an aim; one year later, they squeezed out this concession. That was in 1889. In 1890 they came with soldiers and subdued the people who had accepted them with goodwill. What they received from them was force.

Rand had, without the knowledge of the King, gone to England, got out of the Queen a charter authorizing Rhodes not only to exploit the minerals of our country, but also to rule our country without the consent of the people. This is the treachery that was shown right from the beginning when our country was colonized and the world might as well know the way it all began.

In 1914 there was a war. Two things happened. We were told that the world was faced by a threat from maniacs in Germany who threatened the world with oppression. We came by the thousands and we fought in that war. While we were fighting in 1914, the remaining settlers changed the law and gave majority seats in the Legislative Council in our country to elected members. Elected by whom? By the settlers and no reference was made to the African people. Here we are dealing with a question of consent. We are dealing with a question of who is the person in Southern Rhodesia. If you talk of the peoples of Southern Rhodesia, about whom are you talking, Britain? That is our question to the British. They tell the world and they tell you that the people decided.

We come to 1922. Again the people decided. Twelve thousand white settlers decided the fate of over 2 million people without the courtesy of informing them that 'we, the super-persons, the super-humans, are about to change the status of your country'. One would have expected them to do that at least. They did not. The United Kingdom wanted, for its treasury, either to annex Southern Rhodesia to the Union of South Africa or annex Southern Rhodesia to the United Kingdom by giving the settlers some form of self-government.

The settlers, as you have been told, voted for self-government. It must be emphasized here that it was the settlers, 12,000 of them, who voted. The Chiefs, the people, the indigenous people, were not told. Immediately after that, in 1925, a Commission was set up by an over-anxious settler community anxious that they take everything for themselves. They set up a Commission to investigate the position of land. The recommendations of that Commission were important.

By the Land Apportionment Act, the vicious law in our country which became the basis of exploitation and degradation of our people, our land was divided into two categories, European and African. Southern Rhodesia then had not moved to Europe, it was still in Africa, but we had and we still have European areas in Southern Rhodesia today. Of course, the land that was declared European was that fertile land which the peoples of Southern Rhodesia had – that is, the peoples of the Zimbabwe, that is Southern Rhodesia now; our country is named after Rhodes, but the real name of the country is Zimbabwe, the Kingdom of Monomotapa. Now, those areas which people had inhabited for years were declared European and some remote areas never before inhabited by people were declared African.

Then the depression came between 1933 and the Second World War. This law was not applied. In 1939 we were told again that Hitler was threatening the world I must say here that I am not against Italians or Germans, as people. However, their presence is a fact of real significance in my country. Immediately after the war, our people were moved off their ancestral land and the settler government embarked on an immigration scheme of bringing settlers from Britain, from Germany, from Italy and from a number of European countries. Some of the prisoners of war, most of them Italians, did not go back to Italy. They took all of the lands from which the African people were removed. That is why we are fighting, because we were removed and immediately after the war Germans and Italians took our places.

It was clear that the policies followed by the settlers were racist. I have said, and I must emphasize, that we of the Zimbabwe African Peoples' Union and, indeed, the whole of the African population is not racist; we are not against any person. We are against the oppression of men by men. We never can and never shall tolerate such a policy.

The Germans and Italians are welcome as citizens, pure and simple, in our country. English people are welcome, as is anybody at all. But if they wish to come to a country, as they have done, and assume positions of superhumans, to take all that our people have had for centuries to themselves and call that multiracial government, that has never been seen in the world and in that case they might as well pack up and return from whence they came. We are straightforward in our request in that regard.

In 1953 Britain, again without the people's consent, brought about the federation of Rhodesia and Nyasaland. Why was this federation brought about? Was it because Britain and the white settlers were interested in the economic development of that area? Indeed, that is what the world is being told. The truth, however, is that the white settlers in Southern Rhodesia, having succeeded for over thirty years in running the country at the expense of the African people without their consent, felt insecure when countries like Ghana came into existence. The general slogan of the European politicians in south and central Africa, especially Southern Rhodesia then was, 'We do not want other Ghanas across the Zambesi River. Britain, our father, help us. If you do not, Northern Rhodesia and the Nyasaland will be Ghanas on the borders of a white man's country, Southern Rhodesia. We therefore plead with you, Britain, to give us Northern Rhodesia and Nyasaland.'

Appeal for Unity
FRAIN

> *The FRAIN (Frente Revolucionaria Africana para a*
> *Independencia Nacional) grouped the MPLA (Angola) and the*
> *PAIGC (Guinea Bissau). It was an early version of the CONCP.*
> *At the time of publication of this document, there was some*
> *optimism that the UPA (Angola) would join, under the pressure*
> *of the Pan African movement. This was not to be. This appeal*
> *was signed in Africa in May 1960 by Abel Djassi (Amilcar Cabral),*
> *Hugo Menezes, Lucio Lara, Mario de Andrade, Matias Migueis,*
> *and Viriato da Cruz, who identified themselves 'as militants of*
> *the MPLA and members of the FRAIN'.*

Colonialism, foreign domination in Africa, is seeing its last days. Between the Second All-African Peoples' Conference in Tunis in January 1960, and today, we have come to know that during this year the Congo, the Federation of Mali (Senegal and Sudan), Nigeria, Somalia, and Madagascar will be independent states. Togo has just become independent. Dates have been announced for Sierra Leone and Tanganyika. The right of Kenya to independence has been recognized. . . . The wind of change that is blowing over Africa is running in favour of the liberation revolution of the Angolan people.

With the creation three years ago of the Movimento Anti-Colonialista (MAC), Africans living outside their respective homelands — Cape Verde,

Guinea, Sao Tome, Angola, and Mozambique — launched a united and organized struggle against the common enemy: Portuguese colonialism.

The union in combat of different parties and patriotic movements of all countries under Portuguese domination now has a concrete basis on which it will develop. Since January 1960 the MPLA and the PAIGC have created the Frente Revolucionaria Africana para a Independencia Nacional (FRAIN). FRAIN is open to all patriotic organizations of all African countries still under the Portuguese colonial yoke. . . .

COMPATRIOTS!
ANGOLANS OF ALL SOCIAL STRATA!
CATHOLICS, PROTESTANTS, BROTHERS OF ALL CREEDS!
MEN, WOMEN AND YOUNG PEOPLE!

Our previous struggle has shown concretely that a liberation revolution cannot be the work of one man but only that of the united and organized combat of patriots. The results of the patriotic struggle that has gone on for years *inside Angola* has brought us to the moment of a new phase. This new phase of struggle, in which Angola in struggle is about to enter, requires in our view the urgent creation of a united front of different parties, movements and mass organizations in Angola.

Our Heritage: Portrait of a Great Angolan Queen
MPLA

> *Brief insert in* Angola in Arms *(MPLA), Year 1, No. 1, January 1967.*

Queen Nzinga Mbandi Ngola was born in 1581 in Cabassa, the capital city of the Kingdom of Ngola. When her father Ngola Kiluanji died, Queen Nzinga was already a woman and a mother. From her father she inherited pride, courage, tenacity and hatred for the foreign invader. These qualities added to her prestige when she became Queen of Dongo and Matamba. Her political and warlike genius allied to her high conception of justice serving the ends of her people, conferred upon her an eminent rank in the history of Angola.

Her father had left three daughters and two sons. One of the two sons, Ngola Mbandi, was a bastard. He was ambitious and cunning. After his father's death he weaved an intrigue which finally led to his enthronement. He had the heads of his brothers and nephew (Queen Nzinga's son) as well as those of other high personages, chopped off. Faced with this terror, Nzinga fled the country and went into hiding in Matamba. From here she directed the war for the defence of her people against the Portuguese aggressors. Having found it impossible to subdue Queen Nzinga, the Portuese decided to negotiate peace between the Kingdom of Ngola and Portugal. Later, for purely political reasons, Queen Nzinga decided to be baptized and adopted the name

D. Ana de Sousa, although the name itself was all she retained from her conversion to Catholicism.

Queen Nzinga warred for 30 years against the Portuguese to free her nation. She never accepted Portuguese sovereignty until she died at the age of 82.

The Origins of the Angolan Insurrection
Mario de Andrade

> *From an article by Mario de Andrade (MPLA) that appeared in* Revolution africaine *(Algiers), 74, 27 June 1964, (and reflects on analysis of organizational strengths as of that time). Translated from French.*

The insurrection of the Angolan people has, over the past three years awakened a sense of solidarity in Africa and the rest of the world with the struggle against Portuguese colonialism.

Portugal's refusal to admit the inevitability of independence for the colonized peoples leads to her isolation, while the Western alliance oscillates between its obligations and the needs of its African policy.

One thing is sure: the regime in Lisbon, economically dependent upon the resources of its 'overseas provinces', could not engage itself in a process of *decolonization* which might undermine its structures. Thus it spends its time elaborating vain formulae for survival. Similarly, the alternatives suggested on this subject by certain movements of opposition to Mr. Salazar scarcely move away from the colonial ideology.

However, the liberation movement in Angola, torn apart by political differences in its ranks, is presently [1964 – Eds.] undergoing a crisis whose essential components may well be worth discussing.

There exists at its origin a difference in the way various protagonists acquired their national consciousness.

Furthermore, it should be noted that structural deficiencies and external factors stemming from imperialist plots have hindered the efforts of one of the main organizations to orient the insurrection along revolutionary lines.

And finally, the regional context in which Angola is placed, and particularly the nature of the regime installed in Congo-Leopoldville, add to the complexity of the matter.

It is obvious that the war of liberation is affected by these divisions which beset the nationalist movements. Thus the success or failure of unity in action against the primary enemy, and the establishment of a national front are basic to the future of Angola.

The original distribution of popular support between the MPLA and the UPA, the former being more deeply rooted in the urban areas and the latter in the rural communities bordering the Congo, may have appeared to some observers as being the determining factor in the division of Angolan nationalism. Some went so far as to identify the MPLA as an 'urban party of the elite' and the UPA as the 'party of the radicalized peasant masses'.

The evolution of events, from the beginning of military operations, not only illustrates the falsity of such an assertion, but also that it is impossible to establish a 'class border-line' between the social basis of the two nationalist movements. Especially since both share at present the adherence of the various social strata in Angola, from the forced labourers, the landless peasants, to the *assimilados* – a privileged fringe without real economic power.

In adding our opinion to this picture, we do not wish to re-open a controversial argument, but rather to outline a method of approach.

None of the political machines can claim today to lead by itself all the social strata affected by the insurrection towards revolutionary action. Such is the essence of the matter.

The aggravation of the colonial situation, the acuteness of the forms of exploitation especially noticeable in the practice of forced labor in the rural areas in particular, have caused an exodus of the border populations. This exodus, towards Northern Rhodesia, South West Africa and the river bank areas of the two Congos has gone on for two centuries, and has consequently created a real Angolan diaspora.

The emigrants who settled in Congo-Leopoldville comprise the most stable group, and here always played a major political role.

The settlement of the majority of the emigrants who came from the northern parts of Angola among the Bakongo has shown itself to be a strong factor of solidarity in the fight of the Congolese against Belgian colonization.

One can distinguish two moments in the genesis of their national rebellion. While the first still took the form of a messianic movement, the second was directly political.

It was around 1949 that the prophet Simao Toco began to spread his religious ideas in Congo-Leopoldville. These ideas, known by his name, are in the line of Kibanguism. Tocoism, located in the beginning among the Angolan refugees, eventually gained converts and organized cells in large parts of the north, central and southern parts of the country. This is especially true once Simao Toco, expelled by the Belgian police in January 1950, began to undergo successive persecutions at the hands of the Portuguese colonists, and changes in the locations of his detention.

Just as Kibanguism found its biggest audience among the detribalized peasants in the Congo, so Tocoism awakened a strong current of opposition to forced labour in the plantations of Angola.

The memorandum which 24 'representatives of economic activities' from the district of Uige (Carmona) addressed on March 7, 1957 to the Governor-General of the colony spoke of the influence of disciples of Simao Toco, and complained about the systematic refusal of the peasants to permit their 'voluntary' mobilization for labor on the agricultural plantations.

The Protestant missions (the first Baptist one dating from 1878) took advantage of this climate to encourage and sometimes channel African demands in these areas, since they were very responsive to the propaganda against the official religion of the colonial authorities.

The administration often manifested fears concerning the anti-Portuguese influence of the pamphlets and books distributed by the Protestant missions to the 'native' populations. Confidential circulars seem to acknowledge a striking difference between the native brought up under the influence of the Catholic missions and one brought up by Protestant missions. 'The latter exhibits an insulting arrogance, a peculiar pride manifested in every act of his life. . . . Some of them go as far as to be ashamed of being Portuguese, and speak of themselves as being American or English, on the simple excuse that they belong to an American or English mission.'

Also beginning in 1950, emigration was structured around specific groups, based upon ethnic, cultural or regional affinities. It is the second moment of rebellion. From 1954 on, there appears a real proliferation of these organizations, imitating the model of the Congolese: *Union of Populations of the North of Angola, Aliazo* (Union of the Zombo), *Ngwizani in the Congo,* etc. Only the first one of them, which became in 1958 the *Union of the Populations of Angola* (UPA), later on took positions which resembled a political doctrine.

The declaration of the UPA executive published in 1960 and which is its platform affirms the following in its preface:

> After the liberation of Ghana, Guinea, Cameroun, Togo, the Congo, and Somalia, European colonialism has been in swift retreat. Accordingly, no people in Africa has any longer the right to mark time or to play around with the ruling powers. Thus Portugal must stop dreaming of subjugating millions of Africans indefinitely and must realize, as have all other European states, that the Angolan people and all others under its control will be present at the rendez-vous, having understood that freedom is an inalienable right which the Creator has accorded to all human beings to enjoy in this earthly sojourn.

In the first section, often with well-turned phrases, the text denounces the conditions of colonial exploitation in Angola in order to derive from them the conclusion that 'immediate independence of the territory appears as a normal solution, suitable to all the problems of Angola.'

In its second section, besides appeals directed to the peasants, the unemployed, forced labourers, women, traditional chiefs and youth, it defines the objectives of a struggle for independence, and defines its political positions vis-a-vis the settlers, the Portuguese people and State, African peoples and world public opinion.

Within the framework of the struggle against Portuguese colonialism for the national independence of Angola, this declaration does not, in terms of fundamental options, postulate anything that is inconsistent with the essential points in the program of the MPLA.

But thereupon the UPA, wishing to ignore other political forces in Angola, claims that it covers the gamut of nationalist tendencies in itself and that therefore it *alone* represents the aspirations of the Angolan people.

To overtake, by ignoring them, eventual competitors, this is the tactical shortcut of the UPA leadership. This position has a certain psychological effectiveness.

However, when one looks at it more closely, one discovers the underlying causes of the firm hostility which the UPA maintains against the united front proposed by the MPLA: a traumatism aroused by its limited knowledge of the realities of the country, the intellectual void due to the lack of cadres, and a base of support among masses whose sense of national identification is limited to the horizon of the Bakongo.

The close links between the leaders of the UPA and the Congo has created, in the specific context of imperialist intrigue in Leopoldville, an Angolan nationalism primarily concerned with the immediate securing of large financial support from Western sources. This is nationalism as business. The UPA harmonizes its diplomacy with that of the Congo. The latter, while tolerating officially the existence of an MPLA office [not since 1963 —Ed.] , seeks to deepen and prolong the division amongst the main nationalist forces of Angola.

We will return to this question later.

Encouraged by the positive evolution of the general situation on the continent, Angolan patriots inside the country welcomed any appeal whatsoever to begin direct action that was suggested by 'leaders' outside.

The UPA's logistic advantages due to its base in the Congo, as well as its efforts in mobilizing the Bakongo border populations, were factors which made the UPA in March, 1960, the main beneficiary of the popular insurrection. The orientation to be taken in the war against Portuguese colonialism became a sudden issue. . . .

Since 1957, there was ferocious repression against nationalistic movements in the interior, and the wave of arrests has affected especially the cadres of the MPLA and its sympathizers who worked for the most part among the urban masses. If political clandestinity was a given fact, due to the nature of the Portuguese colonial regime, it was nonetheless the case that the organizational structures of the nationalist movements were not prepared to resist efficaciously the Fascist machine. It thus proved necessary to reconstruct after the dismembering of the internal executive. Two principal realities had to be dealt with by the external delegation of the MPLA, which was reconstituted in 1960:

Firstly, there existed in the country an explosive situation, in which the masses were ready to assume fully their responsibilities in the move to armed action, despite the dispersion of nationalist efforts and the arrest of numerous leaders.

Secondly the UPA had undeniable support among the forced laborers from the Northern regions, and among the Angolan organizations in the Congo. We knew, incidentally, that it was encouraged by various groups to launch military operations immediately.

Prelude to the Revolution
FNLA

From a memorandum presented by the National Liberation Front of Angola (FNLA) to the Commission for the Reconciliation of Angola Nationalist Movements of the OAU which met in Leopoldville (Congo) on 15 July 1963.

The Union of the Populations of Angola was founded on the 10th of July, 1954 in this city of Leopoldville by Angolan emigrants who had taken refuge here as a result of the deplorable living conditions prevailing in Angola.

At that time, the Congo was itself a colonial territory though its living conditions were notably better than those that pertained in our country.

That is not to say that we enjoyed during that period full freedom of action. We had great difficulties to face in organizing our liberation movement.

The first manifestation of our action was marked by the strike that occurred on March 10, 1956 in Angola. This action provoked arrests and deportations of our militants among whom one may count the patriots Figueira Lello and Liborio Nefwane. Portuguese authorities having intercepted some of our tracts, they learned that we were responsible for them and intervened with Belgian colonial authorities in order to bring an end to our activities.

On the 23rd of March, 1956, we were convoked by the Provincial Director of the Criminal Investigation Department, who made us sign a document in which we promised to cease all political activity.

The situation forced us to pursue our action in clandestinity.

At the time of the troubles which broke out in Leopoldville in January, 1959, which led to the arrest of Congolese nationalists, including President Kasa-Vubu, several hundred Angolan emigrants, among whom figured our militants, were arrested. All of our compatriots were extradited to Angola where they were sent to the plantations and placed in forced labour.

Paradoxically, this turned out to be good fortune for us for under our direction our militants formed the cells that were to launch the rebellion of March 15, 1961.

The Peasantry of the South
A. Vakulukuta

*From a statement on the structure, politics and perspectives of
UNITA which appeared in* Kwacha-Angola *(UNITA), Special
Edition, 1972. Translated from French.*

It is not by accident that UNITA has established its first guerilla base in the
southeastern part of the country. For it is there that the peasant masses have
always fiercely resisted first foreign occupation, and then direct colonial
domination. They have always refused to submit to the arbitrary laws and
humiliations inflicted upon the Angolan people by the present status quo,
and have not allowed their land to be expropriated by the landowning colonial
bourgeoisie. They have always responded vigorously to repression and the
punishments of the enemy.

The peasantry of the South were the last to lay down their arms against
expansionist Portugal, for the last murderous campaigns, the military campaigns of Cuamato, Humbe, and Huila, occur in 1919-20, following upon the
previous ones in Cuando, Cubano, Bie, Moxico and Huambo.

It is not without reason that the leaders of UNITA established the party
in this anti-colonial milieu. It is a well-mobilized milieu, from which the revolution may spread to the rest of the country. No-one, not even the Fascist
bourgeoisie who conducts the war, is ignorant of the revolutionary qualities
of the Southern peasants. One has only to arouse their initiative and channel
it to the service of the national and popular revolution, to conduct intelligent
and patient political work aimed at the immediate interests of the elderly and
young, to awaken in them the notion of the conquest of power, of freedom
for their artistic creativity, and of everything that has been taken from them.
It suffices to explain to them the objectives of the revolution.

Development of Nationalism in Mocambique
Eduardo Mondlane

*A statement by the President of FRELIMO, released in Dar es
Salaam on 3 December 1964, and later published in French
in* Presence Africaine, *LIII, ler trimestre, 1965.*

Mocambican nationalism, like practically all African nationalism, was born
of direct European colonialism. Mocambique's most specific source of national
unity is the common experience (in suffering) of the people during the last
one hundred years of Portuguese colonial control. In order to understand the
development of Mocambican nationalism, we must study the main stages of
the development of Portuguese colonialism in our country and note the

15

resulting reaction of the people.

Before I outline these stages of the development of Portuguese colonialism and their relationship to the rise of nationalism, I wish to present a definition of nationalism. By nationalism I mean 'a consciousness on the part of individuals or groups of membership in a nation or of a desire to develop the strength, liberty, or prosperity of that nation'. The above definition applies to nationalism in all circumstances or stages of development of any people. For instance, it might apply to European nationalism as a continental phenomenon, or French, American, Russian, Chinese, Brazilian, etc. — nationalisms as expressions of the aspirations of given ethnic or national entities. The African context in which Mocambican nationalism finds expression might require further refinement of the definition offered above. In view of the recent historical circumstances that have affected the lives of the various peoples within the continent of Africa, it is necessary to add that African nationalism is also characterized by the development of attitudes, activities, and more or less structured programs aimed at the mobilization of forces for the attainment of self-government and independence. In the specific case of Mocambique, these attitudes, activities, and structured programmes, shared by all Portuguese colonies in Africa and possibly by all other remaining peoples not yet free, must include the establishment of military or paramilitary schemes for the final showdown before the actual attainment of independence can be ensured.

If you could bear with me for a few more seconds in connection with these preliminary remarks, I should like to sum up the definition of nationalism offered above in the following manner:

(a) a consciousness on the part of individuals or groups of membership in a nation — in our case, Mocambique.

(b) a desire to develop the strength, liberty, or prosperity of that nation — the concept of FRELIMO (as we are popularly known) pertaining to the future socio-economic structure of the country and how to go about implementing it;

(c) the specific goal of attaining self-government and independence — FRELIMO's political and military program;

(d) a concept of the people's unity — the Mocambican people's desire to rid themselves of Portuguese imperialism and colonialism so as to be completely free to develop their socio-economic structures as they wish; and,

(e) the establishment of more or less permanent political structures for the pursuit of national objectives in cooperation with other African nations.

In reference to African nationalism in general, it is necessary to stress four more points:

(i) that it is a reaction against political controls imposed by Europeans upon the African peoples; and

(ii) that it is a reaction against foreign, especially Western, economic exploitation of the African natural and human resources.

(iii) In those areas of Africa where a combination of European and Asian populations have come to settle alongside the African peoples, African nationalism has also had to include a reaction against local cultural and socio-economic barriers created by members of these non-African communities.

(iv) Concurrent with the rise of African nationalism, there developed another kind of nationalism — cultural nationalism — epitomized by the mushrooming of all sorts of theories concerning African man, labelled 'African personality' by Anglophones and 'Negritude' or 'Africanite' by Francophones.

Mocambique is one of the remnants of an old Portuguese colonial empire that was established during the sixteenth, seventeenth, eighteenth, and nineteenth centuries in Asia, South America, and Africa. In Africa the remnants of this empire still include Angola, Mocambique, Guine (called Portuguese), the Cape Verde Islands, and Sao Tome Island. The largest of these colonies is Angola, although Mocambique has the largest population of them all.

Contacts between Portugal and parts of what is now known as Mocambique began at the end of the fifteenth century, when Vasco da Gama, a well-known Portuguese navigator, reached the island of Mocambique in early March 1498. Since the main interest of the Portuguese kings who had sponsored these trips was to open a route to India that would be safer than the then dangerous Near East land route, for many years the Portuguese satisfied themselves with establishing filling stations along the East African coast, thus leaving the interior untouched. The Portuguese claim that they have been in Mocambique for over four hundred and fifty years, implying that for all that time they have been controlling our country politically. If there is any truth in this Portuguese claim, it has to do with the fact that soon after the first contact with the people of the coastal region of East Africa, the Portuguese, envying the wealth and power possessed by the Arab rulers of the time, plotted, connived, organized whatever forces they could muster, and fought their way into a position of control. This enabled the Portuguese to monopolize the then very rich East African trade in ivory, gold, and precious stones. To accomplish this, the Portuguese took advantage of the rivalries then existent among the sherifs and sheiks of such city states as Pate, Malindi, Kilwa, Zanzibar, Mocambique, Sofala, etc., which were famous for their 'prosperity and elegance'.

At that time, their wealth and cultural refinement were comparable to the best in Europe and Asia. From the reaction of the Portuguese sailors of that time, gleaned from their diaries, it is possible to suggest that East Africa as a whole 'was a world comparable, if not superior, in material culture to Portugal in 1500'. However, political unity among these city states was no easier to achieve at that time than it is now in present-day East Africa. Let me quote Professor James Duffy: 'Political unity among these city states was a transitory burden. Each local prince defended his city's political and commercial independence, and at no time was there an East African nation, although the stronger towns at one time or another dominated their weaker neighbours.'

Even though the Portuguese took advantage of this unfortunate situation, they were never able to impose a lasting political control, except over a very thin coastal strip running from Cape Delgado to the city state of Sofala. By 1700 a resurgence of Islamic influence in this part of Africa had been able to effectively eliminate Portuguese traders and soldiers, as well as scores of towns that they had held from time to time.

From the beginning of the eighteenth century, the Portuguese concentrated on conniving and cajoling their way into control of the rich commerce of the area between Cape Delgado and the Zambezi basin, in an attempt to capture the flow of gold from the famous gold mines of Monomotapa, which the Portuguese had believed to be the proverbial 'King Solomon's Mines'. Again, in this instance, the imperialistic activities of the Portuguese affected an area that included what is today known as Zambia and Zimbabwe or Southern Rhodesia. The capital of Monomotapa's empire was located in Mashonaland and was part of the Makalanga confederacy of that time.

During a period of two hundred years, the Portuguese were able to obtain a great deal of wealth because of the simple fact that they had been able to control the flow of commerce from the interior of the country to the coastal city states and abroad. During the seventeenth and eighteenth centuries, Portuguese authority was firmly enough established in the northern and central parts of Mocambique so that it was possible to introduce Catholic missionaries — first the Dominicans, then the Jesuits, who were the first to introduce Christianity in East Africa. However, whatever success crowned this first missionary effort was almost completely destroyed in the eighteenth century by the corrupting effect of the marriage that had naturally resulted from the association of commercial, religious, and political activities of the Church and the State. It was during this time that the *prazo* system was introduced in Mocambique. *Prazeiros* were Portuguese white and mulatto settlers and land-owners who, not unlike European feudal lords, ruled those Africans who had the misfortune to fall under their authority and control. These Africans' lot was worse than that of slaves. The *prazeiros* often controlled whole districts as personal properties and recognized no law but their own — and only occasionally paid their vassalage to the king of Portugal. Jesuit and Dominican missionaries of the time also came to own vast tracts of land, administering it like any *prazeiro*, collecting head taxes and, when slavery became more profit-able, dealing in slaves. It was out of the *prazo* system that the great land companies, such as Nyasa and Manica e Sofala companies, developed. It can also be presumed that the heartless and peculiarly Portuguese concessionary company system, which typifies the major economic enterprises of Portuguese colonialism, derived its refinements from the *prazo* system of this period.

Corruption in the *prazo* system was so rampant that by the third decade of the nineteenth century even the Portuguese government felt compelled to outlaw it. Among other reasons for its abolition by the Portuguese colonial government, the *prazo* system was notorious for fostering insecurity for person and property, and for the excessive number of Africans who were compelled to leave the area altogether due to the slaving practices of the manor lords. All of this resulted in the almost complete collapse of the Portu-guese administration. However, in order to reimpose Portuguese authority, it was necessary to seek the cooperation of some of the *prazeiros,* which meant their reinstatement; therefore, the vicious circle!

All along, however, the financial benefits that accrued from the slave trade were so great that the *prazeiros* of central Mocambique had become the reservoirs for slaving. It must be noted here, even in passing, that although the slave trade was one of the most characteristic Portuguese economic activities, slavery *per se* in East Africa was practised long before Vasco da Gama touched this coast of Africa. Most of the slaves from East Africa were sold in the Middle East and in South East Asia, including India.

Most of the above colonialistic-imperialistic activities in East Africa took place primarily on the thin coastal strip, involving mostly contacts with the Arabs and the Swahilis, and only very superficial contacts with the bulk of the Bantu-speaking people of present-day East Africa and Mocambique.

The Portuguese conquest of what is now Mocambique originated with the proverbial scramble for Africa, which began in the second half of the nineteenth century. After the partition of Africa at the Berlin Conference of 1884-85, Portugal was impelled to capture and solidify what had been dished out to her. To accomplish this, the Portuguese used every technique known in the history of colonial conquests. Where it was possible, she used infiltration by Portuguese traders, who disguised themselves as simple businessmen interested in the exchange of goods between equals; but later on, after having thoroughly spied upon and mapped out a whole region, they invited in their military forces, which subsequently wiped out whatever resistance might have been put up by the local rulers. At times, the Portuguese used white settlers, who pretended that they needed land to farm, but who, after having been kindly accommodated by the naive traditional rulers, claimed possession of communal lands and forcibly enslaved the African peoples who were originally their hosts. Sometimes even Portuguese missionaries were used as pacifiers of the natives, using the Christian faith as a lullaby, while the Portuguese military forces occupied the land and controlled the people.

Where the traditional political authority was strong and the military machinery was adequate to offer serious resistance to European conquest, the Portuguese were more subtle in their techniques of initial contact. For instance, under these circumstances, the Portuguese were prepared to begin their contacts with strong African states by establishing diplomatic relations, sending Portuguese 'ambassadors' to the courts of the most important traditional rulers. Then, after having sufficiently spied out the internal strengths and weaknesses of the government, they proceeded to attack, using the traditional excuses of 'provocation' or 'protection of the security of the white settlers or missionaries', etc.

This is the way in which the war against the last of the Mocambican traditional empires, the Gaza Empire under Gungunyana, was justified. The war against Emperor Gungunyana began in 1895 and ended in 1898 with the death in battle of General Magigwane and the capture and deportation of the Emperor to Portugal, where he died several years later.

With regard to the kind of government that the Portuguese established after they had subjugated all parts of the country, we have already presented descriptions which have been published elsewhere.

As is clear from the foregoing, the success of the Portuguese in controlling the whole of Mocambique was due mainly to the lack of a cohesive political force to oppose them. Right from the first days of contact with the East African coastal city states in the fifteenth century, when the Portuguese were able, albeit temporarily, to defeat and control many of them, through the sixteenth, seventeenth, and eighteenth centuries, when they captured the main commercial wealth of northern and central Mocambique, up to the nineteenth century, when they proceeded to conquer and keep the present territory of our country, the reaction of our people was fragmentary. It was a piecemeal reaction that encouraged a piecemeal conquest of our people. Even as late as the second decade of this century, in 1917 and 1918 to be exact, when the Makombe of the Barwe — in an attempt to reestablish some of the power of his legendary predecessor King Monomotapa — staged a successful revolt, his success did not last long, for it was not a national Mocambican uprising: it was confined to one or two tribal kingdoms.

Mondlane: Early Days in South Africa
'Spartacus'

> *This appreciation of Dr. Eduardo C. Mondlane was signed by 'Spartacus' in the ANC's* Mayibuye, *III, 4, 14 February 1969.*

Dr. Eduardo C. Mondlane has paid the ultimate price for his unyielding opposition to Portuguese colonialism. His untimely assassination in Dar es Salaam is tragic testament to his success in leading FRELIMO in its armed challenge to Portuguese rule in Mozambique. That Lisbon almost openly and shamefully celebrates his murder confirms anew the services which Dr. Mondlane performed in the anti-colonialist struggle as the first President of FRELIMO. Africa mourns his death, the loss of FRELIMO and the sorrow of the African liberation movement.

The story of Dr. Mondlane's struggle for education and progressive immersion in revolutionary politics highlight both the insuperable obstacles to African advancement within the Portuguese colonial system and the inevitable challenge to that system which must come from those few allowed education within it. Born in 1920 in the Gaza district of Southern Mozambique, Eduardo as a young boy never dreamt of going to school. Yet his widowed mother, the pillar of strength in his family, as in so many broken families in Southern Africa, was determined that he should be the first to obtain education. Thus at the age of eleven, Eduardo Mondlane left his cattle herding and enrolled in one of the few government schools open to Africans.

Transferring two years later to a mission school, Mondlane caught the attention of his teachers who arranged for him to go to Lourenco Marques in 1936 to work for his primary school certificate, the highest academic level open to Africans in Mozambique at the time. Although further academic study seemed closed to Mondlane after he had obtained his primary school certificate, he refused to accept that his education had come to an end. He managed to secure a place in an agricultural school where he completed a course in dry-land farming. For two years Eduardo Mondlane then taught dry-farming in his home district — and thus his continuing interest in the problems of his people on the land.

He had not, however, abandoned his desire for further education. As he had fortunately learned English while in agricultural school, he was able to accept a private scholarship to attend secondary school in the Northern Transvaal, South Africa. Successfully completing matriculation, he then enrolled in the University of the Witwatersrand in Johannesburg in 1948. In South Africa Mondlane experienced the South African version of racism firsthand, yet he was also in Johannesburg at the time that the young militants of the ANC Youth League were organizing their successful campaign to radicalize the parent body in its opposition to *apartheid*. Mondlane directed his political efforts to organizing his countrymen into a Mozambique student association — and as a result the Portuguese authorities intervened to have his South African residence permit revoked. Forced to return to Lourenco Marques after one year of university in Johannesburg, Mondlane was arrested and interrogated. The Portuguese authorities were convinced that Mondlane's embryonic spirit of African nationalism could be stifled and redirected into service of the Portuguese state through direct exposure to the Portuguese motherland. Mondlane was allowed to enroll in the University of Lisbon.

In Lisbon Mondlane formed close associations with the few other students from the Portuguese African colonies. Instead of becoming closer to Portugal they became more antagonistic to her. In spite of close surveillance Mondlane and other African students formed an embryonic anti-Portuguese network from which came many of the leaders who today are in the forefront of the anti-colonialist struggle against Portugal in Africa.

When Mondlane was offered a scholarship to study in America he seized the chance to pursue his higher education outside of Salazar's Portugal. He rapidly completed his B.A. in 1953 and then continued for graduate work in sociology at Northwestern University from where he obtained an M.A. and a Ph.D. From 1957 until 1961 he worked for the United Nations as a research officer on trust territories — thus becoming acquainted with the problems of the independence struggle in other parts of Africa and the world.

Yet Dr. Mondlane's eyes were still fixed upon Mozambique. With the independence of Tanganyika in December, 1961, Mondlane saw new opportunities opening for the creation of a national movement to challenge the Portuguese. He had maintained contact with Mozambican groups outside of the country which had been formed to struggle for independence. Convinced that only a single united body could create the effective organization necessary to challenge the Portuguese, Mondlane worked with other Mozambican patriots to bring all groups together in Dar-es-Salaam in mid-1962. At this meeting it was agreed to dissolve the existing three groups into a new organization, FRELIMO, the Liberation Front of Mozambique. Dr. Mondlane was chosen president of the new organization. Henceforth his educational achievements were to be channelled completely into the struggle for Mozambican freedom.

At its first party congress under Dr. Mondlane's leadership in September, 1962, FRELIMO formulated a far-reaching program for the liberation of Mozambique. The experiences of FRELIMO's leaders under Portuguese colonialism had convinced them that Salazar would never accept the idea of self-determination or negotiation of changes leading towards independence. Accordingly they decided to focus their short-term efforts upon the creation of a direct challenge to Portuguese rule through 1) the setting up of a clandestine political organization within Mozambique and 2) the establishment of a military training program to produce a corps of freedom fighters to undertake armed struggle. Yet the vision of FRELIMO extended beyond the immediate struggle. Centuries of Portuguese neglect had left Mozambique with few literate and trained persons; FRELIMO endorsed a crash educational program at all levels to prepare leadership cadres for the needs of a liberated Mozambique.

Within the matrix set by the September 1962 party congress FRELIMO moved to the start of confrontation with the Portuguese colonial regime. Political organization was extended underground within Mozambique. On September 25, 1964, the first detachments of the FRELIMO freedom fighters opened the initial phase of the armed struggle in northern Mozambique. Advancing slowly against the well-armed and expanded Portuguese forces in Mozambique the FRELIMO guerrillas have freed substantial areas of Mozambique. Within the liberated areas the cadres from FRELIMO-supported schools have led in the establishment of a revolutionary administration which has brought schools, medical services, and economic organization. In 1968 FRELIMO held its first party congress within liberated Mozambique — a practical and symbolic act showing to Mozambicans, the Portuguese, and the world the growing strength of the liberation movement of Mozambique.

Yet the struggle ahead is long and costly — a fact always recognised by Dr. Mondlane. He believed that guerrilla tactics and the administration of liberated Mozambique had to be adapted to the specific problems of the country with careful attention to the elements of the experiences of other liberation struggles as they were relevant. Long before his death he argued that FRELIMO must make no 'facile promises' to the people, 'for it is absolutely essential that they share with us the knowledge that liberation from the Portuguese rule may take many years and many lives'. In this spirit FRELIMO under Dr. Mondlane's leadership advanced the slow, hard struggle against entrenched Portuguese colonialism — and now one of the 'many lives' lost is that of Dr. Mondlane himself. His martyrdom must provide a new spur to all patriots of Southern Africa to achieve the liberation of their peoples.

Guinea: Phases of Portuguese Activity
Amilcar Cabral

From a declaration made by the Secretary-General of the PAIGC to the UN's Special Committee on Territories Under Portuguese Administration, June 1962. Translated from French.

It is necessary to emphasize that the economic activity of the Portuguese in Guinea has been for over 500 years, and still is today, almost exclusively commercial. In its development one may distinguish the following phases:

(1) Portuguese monopoly of commerce (especially that of slaves), at first only sent to European *donatorios* (plantation owners) on the Cape Verde Islands (up to 1530).

(2) Competition from other foreign countries. Settlement by Portuguese tradesmen. Rise of large Atlantic slaving companies which monopolize commerce (1530-1840).

(3) Gradual abolition of the slave trade. Development of research in local products (peanuts). End of the Portuguese monopoly in favor of German and French enterprises (mainly 1840/80-1932).

(4) Portuguese monopoly of commerce, especially of the export trade and shipping. Decrease of non-Portuguese enterprises, concentration of Portuguese monopoly in a handful of enterprises (since 1932).

There is a constant feature characteristic of all these phases: a *redemptive* mode of economy, strongly mono-mercantile. At the beginning, slaves. Today, peanuts.

Herein we relate certain facts which concern the post-slave trade period, up to the establishment of the present political regime. The gradual, eventually definitive abolition of the slave trade upset and disorganized both the economy of 'Portuguese' Guinea and that of the metropole itself. This fact had important consequences for the political evolution of Portugal.

To resolve these problems, the Portuguese tried other forms of commerce and exploitation by developing above all the redemption of local products or those of neighboring areas, which were exported through the port of Bissau. For this reason, they began the penetration of the interior of the country, where they established trading-posts *(factoreries)*.

The research on peanuts, begun in Senegal in 1840, helped the economic development of the colony. Small farmers *(ponteiros)* and non-indigenous merchants stimulated or forced the cultivation of peanuts by the indigenous population. In Bolama and on the shores of the Great River of Buba the peanut cycle had its beginnings and numerous trading-posts were established in these areas.

Portuguese capitalism, scarcely existent, could not, however, compete with non-Portuguese capital which attempted (successfully) to penetrate Africa by every possible means. After the Berlin Conference which brought about the first great partition of the Continent, non-Portuguese enterprises, which had already succeeded in establishing themselves in 'Portuguese' Guinea, monopolized both the internal and external commerce of the country. This was part of the tribute that Portuguese colonialism had to pay to foreign capital in order to maintain its 'presence' in Africa.

Thus, in 1927 again, more than 70% of the exports from 'Portuguese' Guinea were directed to non-Portuguese ports (particularly those of France and Germany), from which an equal proportion of imported merchandise came. We may say that since the end of the last century until the 1930s, 'Portuguese' Guinea was a non-Portuguese colony, administered and *defended* by the Portuguese.

The development of the peanut crop, which occurred mainly at the beginning of this century, opened up the way to soil erosion in 'Portuguese' Guinea, deeply disturbed the lives of the African peoples, to whom it brought the economic, political and social consequences which characterize the present Portuguese rule. Voluntary in the beginning, the result of prodding, it became the chief preoccupation of the administration and thus came in effect to be a mandatory form of cultivation for the rural Africans.

Defeated by the force of arms, the active resistance of the populations to Portuguese penetration and occupation, the development of a peanut monoculture, along with various subsidiary products (such as palm oil, rubber, leather, etc.) — in a redemptive mode — became the basis of 'Portuguese' Guinea's economy and the determining factor in the political situation of its people within the structure of the Portuguese colonial empire. It is fitting to emphasize that even the transfer of the capital from Bolama to Bissau had for its principal cause the erosion of the soil on Bolama Island and Buba Region, with the consequent displacement of the peanut cycle on to Bissau Island and the central areas of the country.

The colonialist-nationalism which, in Portugal, brought the present regime to power, did not undo this situation. Quite the contrary, it did every possible thing to reinforce it, for the exclusive advantage of Portuguese interests.

By establishing discriminatory tariffs to protect commerce between the colonies and Portugal, and by guaranteeing to Portuguese ships, among other things, a monopoly of maritime transport between Portugal and the colonies, the present regime laid the basis for the return of the Portuguese monopoly of commerce in Guinea (Art. 228 — 230 in the Organic Charter of the Portuguese Colonial Empire).

One began to export raw materials exclusively from 'Portuguese' Guinea to Portugal. Unable to make profit, the non-Portuguese commercial enterprises began to leave the country. Peanuts, just as other products of 'Portuguese' Guinea, upon export to Portugal were re-exported to other countries to the profit of Portuguese merchants and to the detriment of the Guinean producer, since the price on the Portuguese market was inferior to that of the world market.

With the eventual development of the peanut-oil industry in Portugal nothing changed in this situation. On the contrary, the increased demands from Portuguese capital (financial, industrial and commercial) imposed new sacrifices on to the Guinean producer now forced to cultivate peanuts and to sell it at prices fixed by the colonial administration.

Cape Verde: Slaves, Poverty and Aridity
Maria Dulce Almada

From a PAIGC statement to the UN's Special Committee on Territories Under Portuguese Administration, June 1962. Translated from French.

The Cape Verde archipelago is located right in the Atlantic Ocean, facing Cap Vert (Senegal), from which it took its name. It comprises ten islands and several islets. It has an area of 3,903 sq. km. Santiago is its largest island, 900 sq. km. in size.

The present population of the Cape Verde Islands is thought to be between 180,000 and 200,000 inhabitants, the majority of whom are Metis and Blacks. The White population is close to 3,000 inhabitants, of whom a considerable part is really cross-bred, since both Metis and Blacks figure in their ancestry. The population of European origin, not cross-bred, is almost exclusively made up by high officials, commercial or industrial entrepreneurs, and of a slight number of commercial employees and skilled workers.

The reference to the Cape Verde Islands dates from the 12th century. They were known to the Arabs, and most probably to the Africans in facing areas of the continent. This all leads one to believe that at the time of the archipelago's discovery *(achamento)* by Portuguese navigators, there did not exist a settled population.

The settlement of the islands, by the establishment of the *donatorio* system (plantations), began in 1466. The early inhabitants were slaves, mostly natives of what is today 'Portuguese' Guinea, and Europeans, the majority of whom were convicts condemned for common or political crimes, and finally of adventurers and prostitutes deported from Portugal.

A slave-trade entrepot in the early stages of the settlement process, the Cape Verde Islands continued as the main slave-trading centre for a long time, a place crowded with Africans taken from the African coast, in order to sell them later to North American, West Indian, Brazilian and even Portuguese plantations. While still remaining a slave entrepot, little by little the plantation system (agricultural exploitation) was introduced in the archipelago. The *donatorios* or their descendants became the owners of the land, which was worked upon by Africans under a slave regime. In 1875, with the liberation of slaves, there was established an agrarian structure which still characterizes the present Cape Verdian economy. The descendants of the seigniors became the large landowners. The slaves or their descendants became the farmers or the sharecroppers.

Five centuries have elapsed since the beginning of the settlement process. The population of the Cape Verde Islands, which has since suffered one of the most lacerating tragedies of colonization, remains in a situation where the possibility of controlling its own destiny is ruled out.

The case of the Cape Verde Islands is similar to that of Brazil, Cuba, Santo Domingo, Haiti, the Guyanas and even North America. Even if one would agree that the Cape Verde Islands had no permanent settlers at the time of their discovery, the fact that Portugal did initiate a process of settlement, including a minority of Europeans, does not necessarily imply that these islands are part of Portugal, no more than Brazil, Cuba, Santo Domingo, Haiti, the Guyanas and the USA are parts of their respective former metropoles.

The African people of the Cape Verde Archipelago, indissolubly tied to the people of 'Portuguese' Guinea, due to historical and blood ties, has acquired the right through centuries of work and suffering to exercise sovereign and free control over all the wealth of the Archipelago — whether natural or created — as well as over their own destiny.

Just like its brother, the people of 'Portuguese' Guinea, just like all the peoples of the Portuguese colonies, the Cape Verdian people have always been denied the opportunity to decide whether or not they want Portuguese nationality, a nationality that has been forced upon them. They are fighting for the right to self-determination, to take their sovereignty from the hands of the Portuguese, to end the unusual suffering which Portuguese domination has always caused, from the days of slavery to those of Fascism, and come to freedom and independence . . .

The Portuguese colonists who took from the Cape Verde Islands everything they were able to take, plundering its natural resources, try to justify the people's suffering by claiming as its cause the Archipelago's *poverty* and the frequent periods of *drought* to which the islands are subjected, as an explanation for the effects of their own action.

By means of facts, figures and even some Portuguese witnesses, it has been proven that the Cape Verde Islands have not only exported very valuable products but have also paid the debts of the Overseas Ministry and of other colonies.

It is pertinent to emphasize that in the economic development plan, launched in 1953 (nearly five centuries after the islands' discovery) there was included an item for 'scientific knowledge of the territory'. This proves how unwarranted is the claim, according to which the Cape Verde Islands are poor, since one cannot conclude of a country's poverty when one does not know it scientifically. In other words, the conclusion that the Islands are poor does not follow from the failure of rare colonial initiatives in the direction of developing the country's economy; as Luis Terry and other scholars of the Cape Verde Archipelago's problems, has realized: 'We must admit that few things have been done — and that these few were done without a plan, continuity or perseverance.'

Furthermore, it is the former Overseas Minister himself, Bacelar Bebiano, who testifies: 'One has to assert that Cape Verde Province is not so sadly poor as one may think. Poverty is an enticing slogan for quite a few things. . . .'

We must also consider that only 12.5% of the Cape Verde Islands surface is cultivated, and that the land does not get anything back out of the revenue it produces, since that part obtained by the landowners is 'spent outside the Archipelago by absentees . . . or invested in local commerce'.

As far as drought is concerned, we must emphasize the fact that if the Cape Verde Islands (due to their geographic situation and the climatic conditions aggravated by an inadequate use of soil) may in actuality be subjected to irregular and relatively low rainfalls, it still does not justify by itself the poverty of the economy. In fact, it rains annually, at least on the agricultural islands. The problem lies rather in the rational utilization of rain supply and in the scientific exploitation of the telluric waters, not to speak of the exploitation of resources other than the agricultural ones.

In the Canary Islands, whose conditions are very similar to those of the Cape Verde Islands, as well as in the semi-arid zones of Asia Minor, Mauritania, Mali and of other countries, the problem of the lack of water has been or is being resolved, so as to allow their respective peoples to further their agricultural development. The Cape Verde Archipelago, which in non-crisis years produced all essential products needed for the supply of its population's needs, indeed enough to export, has much unexploited resources which would allow its people to obtain a life compatible with human dignity and aspirations of progress.

Already in 1891, the Cape Verdian Joao Augusto Martins made the following realistic remarks concerning aridity (cf. 'A Agricultura de Cabo Verde', 1959):

> Aridity is the true cause of the widely-discussed 'famines of Cape
> Verde,' which has long served to excuse the avidity of commerce . . .
> Drought is the logical outcome of the geographical position . . . . It
> is the unfortunate consequence of the fact that there has been no one
> who knows how or wants to remedy the ills by attacking the causes.
> But this in fact has been the tragedy of the Cape Verde Archipelago;
> and it has undoubtedly served as a basis for the most degrading, the
> most demoralizing and undesirable administrative procedures.

The myth of poverty of the Cape Verde Islands, along with the blame attributed to drought, cannot serve to free Portuguese colonialism of the responsibility of the suffering of the Cape Verdian people. As has been clearly stated in the PAIGC's program, this people is aware that the real and sole obstacle to the progress and happiness of the people of Cape Verde Islands is Portuguese colonialism.

The Portuguese colonial presence in the Cape Verde Islands is not only obvious at the political and administrative levels. It is also manifested in the complex of dependency relationships which characterize the relationship between Portugal and the Archipelago, and which maintain the economic and financial life of its people entirely subjected to Portuguese interests in many ways:

(a) Portugal monopolizes the external commerce of the Cape Verde Islands and fixes sale prices in its own interests.

(b) Nearly all imports come from Portugal as a result of high discriminatory taxes for non-Portuguese products.

(c) All financial activity is monopolized by a Portuguese bank, the Overseas National Bank, which has the right to issue the currency of the Cape Verde Archipelago.

(d) The majority of commercial enterprises and the rare industrial ones either belong to Portuguese companies or are directly dependent upon them.

(e) The few Cape Verdian merchants — middle-sized or small — have either made arrangements with the Bank or are simply branches of Portuguese companies.

(f) Almost all rural property of any value, as well as a large part of urban property belonging to Cape Verdians, hold mortgages from the Bank or the Postal Savings Bank which is administered by the Portuguese Overseas Ministry.

(g) The taxes for the undersea cable have long since covered the costs of the metropole. The same is true of the taxes for the port of S. Vicente's fuel supply. The Sal Island's airport is a branch of the Lisbon Airport.

(h) In the exercise of his executive functions, the Governor may not spend over 100,000 Esc. (approximately $3333) without receiving permission from the Portuguese Overseas Ministry.

Such relations of dependence and submission, both financially and economically, illustrate the fact that even the few attempts made by the colonial authorities in the sense of the economic development of the Islands, far from aiming at an improvement in the conditions of life of the people aim instead at defending Portuguese interests in the Archipelago.

It was on behalf of such interests that the islands' soil has been denuded of trees and ruined by an inadequate system of land exploitation incompatible with the agro-climatic conditions. It is on behalf of such interests that one still exports all the coffee, all the *purgueira* and all the castor-oil from the islands to Portugal, as well as forced labour to the *rocas* of S. Tome.

It was equally on behalf of Portuguese interests that no one ever undertook seriously the economic development of the Archipelago, leaving its principal resources unexploited, wasting others and plunging the population into misery as permanent victims of hunger in various ways:

(a) A deliberate discrimination in salary levels has always caused the best officials and technicians from the Cape Verde Islands to leave and attracted instead only incompetent officials or those who were being punished, given the lack of competent officials in Portugal or in the richer colonies.

(b) There was a failure to develop sugar-cane cultivation and allied sugar industries in order to avoid competition with the same in Madeira Island (Portugal), and later with the colonial companies (foreign capital) located in Angola and Mozambique.

(c) The fishing industry was not developed in order to avoid competition with the same in Portugal.

(d) The mineral waters were not developed (particularly those in S. Antao and Brava Island) since their superior quality might have been dangerous to similar enterprises in Portugal.

(e) The exceptional conditions of Porto Grande in S. Vicente Island — one of the best in the Atlantic — were utilized neither in a proper nor in a timely way, in order not to cause a detour for many ships from the port of Lisbon.

(f) No advantage was taken of the natural conditions of the Sal airport either in terms of the nature or extent of work on it, or by establishing taxes which could have attracted aerial navigation, despite the fact that Sal airport has a privileged situation as a port of call for planes flying between Europe and South America, and between Africa and North America. All this, in order to protect the traffic of the Lisbon airport.

(g) There was not a single attempt made to develop or profit from the magnificent natural resources of the Cape Verde Islands to initiate a tourist industry. And this was so in order to defend Portugese tourist interests in Madeira Island and the metropole and to prevent the Cape Verdian people from having new and fruitful contacts with other peoples.

Even if it sounds ridiculous to speak of tourism in a country 'where the internal means of transportation are rare and where there is a lack of adequate harbours,' as the former Overseas Minister, Bacelar Bebiano, has affirmed, it seems relevant to recall the words of the German scholar I. Friedlander (*Beitrage zur Kenntnis der Kapverdischen Inseln,* 1922):

> In Fogo Island I was able to enjoy one of the most surprising landscapes ever . . . . It possesses such a grandiose view that few volcanic landscapes are comparable to it. . . . It undeniably reminds one of an excursion to Vesuvius; but on Fogo Island the proportionate magnitude is indeed so superior that any impression that may originate in the Vesuvius Horse Doors disappears entirely, however useful and beautiful it might have been.

Here are some of the concrete facts which illustrate the permanent *sabotage* to which the development of the Cape Verde Islands has been subjected on the part of Portuguese colonial authorities in defence of Portuguese interests and to the detriment of the interests of the Cape Verdian people. Furthermore, even in 1890, the colony's Governor, J.M. Brandao de Melo, denounced, perhaps despite himself, such sabotage in his report:

> The difficulties which upper strata oppose to any demand for con-cessions are in general so numerous that the claimants become dis-couraged and lose time and money which they could have utilized in the development of industry or in the improvement of fields and their fertilization. In this state of affairs, certain claims remain unresolved by superior authorities, such as the utilization of S. Antao mineral waters. . .

Today the situation remains the same.

But today the Cape Verdian people are more and more aware that the country's poverty is a myth, that drought does not exist in the Cape Verde Islands, that their country's resources — from the soil to mineral waters, from *pouzzolane* to petroleum (whose existence is considered quite probable), from the geographic location to tourism, from animal wealth to the unquestionable worth of the Cape Verdian worker — must be put to work for the progressive evolution of their country.

Sao Tome: Product of Cross-Breeding
CONCP

> *From an information booklet published by the CONCP in Algiers in April 1968. Translated from French.*

The arrival of the Portuguese on the island of Sao Tome dates from 1470. Fifteen years later, Joao da Paiva, to whom the Portuguese monarch had given the island, left with the first nucleus of colonists, having been bestowed such privileges as that of 'being able to make commerce, on firm land, around the five rivers situated beyond the fortress of S. Jorge da Mina'. Thanks to its advantageous location, 'in the middle of the Atlantic, as free as possible from the difficult regions close to the coast', a base or transit-point for the slave-trade came to be established.

The first economic cycle of the archipelago was dominated by the slave-trade and sugar-cane cultivation introduced in 1501.

The cultivation of sugar-cane and the slave-trade developed rapidly. Between 1506 and 1507, there existed already 2,000 slaves on the sugar-cane plantations of both islands, not counting 5-6,000 slaves for sale. In 1517, sugar-cane production was so extensive that it became necessary to enact a 'law on the sale of sugar'.

In both the cities and in the plantations, the relations between Whites and Blacks were established on the basis of a royal decree that 'each colonist must take a woman and give her children'. From the beginning, the plantation owners represented the privileged group who appropriated the land and domestic property. The Black was to supply the labour-power.

Little by little, those of Portuguese descent formed a distinct group — politically and economically influential — who acted, due to their origin, as intermediaries between the two communities.

From the start, large interests shaped the unstable equilibrium of society: the fight between State and Church, for supremacy in commerce and power, and between both of these and the slaves for the liberation of the land.

Sugar-cane cultivation decreased in the second half of the 17th century. In 1601 the exodus of the plantation owners to Brazil began. The development of sugar-cane cultivation in this part of the American continent, the invasions of foreign pirates, and the social climate created by the successive rebellions of the slaves, brought about the decadence of the island's economy. The first cycle thus ended; that of the long fallow period began.

Agriculture now knew a long period of stagnation limited to the cultivation of food-crops (corn, manioc, vegetables and fruit). Merchants lived off the slave-trade and the archipelago functioned as a supply port for the ships going to America and India.

The search for slaves increased the struggle over the ownership of land and the monopoly of transport. England, France, and Holland, which owned colonies devoted to the cultivation of sugar-cane and needed slaves, thus coveted the control by the Portuguese of the archipelago. In 1555 the English attacked the island; in 1641, the Dutch succeeded in occupying it, and in 1709 there was a new assault from the French.

The island ceased to supply the necessary conditions for security of settlement by the Portuguese, and in 1753 the capital was transferred to the island of Principe.

In the beginning of the 19th century the population of the island had dwindled. It was now made up principally of the descendants of Portuguese.

The island's economic revival came with the introduction of coffee in 1800, and that of cocoa in 1822. A new cycle began which constituted a critical stage in the fight for the possession of land and the acquisition of great profits.

The method of introduction of new crops on small landholdings with the aid of new Portuguese capital, the new system of credit introduced by the banks, the impossibility of modernizing agriculture, and political intrigues were factors leading the Portuguese descendants to abandon their way of life, until then similar in all ways to that of the Portuguese, and to identify themselves with the emancipated slaves. Meanwhile we witness the triumph of large property with the establishment of large companies.

The abolition of slavery in 1869 comes at a moment when island agriculture was developing rapidly. The Portuguese farmers faced a terrible dilemma: either to carry out the noble aims of abolition and suddenly set free all the Blacks who until then were slaves, which would constitute the immediate ruin of the colonial economy, or to preserve its structure and form of rule by continuing to rely on slave labour.

Although the Portuguese had declared the abolition of slavery in their colonies, they continued to transport clandestinely new slaves from Accra, Cameroun, Gabon, Angola and Mozambique. This fact rapidly aroused universal hostility and the quick intervention of the anti-slavery powers.

In 1906 Henry Nevinson (see *A Modern Slavery*) denounced slave labour on the cocoa plantations of the archipelago. In 1909, Cadbury, the chocolate manufacturer, himself deeply interested in cocoa development in the former Gold Coast, confirmed Nevinson's statements. More recently, Basil Davidson, John Gunther, James Duffy and other journalists have revealed the humiliating conditions in which slaves were recruited for Sao Tome e Principe.

International public opinion demanded sanctions against Portugal. Since 1909, 'slave cocoa' has been boycotted by English and German importers.

Even if slavery was being regularly unmasked and condemned, it remained nonetheless a fact that Portuguese farmers could not produce cocoa without slave labour. In 1903, the Portuguese government published a decree regulating the emigration of Blacks from Angola, Mozambique and Cape Verde Islands to the plantations of Sao Tome e Principe. It was meant to give the appearance of a 'free' emigration of 'free citizens' from one 'province' to another belonging to the same country. But this 'free' man-power would miraculously replace slave man-power.

Human habitation of the archipelago is quite recent. It is known that the arrival of Joao de Santarem and Pedro Escobar in 1471 marked the first human contact with the two Atlantic islands. Settlement began in 1485 with the French, the Genvese, the Spanish, the deported Portuguese and Jews evicted from Castile, and the Black slaves from Guinea, the Congo and Benin.

The archipelago today has its own population, resulting from the cross-breeding of Whites with Blacks or Africans who remained on the island. It also comprises elements of European and African origin born on the islands, as well as a group of residents from Portugal or from other colonies which is more or less temporary in character.

In the Black population, there can be distinguished the following groups:

(1) Emancipated ones: descendants from former freed slaves;

(2) Angolares: descendants from Angolans, coming undoubtedly from some region on the coast in the 16th century;

(3) Tongas: offspring of slaves born on the plantations. They first appear in the beginning of the modern period of land cultivation.

2. The Road to Armed Struggle

Editors' Introduction

All the national liberation movements in Portuguese and southern Africa started off by seeking to achieve change peacefully, by the pure route of dialogue and persuasion. All without exception found after a while that this route was foreclosed to them by those who held power.

The violence of conquest was repeated in the violence of suppression of protest. Each movement paid its price, found its adherents massacred in the course of a public demonstration or a strike. Each took stock and made the analyses of the nature of their colonial situation we have found in Part I of this book. Each concluded that the only road to national liberation open to them was the road of armed struggle.

It was not that they rejected dialogue. Rather they found regretfully that it was only via armed struggle that one day a real dialogue of colonizer and colonized would be possible, a dialogue rendered possible by the equalizing impact of military combat.

While each movement ended at the same point, each came to it via a different logic and thus each felt it necessary to explain publicly the particular route it has taken.

The decision was particularly hard for the three countries that had a contact with the British parliamentary tradition — South Africa, Namibia and Zimbabwe. It was not that Africans were ever allowed to play a meaningful role in the local parliaments. It was rather that the values and the style of parliamentary struggle were persuasive in the society. Thus the ANC in South Africa had to overcome a long commitment to non-violence. How and why they did so is clear from the successive statements of Chief Luthuli in 1952 and 1964, Nelson Mandela in 1962, and Oliver Tambo in 1968. Furthermore they had to reconcile their views with the ideas and influence of Mahatma Gandhi who developed his theme of *satyagraha* not in India but in South Africa. As for the PAC, it was born in the very resolve to do away with 'equivocation and clever talk' as Mangaliso Sobukwe expressed it.

The thinking of SWAPO was eloquently reflected in the now famous defence of Toivo Ja Toivo during his trial in 1968. In the case of Zimbabwe, both ZAPU and ZANU expressed themselves vigorously and clearly on this issue, a unity of views which enabled them in 1972 to set up a Joint Military

Command.

In many ways, the road was easier for the movements in Portuguese Africa. Since theirs was from the start the path of clandestinity, they had fewer compunctions to overcome. Nonetheless, they did make the effort to see if peaceful reform were possible. Amilcar Cabral explained this in a message to his people in 1965, and later in 1970, he again patiently explained this to a group of US Congressmen. In the case of Angola, the efforts were reflected in the message sent to the Portuguese people in 1960, the letters Agostinho Neto sent from restricted residence in 1960, the interview he gave in 1962, and in an article in an MPLA journal in 1969. As for the UPA, their views were clear from the editorial on the front page of the first issue of their journal in 1962. FRELIMO indicated its position in the message to the Portuguese sent in 1962, followed by the proclamation they issued when they launched the armed struggle.

The Road to Freedom is Via the Cross
Albert Lutuli

> *Public statement by Chief Albert Lutuli in November 1952*
> *when the Government dismissed him from his position as Chief*
> *for refusing to resign from the African National Congress, of*
> *which he was then the President.*

I have been dismissed from the Chieftainship of the Abase-Makolweni Tribe in the Groutville Mission Reserve. I presume that this has been done by the Governor-General in his capacity as Supreme Chief of the 'Native' people of the Union of South Africa save those of the Cape Province. I was democratically elected to this position in 1935 by the people of the Groutville Mission Reserve and was duly approved and appointed by the Governor-General.

Previous to being a chief I was a school teacher for about seventeen years. In these past thirty years or so I have striven with tremendous zeal and patience to work for the progress and welfare of my people and for their harmonious relations with other sections of our multi-racial society in the Union of South Africa. In this effort I always pursued what liberal-minded people rightly regarded as the path of moderation. Over this great length of time I have, year after year, gladly spent hours of my time with such organizations of the Church – and its various agencies such as the Christian Council of South Africa, the Joint Council of Europeans and Africans and the now defunct Native Representative Council.

In so far as gaining citizenship rights and opportunities for the unfettered development of the African people, who will deny that thirty years of my life have been spent knocking in vain, patiently, moderately and modestly at a closed and barred door?

What have been the fruits of my many years of moderation? Has there been any reciprocal tolerance or moderation from the Government, be it Nationalist or United Party? No! On the contrary, the past thirty years have seen the greatest number of laws restricting our rights and progress until today we have reached a stage where we have almost no rights at all: no adequate land for our occupation, our only asset, cattle, dwindling, no security of homes, no decent and remunerative employment, more restriction to freedom of movement through passes, curfew regulations, influx control measures; in short, we have witnessed in these years an intensification of our subjection to ensure and protect white supremacy.

It is with this background and with a full sense of responsibility that, under the auspices of the African National Congress (Natal), I have joined my people in the new spirit that moves them today, the spirit that revolts openly and boldly against injustice and expresses itself in a determined and non-violent manner. Because of my association with the African National Congress in this new spirit which has found an effective and legitimate way of expression in the non-violent Passive Resistance Campaign, I was given a two week limit ultimatum by the Secretary for Native Affairs calling upon me to choose between the African National Congress and the chieftainship of the Groutville Mission Reserve. He alleged that my association with Congress in its non-violent Passive Resistance Campaign was an act of disloyalty to the State. I did not agree with this view. Viewing non-violent Passive Resistance as a non-revolutionary and, therefore, a most legitimate and humane political pressure technique for a people denied all effective forms of constitutional striving, I saw no real conflict in my dual leadership of my people.

I saw no cause to resign from either. This stand of mine, which resulted in my being sacked from the chieftainship, might seem foolish and disappointing to some liberal and moderate Europeans and non-Europeans with whom I have worked these many years and with whom I still hope to work. This is no parting of the ways but 'a launching farther into the deep'. I invite them to join us in our unequivocal pronouncement of all legitimate African aspirations and in our firm stand against injustice and oppression.

Servant of the People

I do not wish to challenge my dismissal, but I would like to suggest that in the interest of the institution of chieftainship in these modern times of democracy, the Government should define more precisely and make more widely known the status, functions and privileges of chiefs. My view has been, and still is, that a chief is primarily a servant of his people. He is the voice of his people. He is the voice of his people in local affairs. Unlike a Native Commissioner, he is part and parcel of the Tribe, and not a local agent of the Government. Within the bounds of loyalty it is conceivable that he may vote and press the claims of his people even if they should be unpalatable to the Government of the day. He may use all legitimate modern techniques to get these demands satisfied. It is inconceivable how chiefs could effectively serve the wider and common interest of their own tribe without cooperating with other leaders of

35

the people, both the natural leaders (chiefs) and leaders elected democratically by the people themselves.

It was to allow for these wider associations and intended to promote the common national interests of the people as against purely local interests that the Government, in making rules governing chiefs, did not debar them from joining political associations so long as those associations had not been declared 'by the Minister to be subversive of or prejudicial to constituted Government'. The African National Congress, its non-violent Passive Resistance Campaign, may be a nuisance value to the Government but it is not subversive since it does not seek to overthrow the form and machinery of the State but only urges for the inclusion of all sections of the community in a partnership in the Government of the country on the basis of equality.

Spirit of Defiance

Laws and conditions that tend to debase human personality — a God-given force — be they brought about by the State or other individuals, must be relentlessly opposed in the spirit of defiance shown by St. Peter when he said to the rulers of his day: 'Shall we obey God or Man?' No one can deny that in so far as non-Whites are concerned in the Union of South Africa, laws and conditions that debase human personality abound. Any chief worthy of his position must fight fearlessly against such debasing conditions and laws. If the Government should resort to dismissing such chiefs, it may find itself dismissing many chiefs or causing people to dismiss from their hearts chiefs who are indifferent to the needs of the people through fear of dismissal by the Government. Surely the Government cannot place chiefs in such an uncomfortable and invidious position.

Will Remain in the Struggle for a True Democracy

As for myself, with a full sense of responsibility and a clear conviction, I decided to remain in the struggle for extending democratic rights and responsibilities to all sections of the South African community. I have embraced the non-violent Passive Resistance technique in fighting for freedom because I am convinced it is the only non-revolutionary, legitimate and humane way that could be used by people denied, as we are, effective constitutional means to further aspirations.

The wisdom or foolishness of this decision I place in the hands of the Almighty.

What the future has in store for me I do not know. It might be ridicule, imprisonment, concentration camp, flogging, banishment and even death. I only pray to the Almighty to strengthen my resolve so that none of these grim possibilities may deter me from striving, for the sake of the good name of our beloved country, the Union of South Africa, to make it a true democracy and a true union in form and spirit of all the communities in the land. My only painful concern at times is that of the welfare of my family but I try even in this regard, in a spirit of trust and surrender to God's will as I see it, to say 'God will provide'.

It is inevitable that in working for freedom some individuals and some families must take the lead and suffer: The Road to Freedom is via the cross. Mayibuye!
Africa! Africa! Africa!

Why We Had to Act
Nelson Mandela

*Excerpt of Mandela's statement to the Court on
22 November 1962.*

Throughout its fifty years of existence the African National Congress, for instance, has done everything possible to bring its demands to the attention of successive South African Governments. It has sought at all times peaceful solutions for all the country's ills and problems. The history of the ANC is filled with instances where deputations were sent to South African Governments either on specific issues or on the general political demands of our people. I do not wish to burden Your Worship by enunciating the occasions when such deputations were sent; all that I wish to indicate at this stage is that, in addition to the efforts made by former presidents of the ANC, when Mr. Strijdom became Prime Minister of this country, my leader, Chief A.J. Luthuli, then President of our organization, made yet another effort to persuade this Government to consider and to heed our point of view. In his letter to the Prime Minister at the time, Chief Luthuli exhaustively reviewed the country's relations and its dangers, and expressed the view that a meeting between the Government and African leaders had become necessary and urgent.

This statesmanlike and correct behaviour on the part of the leader of the majority of the South African population did not find an appropriate answer from the leader of the South African Government. The standard of behaviour of the South African Government towards my people and its aspirations, has not always been what it should have been, and is not always the standard which is to be expected in serious high-level dealings between civilized peoples. Chief Luthuli's letter was not even favoured with the courtesy of an acknowledgement from the Prime Minister's office.

This experience was repeated after the Pietermaritzburg conference, when I, as Secretary of the Action Council, elected at that conference, addressed a letter to the Prime Minister, Dr. Verwoerd, informing him of the resolution which had been taken, and calling on him to initiate steps for the convening of such a national convention as we suggested, before the date specified in the resolution. In a civilized country one would be outraged by the failure of the head of Government even to acknowledge receipt of a letter, or to consider such a reasonable request put to him by a broadly representative collection of important personalities and leaders of the most important community of the country, of the most numerous community of the country. Once again, Government standards in dealing with my people fell below what the civilized world would expect. No reply, no response whatsoever, was received to our letter, no indication was even given that it had received any consideration whatsoever. Here we, the African people, and especially we of the National Action Council, who had been entrusted with the tremendous responsibility of safeguarding the interests of the African people, were faced with this conflict between the law and our conscience. In the face of the complete failure of the Government to heed, to consider, or even to respond to our seriously proposed objections and our solutions to the forthcoming Republic, what were we to do? Were we to allow the law, which states that you shall not commit an offence by way of protest, to take its course and thus betray our conscience and our belief? Were we to uphold our conscience and our beliefs to strive for what we believe is right, not just for us, but for all the people who live in this country, both the present generation and for generations to come, and thus transgress against the law? This is the dilemma which faced us and in such a dilemma, men of honesty, men of purpose and men of public morality and of conscience can only have one answer. They must follow the dictates of their conscience irrespective of the consequences which might overtake them for it. We of the Action Council, and I particularly, as Secretary, followed my conscience.

If I had my time over I would do the same again, so would any man who dares call himself a man. We went ahead with our campaign as instructed by the Conference and in accordance with its decisions.

I wish again to return to the question of why people like me, knowing all this, knowing in advance that this Government is incapable of progressive democratic moves, so far as our people are concerned, knowing that this Government is incapable of reacting towards us in any way other than by the use of overwhelming brute force, why I, and people like me, nevertheless, decide to go ahead to do what we must. We have been conditioned to our attitudes by the history which is not of our making. We have been conditioned by the history of White Governments in this country to accept the fact that Africans, when they make their demands strongly and powerfully enough to have some chance of success, will be met by force and terror on the part of the Government. This is not something we have taught the African people, this is something the African people have learned from their own bitter experience. We learned it from each successive Government. We learned it from the Government of General Smuts at the time of two massacres of our people: the 1921 massacre in Bulhoek when more than 100 men, women and children were killed, and from the 1923 massacre — the Bondelswart massacre in South West Africa, in which some 200 Africans were killed. We have continued to learn it from every successive Government.

Government violence can do only one thing and that is to breed counter-violence. We have warned repeatedly that the Government, by resorting continually to violence will breed, in this country, counter-violence amongst the people, till ultimately, if there is no dawning of sanity on the part of the Government – ultimately, the dispute between the Government and my people will finish up by being settled in violence and by force. Already there are indications in this country that people, my people, Africans, are turning to deliberate acts of violence and of force against the Government, in order to persuade the Government, in the only language which this Government shows, by its own behaviour, that it understands.

Elsewhere in the world, a Court would say to me 'You should have made representations to the Government'. This Court, I am confident, will not say so. Representations have been made, by people who have gone before me, time and time again. Representations were made in this case by me; I do not want again to repeat the experience of those representations. The Court cannot expect a respect for the processes of representation and negotiation to grow amongst the African people, when the Government shows every day, by its conduct, that it despises such processes and frowns upon them and will not indulge in them. Nor will the Court, I believe, say that, under the circumstances, my people are condemned forever to say nothing and to do nothing. If the Court says that, or believes it, I think it is mistaken and deceiving itself. Men are not capable of doing nothing, of saying nothing, of not reacting to injustice, of not protesting against oppression, of not striving for the good society and the good life in the ways they see it. Nor will they do so in this country.

Perhaps the Court will say that despite our human rights to protest, to object, to make ourselves heard, we should stay within the letter of the law. I would say, Sir, that it is the Government, its administration of the law, which brings the law into such contempt and disrepute that one is no longer concerned in this country to stay within the letter of the law. I will illustrate this from my own experience. The Government has used the process of law to handicap me, in my personal life, in my career and in my political work, in a way which is calculated, in my opinion, to bring about a contempt for the law. In December, 1952, I was issued with an order by the Government, not as the result of a trial before a Court and a conviction, but as a result of prejudice, or perhaps Star Chamber procedure behind closed doors in the halls of Government. In terms of that order I was confined to the Magisterial district of Johannesburg for six months and, at the same time, I was prohibited from attending gatherings for a similar period. That order expired in June 1953, and three months thereafter, again without any hearing, without any attempt to hear my side of the case, without facing me with charges or explanations, both bans were renewed for a further period of two years. To these bans a third was added: I was ordered by the Minister of Justice to resign altogether from the African National Congress and never again to become a member of to participate in its activities. Towards the end of 1955, I found myself free and able to move around once again, but not for long. In February 1956, the bans were again renewed, administratively, again without hearing, this time for five years. Again, by order of the Government, in the name of the law, I found myself restricted and isolated from my fellow men, from people who think like me and believe like me. I found myself trailed by officers of the Security Branch of the Police Force wherever I went. In short I found myself treated as a criminal — an unconvicted criminal. I was not allowed to pick my company, to frequent the company of men, to participate in their political activities, to join their organizations. I was not free from constant police surveillance. I was made, by the law, a criminal, not because of what I had done, but because of what I stood for, because of what I thought, because of my conscience. Can it be any wonder to anybody that such conditions make a man an outlaw of society? Can it be wondered that such a man, having been outlawed by the Government, should be prepared to lead the life of an outlaw, as I have led for some months, according to the evidence before this Court?

It has not been easy for me during the past period to separate myself from my wife and children, to say goodbye to the good old days when, at the end of a strenuous day at an office, I could look forward to joining my family at the dinner-table, and instead to take up the life of a man hunted continuously by the police, living separated from those who are closest to me, in my own country, facing continually the hazards of detection and of arrest. This has been a life infinitely more difficult than serving a prison sentence. No man in his right senses would voluntarily choose such a life in preference to the one of normal, family, social life which exists in every civilized community.

But there comes a time, as it came in my life, when a man is denied the right to live a normal life, when he can only live the life of an outlaw because the Government has so decredd to use the law to impose a state of outlawry upon him. I was driven to this situation, and I do not regret having taken the decisions that I did take.

On the Rivonia Trial
Albert Lutuli

> *Statement issued on 12 June 1964 when Nelson Mandela,*
> *Walter Sisulu and six other leaders were sentenced to life*
> *imprisonment in the 'Rivonia Trial'.*

Sentences of life imprisonment have been pronounced on Nelson Mandela, Walter Sisulu, Ahmed Kathrada, Govan Mbeki, Dennis Goldberg, Raymond Mhlaba, Elias Motsoaledi and Andrew Mlangeni in the 'Rivonia trial' in Pretoria. Over the long years these leaders advocated a policy of racial co-operation, of goodwill, and of peaceful struggle that made the South African liberation movement one of the most ethical and responsible of our time. In the face of the most bitter racial persecution, they resolutely set themselves against racialism; in the face of continued provocation, they consistently chose the path of reason. The African National Congress, with allied organisations representing all racial sections, sought every possible means of redress for intolerable conditions, and held consistently to a policy of using militant, non-violent means of struggle. Their common aim was to create a South Africa in which all South Africans would live and work together as fellow-citizens, enjoying equal rights without discrimination on grounds of race, colour or creed.

To this end, they used every accepted method: propaganda, public meetings and rallies, petitions, stay-at-home-strikes, appeals, boycotts. So carefully did they educate the people that in the four-year-long Treason Trial, one police witness after another voluntarily testified to this emphasis on non-violent methods of struggle in all aspects of their activities.

But finally all avenues of resistance were closed. The African National Congress and other organisations were made illegal; their leaders jailed, exiled or forced underground. The government sharpened its oppression of the peoples of South Africa, using its all-white Parliament as the vehicle for making repression legal, and utilising every weapon of this highly industrialised and modern state to enforce that 'legality'. The stage was even reached where a white spokesman for the disenfranchised Africans was regarded by the Government as a traitor. In addition, sporadic acts of uncontrolled violence were increasing throughout the country. At first in one place, then in another, there were spontaneous eruptions against intolerable conditions, many of these acts increasingly assumed a racial character.

The African National Congress never abandoned its method of a militant, non-violent struggle, and of creating in the process a spirit of militancy in the people. However, in the face of the uncompromising white refusal to abandon a policy which denies the African and other oppressed South Africans their rightful heritage — freedom — no one can blame brave just men for seeking justice by the use of violent methods; nor could they be blamed if they tried to create an organised force in order to ultimately establish peace and racial harmony.

For this, they are sentenced to be shut away for long years in the brutal and degrading prisons of South Africa. With them will be interred this country's hopes for racial cooperation. They will leave a vacuum in leadership that may only be filled by bitter hate and racial strife.

They represent the highest in morality and ethics in the South African political struggle; this morality and ethics has been sentenced to an imprisonment it may never survive. Their policies are in accordance with the deepest international principles of brotherhood and humanity; without their leadership, brotherhood and humanity may be blasted out of existence in South Africa for long decades to come. They believe profoundly in justice and reason; when they are locked away, justice and reason will have departed from the South African scene.

This is an appeal to save these men, not merely as individuals, but for what they stand for. In the name of justice, of hope, of truth and of peace, I appeal to South Africa's strongest allies, Britain and America. In the name of what we have come to believe Britain and America stand for, I appeal to those two powerful countries to take decisive action for full-scale action for sanctions that would precipitate the end of the hateful system of apartheid.

I appeal to all governments throughout the world, to people everywhere, to organisations and institutions in every land and at every level, to act now to impose such sanctions on South Africa that will bring about the vital necessary change and avert what can become the greatest African tragedy of our times.

Call to Revolution
Oliver Tambo

Excerpt from New Year Message from the Acting President-General of the ANC (South Africa) on 1 January 1968.

We have not embarked on our present struggle lightly. We know that the revolution in South Africa will be a long and bitter one calling for maximum sacrifices from all lovers of freedom. Yet our national organization with full support of the vast majority of the nation has chosen this path as essential if we are to lead our country out of the nightmare of White oppression.

The founders of our nation – Seme, Makgatho, Montsioa, Mangena, Mapikela, Plaatje, Dube and others – taught us that the African people were conquered because the Europeans had the guns and were better organised. In addition, our forefathers fought separately and divided. In this way the Whites were able to defeat our peoples one by one. Therefore we had to concentrate first on removing the divisions among ourselves and creating a single African nation owing allegiance to one organization – the African National Congress.

Throughout the last 55 years the ANC has sacrificed everything in the cause of African unity. In addition our people fought in many different ways against oppression and for freedom.

The White government of South Africa treated all the demands and struggles of our people with contempt, because they had armed might on their side. All peaceful methods of drawing attention to our grievances were ruthlessly abolished. The methods used to crush the national strike of May 1961 showed that the White minority was determined to maintain itself in power by force.

It was then clear that the African and other oppressed people could not hope to achieve their freedom except by organizing their own liberation army and arming the masses to fight a revolutionary war of liberation.

Revolution calls for supreme vigilance, organization and capacity to sacrifice. The movement needs men and women willing to fight and to perform all the tasks of war. In the political sphere we need organizers, propagandists and activists who will spread the message of struggle all over the country, in towns, rural areas and farms. Men and Women, Students, Workers, Peasants, religious people – all must join the struggle and find a place in it.

Special responsibility in the revolution will rest on our splendid youth who have already shown that they are capable of great deeds. The armed struggle will require that our young men and women prepare themselves to learn the arts and skills of war and then to fight with arms in hand for freedom. This will be a great challenge to the Youth, on whom the nation depends for victory in the revolution.

We in the African National Congress do not imagine that the defeat of imperialism in Southern Africa will be quick or easy. We realise it will be longdrawn and bloody. But we are confident of the final outcome. As our forces drive deeper into the south, we have no doubt that they will be joined not by some but by the whole African nation; by the oppressed minorities, the Indian and Coloured people; and by an increasing number of White democrats.

The battle lines have been drawn up. There can be but one result: victory over the fascist oppressors and the establishment of a democratic state in South Africa! Towards this victory we will fight to the bitter end. Our battle cry is and shall continue to be:

Victory or Death! We Shall Win!
Long Live The Armed Struggle of the People for Freedom
Amandla Ngawethu! Maatla Ke A Rona!

From Gandhi to Mandela
ANC

Article in Sechaba *(ANC), III, 5, May 1969, written in commemoration of the 75th Anniversary of the formation of the Natal Indian Congress by Mahatma Gandhi.*

Where the choice is set between cowardice and violence I would advise violence. I praise and extol the serene courage of dying without killing. Yet I desire that those who have not this courage should rather cultivate the art of killing and being killed, than basely to avoid the danger. This is because he who runs away commits mental violence; he has not the courage of facing death by killing. I would a thousand times prefer violence than the emasculation of a whole race. I prefer to use arms in defence of honour rather than remain the vile witness of dishonour. (Mahatma Gandhi, Declaration on question of the use of violence in defence of rights, *Guardian,* 16 December 1938).

At the beginning of June 1961, after a long and anxious assessment of the South African situation, I, and some colleagues, came to the conclusion that as violence in this country was inevitable, it would be

unrealistic and wrong for African leaders to continue preaching peace and non-violence at a time when the Government met our peaceful demands with force. This conclusion was not easily arrived at. It was only when all else had failed, when all channels of peaceful protest had been barred to us, that the decision was made to embark on violent forms of political struggle, and to form Umkonto We Sizwe [The Spear of the Nation]. We did so not because we desired such a course, but solely because the Government had left us with no other choice.
(Nelson Mandela, in his speech during the Rivonia Trial, 1963-64).

This year the world joins in commemorating the centenary of one of the greatest men that ever lived — Mohandas Karamchand Gandhi. It is also the 75th year of the foundation by Gandhi of the Natal Indian Congress, which was later part of the South African Indian Congress. All its main leaders are virtually proscribed by the Fascist government of South Africa. It is a commentary on the situation in South Africa that it will constitute a serious risk to the people of our country to endeavour to pay any proper homage to the memory of Mahatma Gandhi because of possible retaliation by the government. The ruling Fascist party has always hated everything Gandhi ever stood for.

It is only natural that in this anniversary most attention was to be paid to the role and contribution of Mahatma Gandhi to the independence of mighty India. Yet no South African can forget the year 1893 when Gandhi landed at Durban. The future Mahatma was a young, foppishly dressed, English-trained barrister who had come to South Africa to handle his first big civil case. It did not take long for Gandhi to discover that he was a member of an oppressed community and he was treated to all the insults and even beatings that non-whites were subjected to.

He was about to return to Indian in 1894 when, at the farewell party held in his honour someone handed him a copy of the Natal Mercury. The Natal Legislative Assembly had been debating a new law to disenfranchise Indians. Gandhi agreed to stay in South Africa a little longer to help fight this new law. As it happened he was to remain in the country another twenty years before he returned to India in 1914.

The Legacy of Gandhi

Like all great historical figures, Mahatma Gandhi was a very controversial man. For centuries men will try and assess his true legacy. What is certain is that he moved millions and millions of people to act for freedom and dignity against imperialism. Gandhi himself considered his work a 'search for truth'; he called his autobiography *The Story of My Experiments with Truth*. It is unnecessary for our purposes to examine Gandhi's philosophy, which derived largely from his religious beliefs. The main field of Gandhi's activity was politics; it is here that the role of the Mahatma is to be sought.

Space does not allow us to give an account of Gandhi's struggles in South Africa. But he led the Indian people in demonstrations, marches, strikes and passive resistance campaigns which involved courting imprisonment. Gandhi himself did not like the phrase 'passive resistance' and argued strongly against its use to refer to campaigns he led. He preferred the word 'Satyagraha' which meant soul-force. The real point is that he organised the masses of the people in struggles which had to be strictly non-violent. There is no doubt that Gandhi's campaigns both in South Africa and India showed that there was tremendous potential in his method for rousing the masses and organising them. Yet the method also caused undue power to be placed in the hands of the leadership to curb and take away the initiative of the masses if they so wished. Mass pressure combined with negotiation and compromise seemed the essence of the Gandhian political method. To disarm the masses in the face of an enemy determined to rule by force is a problem that Gandhi never really resolved except by extremely abstruse reasoning.

Violence Not Ruled Out

Perhaps it was when confronted by such phenomena as fascism and imperialism that Gandhi had to concede that there were circumstances in which violent struggle would be justifiable. It is overwhelmingly in the literature of the imperialist world that one finds unqualified non-violence as the specific contribution of Gandhi to political method. No doubt we will be hearing nothing else from the imperialists during this centenary year.

But Gandhi himself felt that violence was preferable to cowardice and dishonour. More than this no serious revolutionary has ever put forward. Every freedom fighter would prefer to achieve liberty and social progress by peaceful means and history has proved that the masses have generally been patient almost to a fault before resorting to armed struggle.

After the departure of Gandhi to India in 1914 a deep void existed in the Indian political scene; the African National Congress had been formed two years earlier. Although he had been in the country twenty years' Gandhi's links with the African people had been slight. Years later Gandhi was to express regret at this. On the other hand some revolutionaries have felt that it was not an entirely unhappy mistake as it meant the African liberation movement never absorbed some of the more unacceptable aspects of Gandhian philosophy.

But even among the Indian people the absence of Gandhi left a vacuum which was filled by an opportunistic leadership. The militant mass activities were abandoned. In their place were endless conferences, compromises, court cases and retreats.

It is the events in India which now became the centre of attraction. It was from there that a new generation of South African politicians gained the inspiration to resume once more the Gandhi tradition. Of these young men the most outstanding was Yusuf Dadoo, a well-known Communist, whose assumption of leadership in the South African Indian Congress Mahatma Gandhi himself approved against the protests of conservative elements in the community. In fact Dr. Dadoo was for many years Gandhi's personal correspondent on South African affairs. Another was Dr. G.M. Naicker, President of the Natal Indian Congress, who has been and still is a staunch Gandhite.

The historic victory over fascism by the Soviet Union and other countries in the Second World War laid the basis for the great advance to national liberation and independence in India, China and many countries of the third world. The Dadoo-Naicker leadership of the South African Indian Congress had a platform which differed somewhat from that of Mahatma Gandhi thirty years earlier. Yet it was widely acclaimed as a return of the Gandhi tradition. The SAIC now called for unity of all the oppressed people in South Africa, militant mass struggle and international solidarity with all peoples fighting for progress in the world. In 1946 the Passive Resistance struggle was launched by the SAIC against the so-called Ghetto Act which introduced restrictions on the ownership of land by Indians. Thousands participated in this campaign. Although there was much admiration for the Indian community the other oppressed people did not participate in the campaign. In the same year the great miners' strike of Africans took place which helped to remove the sense of isolation of the SAIC campaign.

From then it followed naturally that the trend should more and more lead to co-operation among the oppressed. In 1947 the leaders of the African National Congress and the SAIC signed a pact of co-operation on common issues. This was cemented in the great campaigns for the Defiance of Unjust Laws and the Congress of the People. In 1955 the Freedom Charter became the common programme of all the progressive organisations in South Africa.

During the discussions on the campaign for the Defiance of Unjust Laws there had been some debate on whether or not the Gandhi ideas and methods were being followed as a principle. In the result the Gandhi methods of civil disobedience, hartal, forms of mass organisation were borrowed from. But the ideas of Satyagraha in the Gandhian mould were rejected as not being in accord with the specific situation.

The attitude of the Fascists to any forms of struggle including those of Gandhi were clearly indicated in the monstrous Suppression of Communism Act of 1950. It was 'communism' in South Africa to prosecute any struggle by the kind of methods used by Gandhi and the penalties for 'advocating' such methods carried a penalty of ten years' imprisonment. As more and more repression was forced on the people of South Africa the question of new forms of struggle came to the fore.

It was Nelson Mandela, now serving life imprisonment on Robben Island, who gave clear and public voice to the widespread feeling that non-military methods of struggle had reached the end of their tether. This was in May 1961. By December of that year Umkonto We Sizwe (the Spear of the Nation) announced its formation. The preparations for armed struggle began which culminated in the beginning of guerrilla war in Zimbabwe in August 1967. The guerrilla war will gradually develop until the whole of Southern Africa becomes a theatre of fierce armed revolutionary wars.

Gandhi Contradicted?
The main blow of the Gandhian campaigns was directed at those forces which

dominate other people. He was a Nationalist and patriot. Yet he showed considerable concern for the conditions and welfare of the village peasants of India. Many of his ideas seemed to lack revolutionary consistency although it is now suggested that he was limited by the forces and colleagues who surrounded him in the leadership of the Indian Congress. He stood for unity and refused to take up any attitude of hostility to ideas which he did not accept such as Communism.

In the light of his life and work the South African revolutionaries consider that in taking up arms against the fascists they are not acting in contradiction to Gandhi. On the contrary the armed struggle is a challenge to all those who prefer freedom to cowardice to join in the fight.

When Gandhi died at the hands of a religious fanatic in 1947, Jawaharlal Nehru said 'a light had gone out'. For the people of South Africa who had special links with Gandhi the tragedy had a particular poignancy.

Today under the shadow of the Fascist terror machine a few people might repair to the settlement at Phoenix, Inanda, just outside Durban. Some cultural activity on a small scale might be arranged. It is not easy to imagine more happening. With thousands of activists and leaders imprisoned, and countless others underground and fighting as guerrillas, the anniversary of Mahatma Gandhi might pass by with barely a ripple in South Africa. This will be a purely surface condition. If the masses were to be free to do so they would commemorate the life of Mahatma in a fitting manner. We have not forgotten his example.

The State of the Nation
Mangaliso Sobukwe

An address by the President of the Pan-Africanist Congress of Azania (South Africa) three months after the founding of the PAC in July 1959.

Mr. Speaker Sir, Sons and Daughters of Afrika: just over three months ago, on the 6th April, we met in the Communial Hall in Orlando, Johannesburg, to launch the ship of freedom — the Pan Africanist Congress. On that historic day, the African people declared total war against white domination, not only in South Afrika but throughout the continent. On that day there entered into the maelstrom of South African politics an organization dedicated to the cause of African emancipation and independence; an organisation committed to the over-throw of white supremacy and the establishment of an Africanist Socialist Democracy.

Oppressed Versus Oppressor
It is just over three months that the Pan Africanist Congress has been born,

but within that short space of time she has successfully pinpointed the basic assumption in our struggle, namely that:

(1) The illiterate and semi-literate masses of the African people are the key, the core and cornerstone of the struggle for democracy in this country.

(2) African nationalism is the only liberatory creed that can weld these masses who are members of heterogeneous tribes into a solid, disciplined and united fighting force; provide them with a loyalty higher than that of the tribe, and give them formal expression to their desire to be a nation.

(3) The struggle in South Afrika is part of the greater struggle throughout the continent for the restoration to the African people of the effective control of their land. The ultimate goal of our struggle, therefore, is the formation of a United States of Afrika.

These pronouncements have struck a responsive chord in the hearts of the Sons and Daughters of the land, and awakened the imagination of the youth of our land while giving hope to the aged who for years have lived in the trough of despair. Indeed, the aged can now truly say, 'Lord now lettest Thou thy servant depart in peace, according to Thy will, for mine eyes have seen Thy salvation'.

The issues are clear-cut. The Pan Africanist Congress has done away with equivocation and clever talk. The decks are cleared, and in the arena of South African politics there are today only two adversaries: the oppressor and the oppressed, the master and the slave. We are on the eve of a continental showdown between the forces of evil and the forces of righteousness; the champions of oppression and the champions of freedom. Realising this, the oppressor is panic-stricken and is making feverish preparations for a last-ditch stand in defence of white supremacy. On the other hand, the forces of freedom are gathering strength from day to day, disciplining, nerving and steeling themselves for the imminent struggle.

Afrika for the Africans

Once again, as in 1949, the African people are waiting expectantly and eagerly the emergence of a bold and courageous programme from the PAC — an organisation that has its roots among the masses, and whose leadership comes from their loins. Not only has PAC succeeded in raising the eyes of our people above the dust of immediate conflict to the genuine democracy that lies beyond the stormy sea of struggle, but it has also imparted a meaning and a purpose to their struggle. The African people, therefore, are awake! They are waiting; waiting eagerly and expectantly; waiting for the call; the call to battle — to battle for the reconquest of the continent of Afrika which for over 300 years has been the prostitute of the philanderers and rakes of western capitalism. *'Mayibuye i Afrika'*, that is the cry ringing throughout the continent. Afrika for the Africans! *Izwe lethu — i Afrika!* Those are the words that spell the doom of white supremacy in Afrika.

Position in the Continent

Throughout the continent of Afrika the struggle is being relentlessly waged against the historical anachronisms of imperialism, colonialism and white supremacy. Precious African blood is flowing in Algeria where the Sons and Daughters of Afrika, under the courageous leadership of Ferhat Abbas of the government of Free Algeria, are paying the supreme sacrifice for the recovery of the destroyed shrines.

Greater and greater efforts are being made by the independent countries of Afrika to mould, shape and assert the African personality, and to lay the foundations for a United States of Afrika. Just recently the heads of the States of Ghana, Guinea and Liberia met in conference to discuss methods of furthering the cause of Pan Africanism.

In Tanganyika, Nyerere is fighting for the revision of the multiracial constitution imposed on the African people by imperialist Britain, and is pressing for the practical application of the democratic principle of 'one man one vote'. In Uganda, as our Bulletin stated, 'British imperialism is locked in mortal combat with African nationalism'. In Central Afrika tension is high and there is clear evidence that in the struggle between Kamuzu Banda and Roy Welensky Banda will emerge triumphant. In fact, the signs are that not only Nyasaland but Northern Rhodesia as well, will secede from the unholy federation of Welensky and Lennox-Boyd.

South Afrika

Throughout Afrika, then, the forces of white supremacy are in retreat before the irresistible march of African nationalism. This is the era of African emancipation. Afrika holds the stage today. For the first time, positive action is being taken by the world against the inhuman policies of South Africa's white, foreign minority governments. And the countries that have taken the lead in this world-wide boycott of South African goods are the countries of Afrika and those governed by people of African descent. And in South Africa, what is the position? Well you all know, that there has been talk from certain quarters of 'hitting the nationalists in the stomach'. We would have used the word 'belly', but responsible, moderate leaders, you see, do not use such ugly words! There was such talk then, and lists were prepared. But immediately one so-called 'nationalist concern' made certain sectional trade union concessions, it was no longer a nationalist-controlled firm, and its products were no longer nationalist products. The old, meaningless stunts are still being used by certain quarters. But there is the boycott of beerhalls launched by the courageous women of Durban — a movement originating from the masses and controlled by them. Nobody doubts its success. The evidence is there for all to see. If their 'friends' do not interfere with the Durban women they will undoubtedly achieve their goal — of acquiring for the Africans of Durban the status of human beings. There is also the potato boycott which, while commanding the active support of all Africans because of the atrocious evil perpetrated by white farmers against African convict labourers, has unfortunately been handled by the quarters aforementioned. The result has been that those quarters, which fear the militancy of the African people more than they loathe oppression, are hoping and praying that the boycott will fizzle out before they are compelled to call it off.

What of the Pan Africanist Congress?
We are met here today to commemorate our National Heroes' Day. We are, today, going down the corridor of time and renewing our acquaintance with the heroes of Africa's past — those men and women who nourished the tree of African freedom and independence with their blood; those great Sons and Daughters of Afrika who died in order that we may be free in the land of our birth. We are met here, today, to rededicate our lives to the cause of Afrika, to establish contact, beyond the grave, with the great African heroes and to assure them that their struggle was not in vain. We are met here, Sons and Daughters of our beloved land, to drink from the fountain of African achievement, to remember the men and women who begot us, to remind ourselves of where we come from and to restate our goals. We are here to draw inspiration from the heroes of Thaba Bosiu, Isandlwana, Sandile's Kop, Keiskama Hoek and numerous other battlefields where our forefathers fell before the bullets of the foreign invader. We are here to draw inspiration from the Sons and Daughters of Afrika who gave their all to the cause and were physically broken in the struggle. We are met here, Sons and Daughters of Afrika, to take a trowel in our right hand and a shield and sword in our left, to commence the tremendous task of rebuilding the walls of Afrika!

We are gathered here, today, to reiterate our resolve to declare total war against the demi-god of white supremacy. We are here to say Afrika must be free and will be free by 1963. We are here to serve an ultimatum on the forces of oppression. We are here to make an appeal to African intellectuals and businessmen, African urban and rural proletariat to join forces in a determined, ruthless, and relentless war against white supremacy. We say to waverers and fence-sitters: *Choose Now,* tomorrow may be too late. Choose now, because very soon we shall be saying, with biblical simplicity, that He who is not with Us is against Us!

Pan Africanist Congress Programme
The decks are cleared! The battle must be joined! Therefore, Sons and Daughters of the soil, in the name of the National Working Committee of the Pan Africanist Congress, I announce the Status Campaign — a campaign which once launched, will not be called off until our goal is achieved. This is an unfolding and expanding campaign, involving the political, economic and social status of the African. It is all-embracing and multi-frontal, but is itself part of our unfolding and expanding, dynamic nation-building programme. Details of the campaign have already been circulated to all regions, with specific instructions that branches be encouraged to discuss the campaign freely and frankly. I shall, therefore, not outline the campaign here, but shall deal instead with the objectives of the campaign.

Mental Revolution
We have stated in the past, in all our documents, that whatever campaign is

launched by any liberatory movement worth the name, must at all times be related to the ultimate objectives and must assist in building the fighting capacity of the masses.

For over three hundred years, the white foreign ruling minority has used its power to inculcate in the African a feeling of inferiority. This group has educated the African to accept the *status quo* of white supremacy and black inferiority as normal.

It is our task to excise this slave mentality, and to impart to the African masses that sense of self-reliance which will make them choose 'to starve in freedom rather than have plenty in bondage'; the self-reliance that will make them prefer self-government to the good government preferred by the ANC's leader.

It must be clearly understood that we are not begging the foreign minorities to treat our people courteously. We are calling on our people to assert their personality. We are reminding our people that they are men and women with children of their own and homes of their own, and that just as much as they resent being called *kwedini* or *mfana* or *moshemane* by us — which is what 'boy' means — they must equally resent such terms of address by the foreigner. We are not hoping for a change of heart on the part of the Christian oppressor. We are reminding our people that acceptance of any indignity, any insult, any humiliation, is acceptance of inferiority. They must first think of themselves as men and women before they can demand to be treated as such. The campaign will free the mind of the African — and once the mind is free, the body will soon be free. Once white supremacy has become mentally untenable to our people, it will become physically untenable too — and will go. I am absolutely certain that once the Status Campaign is launched, the masses will themselves come forward with suggestions for the extension of the area of assault — and once that happens, the twilight of white supremacy and the dawn of African independence in this part of the continent, will have set in.

Soft Campaign?

Certain quarters have accused us of being concerned more with our status, with being addressed as 'Sirs' and 'Madam' than with the economic plight of the African people. Our reply is that such accusations can come only from those who think of the African as an economic animal — a thing to be fed — and not as a human being. It is only those who have been 'herrenvolkenised' by their 'herrenvolk' environment, people who have no idea whatsoever of the African personality, who can expect us to be lick-spittles in order to get more crumbs from the oppressor's table.

Others, again, have said that we have chosen a 'soft campaign', without any risks, because we fear to challenge apartheid totally. Let it be clear that we are not fighting just apartheid. We are fighting the whole concept of white supremacy. And we are fully aware of the nature and the size of our task. And we will not shirk it. Right from the beginning of the campaign, the leaders will be in front. They will picket the concerns that are to be boycotted. And they will do so under our slogan of 'no bail, no defence, no fine'. And that slogan will not be changed until we land on the shores of freedom and independence.

Clarion Call

We therefore call, first of all, on the members of PAC, who are the hard core, the advance guard, that must lead the struggle, and on the African people in general. All of them, without exception must wait for the call. They will be kept informed of every step we take. And when the call comes, we expect them to respond like a disciplined people. There is plenty of suffering ahead. The oppressor will not take this lying down. But we are ready. We will not go back. Come what may. This campaign will be maintained, unfolded and expanded until Masiza's question is answered: *'Koda kube nini Nkosi zonk'izizwe zisinyasha phantsi kweenvawo?* (Until when, oh Lord, will all nations trample us under foot?) — until we can answer 'No more'. We will go on, Sons and Daughters of Afrika, until in every shanty, in every bunk in the compounds, in every hut in the deserted villages, in every valley and on every hill-top, the cry of African freedom and independence is heard. We will continue until we walk the streets of our land as free men and women, our heads held high. We will go on until the day dawns when every person who is in Afrika will be an African, and a man's colour will be as irrelevant as is the shape of his ears. We will go on, steadfastly, relentlessly and determinedly until the cry of 'Afrika for the Africans, the Africans for humanity and humanity for God' becomes a reality; until government of the Africans by the Africans for the Africans is a *fait accompli.*

We will not look back; we will not deviate. And as the heat of oppression mounts we shall become purer and purer, leaving all the dross of racialism and similar evils behind, to emerge as a people mentally and physically disciplined, appreciative of the fact that:

> There is only one man in all the world,
> And his name is All men.
> There is only one woman in all the world,
> And her name is All women!

Sons and Daughters of Afrika, we are standing on the threshold of a historic era. We are about to witness momentous events. We are blazing a new trail and we invite you to be, with us, creators of history. Join us in the march to freedom. March with us to independence. To independence now. Tomorrow the United States of Afrika.
IZWE LETHU!

South Africa, Intruder in Our Country

Toivo Hermann Ja Toivo

*Statement by SWAPO member, Accused No. 24, during the
trial of South West Africans in Pretoria, 1 February 1968.*

My Lord:

We find ourselves here in a foreign country, convicted under laws made by
people whom we have always considered as foreigners. We find ourselves
tried by a Judge who is not our countryman and who has not shared our
background.

When this case started, Counsel tried to show that this court had no
jurisdiction to try us. What they had to say was of a technical and legal
nature. The reasons may mean little to some of us, but it is the deep feeling
of all of us that we should not be tried here in Pretoria.

You, my Lord, decided that you had the right to try us, because your
Parliament gave you that right. That ruling has not and could not have changed
our feelings. We are Namibians and not South Africans. We do not now, and
will not in the future, recognize your right to govern us; to make laws for us
in which we had no say; to treat our country as if it were your property and
as if you were our masters.

We have always regarded South Africa as an intruder in our country. This
is how we have always felt and this is how we feel now, and it is on this basis
that we have faced this trial.

I speak of 'we' because I am trying to speak not only for myself, but for
others as well, and especially for those of my fellow accused who have not had
the benefit of any education. I think also that when I say 'we', the overwhelming majority of non-white people in South West Africa would like to
be included.

We are far away from our homes; not a single member of our families has
come to visit us, never mind be present at our trial. The Pretoria Gaol, the
Police Headquarters at Gompol where we were interrogated and where
statements were extracted from us, and this court are all we have seen in
Pretoria. We have been cut off from our people and the world. We all
wondered whether the headmen would have repeated some of their lies if our
people had been present in court to hear them.

The South African Government has again shown its strength by detaining
us for as long as it pleased, keeping some of us in solitary confinement for
300 to 400 days and bringing us to the capital to try us. It has shown its
strength by passing an act especially for us and having it made retrospective.
It has even chosen an ugly name to call us by. One's own are called patriots,
or at least rebels; your opponents are called terrorists.

A court can only do justice in political cases if it understand the position
of those that it has in front of it. The state has not only wanted to convict
us, but also to justify the policy of the South African Government. We will
not even try to present the other side of the picture, because we know that a

court that has not suffered in the same way that we have cannot understand us. This is perhaps why it is said that one should be tried by one's equals. We have felt from the very time of our arrest that we were not being tried by our equals but by our masters, and that those who have brought us to trial very often do not even do us the courtesy of calling us by our surnames. Had we been tried by our equals, it would not have been necessary to have any discussion about our grievances. They would have been known to those set to judge us.

It suits the Government of South Africa to say that is ruling South West Africa with the consent of its people. This is not true. Our organization, the South West African People's Organization, is the largest political organization in South West Africa. We considered ourselves a political party. We know that whites do not think of blacks as politicians — only as agitators. Many of our people, through no fault of their own, have had no education at all. This does not mean that they do not know what they want.

A man does not have to be formally educated to know that he wants to live with his family where he wants to live, and not where an official chooses to tell him to live; to move about freely and not require a pass; to earn a decent wage; to be free to work for the person of his choice for as long as he wants; and finally, to be ruled by the people that he wants to be ruled by, and not by those who rule him because they have more guns than he has.

Our grievances are called 'so-called' grievances. We do not believe South Africa is in South West Africa in order to provide facilities and work for non-whites. It is there for its own selfish reasons. For the first forty years it did practically nothing to fulfill its 'sacred trust'. It only concerned itself with the welfare of the whites.

Since 1962 because of the pressure from inside by the non-whites and especially my organization, and because of the limelight placed on our country by the world, South Africa has been trying to do a bit more. It rushed the Bantustan Report so that it would at least have something to say at the World Court.

Only one who is not white and has suffered the way we have can say whether our grievances are real or 'so-called'.

Those of us who have some education, together with our uneducated brethren, have always struggled to get freedom. The idea of our freedom is not liked by South Africa. It has tried in this court to prove through the mouths of a couple of its paid Chiefs and a paid official that SWAPO does not represent the people of South West Africa. If the Government of South Africa were sure that SWAPO did not represent the innermost feelings of the people of South West Africa, it would not have taken the trouble to make it impossible for SWAPO to advocate its peaceful policy.

South African officials want to believe that SWAPO is an irresponsible organization that resorts to the level of telling people not to get vaccinated. As much as white South Africans may want to believe this, this is not SWAPO. We sometimes feel that it is what the Government would like SWAPO to be. It may be true that some member or members of SWAPO somewhere refused to do this. The reason for such refusal is that some people in our part of the world have lost confidence in the governors of our country and they are not prepared to accept even the good that they are trying to do.

Your Government, my Lord, undertook a very special responsibility when it was awarded the mandate over us after the First World War. It assumed a sacred trust to guide us towards independence and to prepare us to take our place among the nations of the world.

We believe that South Africa has abused that trust because of its belief in racial supremacy (that white people have been chosen by God to rule the world) and apartheid. We believe that for fifty years South Africa has failed to promote the development of our people. Where are our trained men? The wealth of our country has been used to train your people for leadership and the sacred duty of preparing the indigenous people to take their place among the nations of the world has been ignored.

I know of no case in the last twenty years of a parent who did not want his child to go to school if the facilities were available, but even if, as it was said, a small percentage of parents wanted their children to look after cattle, I am sure that South Africa was strong enough to impose its will on this, as it has done in so many other respects. To us it has always seemed that our rulers wanted to keep us backward for their benefit.

1963 for us was to be the year of our freedom. From 1960 it looked as if South Africa could not oppose the world for ever. The world is important to us. In the same way as all laughed in court when they heard that an old man tried to bring down a helicopter with a bow and arrow, we laughed when South Africa said that it would oppose the world. We knew that the world was divided, but as time went on it at least agreed that South Africa had no right to rule us.

I do not claim that it is easy for men of different races to live at peace with one another. I myself had no experience of this in my youth, and at first it surprised me that men of different races could live together in peace. But now I know it to be true and to be something for which we must strive.

The South African Government creates hostility by separating people and emphasizing their differences. We believe that by living together, people will learn to lose their fear of each other. We also believe that this fear which some of the whites have of Africans is based on their desire to be superior and privileged and that when whites see themselves as part of South West Africa, sharing with us all its hopes and troubles, then that fear will disappear. Separation is said to be a natural process. But why, then, is it imposed by force, and why then is it that whites have the superiority?

Headmen are used to oppress us. This is not the first time that foreigners have tried to rule indirectly — we know that only those who are prepared to do what their masters tell them become headmen. Most of those who had some feeling for their people and who wanted independence have been intimidated into accepting the policy from above. Their guns and sticks are used to make people say they support them.

I have come to know that our people cannot expect progress as a gift from anyone, be it the United Nations or South Africa. Progress is something we shall have to struggle and work for. And I believe that the only way in which we shall be able and fit to secure that progress is to learn from our own experience and mistakes.

Your Lordship emphasized in your judgment the fact that our arms come from communist countries, and also that words commonly used by communists were to be found in our documents. But my Lord, in the documents produced by the state there is another type of language. It appears even more often than the former. Many documents finish up with an appeal to the Almighty to guide us in our struggle for freedom. It is the wish of the South African Government that we should be discredited in the western world. That is why it calls our struggle a communist plot; but this will not be believed by the world. The world knows that we are not interested in ideologies.

We feel that the world as a whole has a special responsibility towards us. This is because the land of our fathers was handed over to South Africa by a world body. It is a divided world, but it is a matter of hope for us that it at least agrees about one thing — that we are entitled to freedom and justice.

Other mandated territories have received their freedom. The judgment of the World Court was a bitter disappointment to us. We felt betrayed and we believed that South Africa would never fulfil its trust. Some felt that we would secure our freedom only by fighting for it. We knew that the power of South Africa is overwhelming, but we also knew that our case is a just one and our situation intolerable — why should we not also receive our freedom?

We are sure that the world's efforts to help us in our plight will continue, whatever South Africans may call us.

We do not expect that independence will end our troubles, but we do believe that our people are entitled — as are all peoples — to rule themselves. It is not really a question of whether South Africa treats us well or badly, but that South West Africa is our country and we wish to be our own masters.

There are some who will say that they are sympathetic with our aims, but that they condemn violence. I would answer that I am not by nature a man of violence and I believe that violence is a sin against God and my fellow men. SWAPO itself was a non-violent organization, but the South African Government is not truly interested in whether opposition is violent or non-violent. It does not wish to hear any opposition to apartheid. Since 1963, SWAPO meetings have been banned. It is true that it is the tribal authorities who have done so, but they work with the South African Government, which has never lifted a finger in favour of political freedom. We have found ourselves voteless in our own country and deprived of the right to meet and state our own political opinions.

Is it surprising that in such times my countrymen have taken up arms? Violence is truly fearsome, but who would not defend his property and himself against a robber? And we believe that South Africa has robbed us of our country.

I have spent my life working in SWAPO, which is an ordinary political party like any other. Suddenly we in SWAPO found that a war situation had arisen and that our colleagues and South Africa were facing each other on the field of battle. Although I had not been responsible for organizing my people militarily and although I believed we were unwise to fight the might of South Africa while we were so weak, I could not refuse to help them when the time came.

My Lord, you found it necessary to brand me as a coward. During the Second World War, when it became evident that both my country and your country were threatened by the dark clouds of Nazism, I risked my life to defend both of them, wearing a uniform with orange bands on it.

But some of your countrymen, when called to battle to defend civilization, resorted to sabotage against their own fatherland. I volunteered to face German bullets, and as a guard of military installations, both in South West Africa and the Republic, was prepared to be the victim of their sabotage. Today they are our masters and are considered the heroes, and I am called the coward.

When I consider my country, I am proud that my countrymen have taken up arms for their people and I believe that anyone who calls himself a man would not despise them.

In 1964 the ANC and PAC in South Africa were suppressed. This convinced me that we were too weak to face South Africa's force by waging battle. When some of my country's soldiers came back I foresaw the trouble there would be for SWAPO, my people, and me personally. I tried to do what I could to prevent my people from going into the bush. In my attempts I became unpopular with some of my people, but this, too, I was prepared to endure. Decisions of this kind are not easy to make. My loyalty is to my country. My organization could not work properly – it could not even hold meetings.

I had no answer to the question 'Where has your non-violence got us?' Whilst the World Court judgment was pending, I at least had that to fall back on. When we failed, after years of waiting, I had no answer to give to my people.

Even though I did not agree that people should go into the bush, I could not refuse to help them when I knew that they were hungry. I even passed on the request for dynamite. It was not an easy decision. Another man might have been able to say 'I will have nothing to do with that sort of thing'. I was not, and I could not remain a spectator in the struggle of my people for their freedom.

I am a loyal Namibian and I could not betray my people to their enemies. I admit that I decided to assist those who had taken up arms. I know that the struggle will be long and bitter. I also know that my people will wage that struggle, whatever the cost.

Only when we are granted our independence will the struggle stop. Only when our human dignity is restored to us, as equals of the whites, will there be peace between us.

We believe that South Africa has a choice – either to live at peace with us or to subdue us by force. If you choose to crush us and impose your will on us then you not only betray your trust, but you will live in security for only so long as your power is greater than ours. No South African will live at peace in South West Africa, for each will know that his security is based on force and that without force he will face rejection by the people of South West Africa.

My co-accused and I have suffered. We are not looking forward to our imprisonment. We do not, however, feel that our efforts and sacrifices have been wasted. We believe that human suffering has its effect even on those who impose it. We hope that what has happened will persuade the whites of South Africa that we and the world may be right and they may be wrong. Only when white South Africans realise this and act on it will it be possible for us to stop our struggle for freedom and justice in the land of our birth.

The Algerian Example
ZAPU

> *Article by ZAPU in* Zimbabwe Review *(Lusaka),*
> *13 August 1966.*

The Rhodesian situation is not very different from the Algerian one before the French colonialists were defeated by the oppressed masses of that country after seven years of a bloody struggle.

The leader of the people of Zimbabwe, Mr. Joshua Nkomo, said many a time that if the British Government continued shirking its responsibilities over the 4,000,000-plus Africans of Southern Rhodesia, these oppressed people would just have to use the same methods which were employed by the Algerians against the French from 1954 to 1961.

Nobody in his or her right senses can say that we have not tried our utmost to avert this course of action. Our leader, Joshua Nkomo, went to the United Nations, the Commonwealth and other international forums (to say nothing about his numerous representations to the British Government) to appeal for a peaceful solution to the issue but all in vain because of the British Government's constant vacillation, procrastination and lack of fair play.

Our fellow Africans in Zambia and elsewhere have been at pains to achieve exactly the same object as we want by peaceful means but their efforts have been frustrated by the British Government. The writing is now clear on the wall – *Fight it out if you want majority rule in your country.* This writing, by Harold Wilson, is in big block letters for all of us to see. We have seen it clearly.

Of course Britain's Harold Wilson will never give us the material with which to fight the British minority settlers in Southern Rhodesia just as Charles de Gaulle did not arm the Algerians against French settlers in Algeria. The Algerians had to get arms and other things from those people who wished them well in their fight for freedom.

Some of the 4,000,000 people of Zimbabwe will just have to use sticks, stones and spears. But we must of necessity have some who are well equipped to challenge the machine-gun and rifle fire of the forces of the British settler regime in our country. With full material aid, co-operation and other facilities from our friends and sympathisers, *there is absolutely no reason why our struggle should take longer than the Algerian one.* After all, there were one million French settlers in Algeria whereas there are only about 200,000 British settlers in Rhodesia. It must, of course, be remembered all the time that not all of these British settlers are enemies of the 4,000,000 people of Zimbabwe.

Mr. Nkomo declared in 1962: 'We are not different from the people of Algeria. If, therefore, we fail to achieve our goal by peaceful means, we will resort to the same methods which were used by the Algerians against their oppressors.'

By What Methods?
ZANU

An editorial by ZANU in Zimbabwe News *(Lusaka), VI, 8, August 1972.*

Whenever they have the chance, governments of many western countries never tire of repeating that they too are for the liberation of the peoples of Angola, Namibia, Zimbabwe, Mozambique, South Africa and Guinea-Bissau. But they are quick to add that they want liberation to be achieved through peaceful struggle. They oppose armed struggle. At the United Nations they oppose any resolutions that do not agree with their views on peaceful methods of struggle. And they never fail to exploit opportunities that may arise to sermonize Caetano, Vorster and Smith on the evils of racial discrimination, apartheid and colonialism.

But how does their record stand up to the test of peaceful struggle? Does it live up to their declared commitment to it? The answer is a clear 'no'.

Over the years many of these countries have shown that they pay only lip service to peaceful struggle. They use the language and the cloak of peaceful struggle to mask their support for, and cooperation with the racist and colonial regimes in southern Africa.

The breaking of UN sanctions by the United States which is now importing chrome from Rhodesia; the continuing sale of arms to South Africa by, in particular, Britain and France in defiance of UN resolutions; the refusal by West German and by British firms to withdraw from the construction of the Cabora Bassa dam in Mozambique in spite of world-wide demands that they withdraw; the sabotaging of the general boycott of South African goods by nearly all western countries; the relentless efforts by many of these countries to re-admit South Africa and Rhodesia into the Olympic Games – all these are but a few among numerous examples of the tongue-in-cheek attitude that most western countries adopt to peaceful struggle. It is nonsense to say that they support this form of struggle when they sabotage action in support of that struggle.

Indeed, western economic involvement in unliberated Africa – the white south – increases every year. Companies from NATO countries are selling more goods and investing more capital in the white-ruled south. This means that they have powerful economic and political interests in the defence of enslaved Africa; they have a stake in colonialism, racism and apartheid. And in turn, Rhodesia, South Africa and Portugal are making sure that the west defends that stake – they intensify the suppression, repression and oppression of the indigenous peoples. This is why most western countries flout sanctions and embargos against the white south and sabotage world-wide efforts to isolate the racist regimes politically, culturally and socially. In a nutshell, the west does not want enslaved Africa to be liberated either by armed struggle or by peaceful struggle. It is fair to say that their record shows that most western governments would welcome it that white rule should last indefinitely.

But Africa cannot allow this. This means that independent Africa will have to carry the chief burden of enforcing sanctions and embargos while the oppressed people in Angola, Namibia, South Africa, Zimbabwe, Mozambique and Guinea-Bissau bear the brunt of the armed struggle. The two struggles complement each other, with the armed struggle being the main struggle. And the time has come for Africa to put teeth into the peaceful struggle. She must now take measures that will force western companies which break sanctions and embargos to choose between the huge market of independent Africa and the comparatively small market of the white south.

Several methods present themselves. African states could take over or nationalize the subsidiaries of companies which operate in their countries and which are extensions of western companies which break sanctions and embargos. Secondly, they could make it a condition that any company wishing to set up shop in an independent African country should first declare its position towards the white south. The company could be required to declare that it is not operating in the white south before it is allowed to carry on business operations. Lastly, companies already established both in an independent African country and in the racist south could be given time limits by the end of which they would be required to have decided either to confine their operations in independent Africa only or to quit.

We believe that these methods, which could be put into effect in planned stages, offer perhaps the only efficacious means of putting teeth into peaceful struggle to a continent as yet militarily weak. And without legal powers to prosecute offending companies within the western countries the only practical action available to independent Africa is economic action within the continent itself. Time and events have proved that appeals to western countries and to the United Nations to enforce sanctions and embargos are not enough. And calls on western companies not to invest in the white south have fallen largely on deaf ears. Africa needs to supplement these calls and appeals with independent action of her own, and she has the political power to do so.

It can safely be said that those western countries and firms which are breaking sanctions and embargos are doing so in the conviction that their political and economic interests in independent African countries will not suffer. They believe that Africa cannot hit back; hence they sabotage peaceful struggle. Africa's duty here is to drive home to all firms and countries of the west that they can and will suffer for working against her political and security interests.

These methods have powerful advantages too. The first is that they would go a long way to liberate Africa economically while at the same time helping to liberate the white south politically. They would help to Africanise the economy of each African state concerned regardless of the political ideology of that state. Every subsidiary of a western company which is breaking sanctions or embargos and which an African country would take over on that account would make that country's control over its economy stronger still. And every company which would prefer to do business in an independent African country to the exclusion of operating in the white south would make the white south be starved of investment by that much. Secondly, independent Africa would be effecting those methods in support of the United Nations.

In fact their use for political ends is not new. Several African countries have already used one or other of them, or all of them. Zambia, for instance, took over a subsidiary of certain companies which are taking part in the construction of the Cabora Bassa dam in defiance of international opinion. What would be new is that African states would be coordinating, intensifying and expanding the use of these methods for continental liberation. African nations would also be linking up this form of struggle with, for example, the struggles of certain church bodies in many western countries which are waging a campaign — with some success — for the withdrawal of church investments from companies that are operating in the white south or companies that are breaking sanctions or embargos. The African nations' struggle would reinforce, in a practical way, the efforts of millions of people in the west who belong to church bodies and to other organizations engaged in similar peaceful struggles and who all oppose racist rule and colonial domination. In the third-world and elsewhere, Africa would almost certainly trigger chain-reactions of support from many nations. The tremendous international support received over the expulsion of Rhodesia from the Olympic Games forcefully demonstrated this kind of support.

Technical know-how and technology are no longer the monopoly of companies that break sanctions and embargos. The construction of the Tanzam railway and of many other complicated engineering jobs in other parts of Africa show that independent Africa can, if she so desires, get required help from countries as far apart as Sweden and India or China and Yugoslavia. Some of these countries being developing nations themselves but having a technology more advanced than that found in most African countries and having also once suffered colonial and foreign domination, would be in a better position to understand Africa's aspirations and problems. There are countless other sources for transistor batteries should African states decide to take over the business assets of Union Carbide (Ucar batteries) which is breaking sanctions against Rhodesia. Some of the sources may be found even in the west itself!

The struggle for the political liberation of the white south will be protracted. It is precisely companies like Foote Minerals and Union Carbide, and their political faces like the Nixon Administration, which will make the liberation struggle long, difficult and bloody. Yet Union Carbide is basking in the sunshine of huge profits which it siphons from independent Africa's enormous market! For how long will independent Africa continue to enrich such firms while they, at the same time, provide Smith, Vorster and Caetano with the wherewithal to oppress, suppress, repress, restrict and detain without trial jail, rape, maim and kill black people in Mozambique, Angola, Guinea-Bissau, Zimbabwe and South Africa? For how long must independent Africa continue to face threats to her security — and actually suffer military attacks — from the white south while it permits the very fountain-heads of those threats and attacks to operate on its continent? The Nixon Administration falsely claims that it is breaking sanctions in order to build up stocks of chrome for defence purposes. But what about the defence of Africa?

An Historic Lesson: Pijiguiti
Amilcar Cabral

> *A radio message to the people of Guinea and Cape Verde*
> *Islands and to members of the armed forces of the PAIGC,*
> *sent by Amilcar Cabral, Secretary-General, on 3 August 1965,*
> *the 6th anniversary of the massacre of Pijiguiti. Published in*
> Libertacao, *journal of the PAIGC, in the supplement to No. 57,*
> *August 1965.*

Exactly six years ago, on 3 August 1959, the Portuguese colonialists committed one of the greatest crimes against our defenceless population. On the wharfs of Pijiguiti, in the port of Bissau, the agents of the Portuguese colonialists (troops, police, and some armed settlers) shot and killed, in less than a half hour, 50 African workers on strike and wounded more than a hundred. . . . .

The massacre of August 3 was, however, more than a crime by the Portuguese colonialists, more than an act of patriotic heroism on the part of our working people. The events of August 3 were an historic lesson for our African people and for the leadership of our party.

In truth, the massacre on the quays of Pijiguiti showed our people and our national party the true path to pursue in our liberation struggle. With the glorious and useful sacrifice of the workers assassinated in Pijiguiti, we learned that, faced with the criminal character and lack of scruples of the Portuguese colonialists, we have to mobilize our people, both in Guinea and Cape Verde, unite them around our party, organize them, and prepare them for the struggle. We learned also that our struggle must not be waged in the cities and that, faced with the arms of the Portuguese colonialists, the only form of struggle we can wage is *armed struggle.*

A Situation of Permanent Violence
Amilcar Cabral

> *Excerpt of testimony by the Secretary-General of the PAIGC*
> *to the Subcommittee on Foreign Affairs of the US House*
> *of Representatives, chaired by Rep. Charles C. Diggs, Jr.,*
> *on 26 February 1970.*

We tried during the years of 1950, 1953, 1954, 1955 and 1956 to convince the Portuguese Government that it was necessary to change. In that moment, even we didn't think about independence. We hoped in that moment to change, to have civil rights, to be men, not treated like animals in general, because the Portuguese divided us into two groups, the indigenous people and the assimilado people.

At that moment, after the adoption of the resolution in the United Nations granting independence for all colonies the Portuguese changed a little on paper, but not in practice.

We wanted at that moment, when we were beginning to demand our rights, to pass from the situation of Portuguese of second class to Portuguese like Portuguese. We received, as answer, only repression, imprisonment, torture and in 1959 after the creation of our party, when we called a strike in the Port of Bissau, the Portuguese troops killed about 50 workers in 20 minutes and wounded more than 100. This massacre showed us that it was not well, it was not good, it was not intelligent to fight against the Portuguese with empty hands.

We didn't want, absolutely not, to resort to violence, but we realized that the colonial Portuguese domination was a situation of permanent violence. Against our aspirations they systematically answered with violence, with crimes, and we decided in that moment to prepare ourselves to fight.

In that moment, as you know, sir, Africa began to become independent. The 'wind of change' was blowing over Africa. The other colonial powers decided to decolonialize. Portugal signed the United Nations Charter and later Portugal voted for the proclamation of the right for independence of all people.

But Portugal never accepted to apply this international decision. Portugal insisted, the Portuguese Government insisted that we were provinces of Portugal.

If in the beginning of our colonial life we were exactly like the Portuguese, we had all the rights the Portuguese had, maybe it would be possible to convince us that we were Portuguese in the Portuguese provinces. But in our country we never had rights, the minimum rights of man, and in that moment it was very late to convince us that our country was a Portuguese province.

We saw Africa beginning with independence, in many African states, and we decided to do our best also to get our right to self-determination and independence. That is the reason for 7 years of fighting.

We have liberated more than two-thirds of the country. In the liberated areas of our country, facing the Portuguese bombs, we are trying to build a new life. In the liberated areas, for example — I can tell you that all of this has been confirmed by journalists and filmmakers and writers, like some men from Sweden and other countries that have been in our country for 1, 2, or more months. We have organized the education, the services of education. We have now more than 130 schools. The Portuguese, in all Guinea, in the time of colonialism, had 45 missionary schools, so-called elementary schools, and 11 official schools.

We have now about 15,000 children in the schools. Before, in my country there were only 2,000 children, but the indigenous people; that is, 99.7% of the population, couldn't go to their official schools, only to the missionary schools.

Now, in our country, we have established in the liberated areas, in spite of the bombing, permanent bombing by Portuguese planes, four hospitals — not very nice hospitals, but what we can do in this stage of our life. We have trained nurses during these years, more than 250 nurses, men and women. We have more than 100 sanitary posts in order not only to assist the wounded or sick fighters, but to assist the population of the liberated regions.

We have organized and developed in the liberated regions, our party, our political organization, our administration, and in this moment we can say that our country is like a state of which a part of the national territory is yet occupied by the colonial forces.

Portugal controls only the urban centres and some little parts in the countryside. We control the major part of the countryside, and in the contested regions we are fighting each day in order to complete the liberation of our country.

One can ask how Portugal, an underdeveloped country also, one of the most backward in Europe which has some regions with more than 46% of illiterates — I am referring to official figures — how can Portugal fight all of these colonial wars in my country, in Angola and in Mozambique?

The Portuguese people are progressively realizing that colonial wars are not only against the African people, but also against their own interests.

We think that with this war the Portuguese Government is losing or making it possible to lose one of the best chances Portugal has in history, because our hopes were and still are, in spite of all the crimes against our people, that we could, in independence, like an African people, develop the best relations with Portugal, even to study and to decide together some problems concerning the development of our country and the progress of our peoples.

Message to the Portuguese People
MPLA

> *In June 1960 the MPLA sent this open message to the Portuguese people. It was signed on behalf of the Executive Committee by Viviato Cruz, Mario de Andrade, and Lucio Lara.*

The MPLA directs this message to the Portuguese people in the spirit of the love of liberty, fraternity, and universal peace. . . .

The Angolan people and the MPLA are not fighting Portugal. Respect for the survival, liberty, and aspiration to progress of Portugal is one of the fundamentals of the survival, liberty, and progress that the Angolan people and the MPLA seek for Angola.

The Angolan people and the MPLA are not fighting Portugal. We do not believe that this people which, throughout its history and faced with invaders and oppressors, offered the example of struggle through love of liberty, wishes today to sanction wars and massacres that will lead its sons to death for the exclusive benefit of a handful of exploiters.

The Angolan people and the MPLA are struggling rather, and will struggle until final victory, against Portuguese colonialists. The history and experience of contemporary struggles between colonialists and colonized peoples has always shown that, confronted with the freedom struggle of oppressed peoples, colonialists of a given country do not all have the same reaction, adopt the same tactics or approve unanimously the same way of handling the colonial problem.

Under the irresistible pressure of the struggle of colonial peoples, two viewpoints tend to emerge among the colonialist group: those who are obstinate and those who are partisans of negotiations . . . .

In our era, no colonizing country can win a colonial war . . . . The Angolan people and the MPLA propose the liquidation of Portuguese colonialism by peaceful, democratic means, by negotiation . . . .

An honest analysis of the situation in Portugal and its colonies can only lead to the conclusion that Portuguese colonialism is a proven enemy of the colonized peoples and of the Portuguese people themselves. A people that oppresses another people cannot truly be free . . . .

Colonialism is our common enemy. The Angolan people and the MPLA do *not* struggle therefore for a *renovation* of the empire or of Portugal overseas, but for the complete liquidation of the colonial system in Angola and for the winning of the effective exercise of the right to self-determination . . . .

Letters to the Minister
Agostinho Neto

> *Three letters sent to the Minister of Overseas Portugal, Lisbon, in 1960-61 by Agostinho Neto, later President of the MPLA, from forced residence in Ponta do Sol (Cape Verde Islands)*

Ponta do Sol, November 30, 1960

Excellency:

I, Antonio Agostinho Neto, physician, married, native of Icolo and Bengo, Angola, arrested in Luanda by the PIDE on the 8th day of June of the current year, accused of 'subversive activities against the external security of the State' and transferred to the Lisbon Prison on the 8th day of August of the same year and then deported to the island of Santo Antao where I arrived on October 19 of the same year, accompanied by my wife and young son.

'Because of pressing public service requirements,' I was appointed interim second-class physician of the Department of Health of Cape Verde, placed as Deputy of Health of the city of Maria Fia, with a monthly salary of 540,000 Cape Verde escudos, plus an allowance of 600.00 Cape Verde escudos from the Sinagoga Leprosaurium on this island, aside from the partly furnished house assigned to the Deputy of Health.

Against my will, I had to accept the post to which I was appointed, in order to guarantee the minimum necessary to sustain my family, since it is impossible to subsist here with just the income from the free clinic, because the people are extremely poor.

Notwithstanding my five months of inactivity with no income, being forced to close my practice in Luanda because of my imprisonment, I had to put up a bond of two thousand five escudos during my move to the Island of Santo Antao and until I assumed remunerated duties.

Thus:

	Hotel do Atlantico on the island of Sal	571$00
	Pensao Chave d'Ouro in S. Vicente	178$00
	Municipal Inn in this city	2,034$00
	Transportation of luggage, etc.	111$50
		2,885$00

(I am enclosing vouchers)

Being confronted by this situation, I do not consider my problem solved and appeal to Your Excellency once again to provide a satisfactory solution promptly, releasing me from the police restrictions imposed upon me on this island.

In that connection, I cabled Your Excellency on October 22 and my attorney filed a petition at the beginning of this month for my transfer to Angola or the issuance of a passport to go abroad with my family.

Your Excellency replied to me through the local District Administrator, who verbally informed me of police decisions barring me from changing residence, compelling me to report to said Administrator on the 1st day of each month, prohibiting participation in demonstrations or affairs of a political nature, etc. Said functionary further informed me of Your Excellency's recommendation to the effect that I should refrain from complaining about my situation, for in the opinion of Your Excellency, I was treated with much 'condescension'.

However, there is no order published in the Diario do Governo (Official Gazette) requiring my residence on this island and limiting the time of this punishment, as would be normal, and without the latter, I am completely at the mercy of the PIDE.

Furthermore, there is no guarantee of employment once the interim period of one year expires.

I should like to rejoin my family and enjoy complete freedom to practise my profession outside of the Department of Health whose organization and posts are not encouraging for reasons I need not enumerate; those reasons simply add to my concern about the way in which my case was handled.

On the other hand, I feel that no contribution whatever is made toward political clarification of the problem of Angola by my exile nor by the systematic violent repression of those who in one way or another express themselves in favour of solutions to problems that are becoming more and more acute among the people of Angola and are reflected throughout the world.

The affection and sympathy with which I and my wife have been received here on every level of the population and the material and moral aid we have received simply prove that our problem is not only understood in Angola and in Metropolitan Portugal and in other parts of the world, but touches the heart of every sensitive person.

This is to be contrasted with the brutality with which we were treated at Lisbon Airport by PIDE agents who not only tried to prevent us from taking leave of our relatives and acquaintances, but also treated them roughly.

In spite of the coarse words and attitudes of the PIDE people, the friendly demonstration of Africans at the airport was very comforting to me and my family because of their courage and humanity.

I and my wife now aspire to complete freedom and wish to live worthy lives without being subject to the arbitrary will of the police organization, as is the case with out present pseudo-liberty.

I therefore petition Your Excellency to permit our immediate return to Angola or else our departure abroad.

Respectfully,   Sgd.: Agostinho Neto

Second Petition

Excellency:

After nearly three months of exile on this island in the company of my wife and minor son, an abnormal situation continues even though prison bars have been replaced by the waters of the sea around us.

For this reason, added to the fact that I have received no answer to my letter of last month addressed to Your Excellency, I again file a petition in the hope that the grounds for my deportation may have ended; but if the objective of the Government is to separate me from my relatives, from my friends and from my fellow-countrymen in Angola and in Metropolitan Portugal, why cannot I and my family go into exile abroad to live in dignity and freedom?

In fact, without a publicly announced legal decision ordering my residence on this island and without a time limit for the punishment being inflicted on me, I fail to understand the objective of such penalty. The Government decided to release me after having kept me in prison from June 8 to October 15, 1960 without having me sentenced by the Courts of Angola to the heavy penalties imposed on other Angolans accused of activities similar to those for which I was arrested (3 to 10 years imprisonment and security restrictions), there being no record of such penalties in the Portuguese plenary courts. The Government decided to grant me the post of Deputy of Health of this island at a salary of 6,000$00 monthly. These facts indicate apparent benevolence.

But it also decided to prevent my return to my native land, Angola, or to go abroad where I could live without police vigilance, which is always disagreeable, whether the agents are discreet or bare-faced, in a walled prison or on an open island.

It further decided to keep me under control, with all of the consequences thereof: letters and newspapers that never arrive, restrictions, humiliating obligations, etc.

The Government certainly cannot believe that by subjecting me to physical, moral and economic pressures, it can change my way of thinking. This way of thinking is based on problems involving the people of my land, a people I would like to see made happy, and it cannot be changed by the pressures exerted against me.

It can do nothing to stop me from thinking that a problem exists in Angola, a problem which requires a solution and on which I would give an opinion, if the Government were willing and it were somehow helpful and if I were entirely free.

That problem of Angola, experienced by the people of my land, widely recognized in sessions of the U.N. General Assembly and in other international conferences, known throughout the world, should not be regarded in so cursory a fashion, as has been the case, in Portuguese media authorized to offer opinions, however unenlightened they may be.

It is because of that problem that I was deported, as well as Reverend Joaquim Pinto de Andrade to the island of Principe, and it is because it exists that hundreds of Angolans are in prisons in Angola.

In view of these sad facts, after one of my brothers, Dionisio da Silva Neto, was arrested by the PIDE on December 5, 1960 in Luanda, when repression touches my relatives, friends and fellow-countrymen, aside from myself and I listen to the Assistant Director of the PIDE of Luanda stating with deep-seated hatred that 'if there should be independence, it will be an independence of whites, as occurred in Brazil!' (sic), I cannot help continuing to think of improvement of the living conditions of my people, conditions for which politics are essential.

When the Assistant Director of the PIDE calls me 'his black' and then utters the words quoted above, I cannot help thinking of the factors responsible for such nonsensical talk in days as wonderful as those the world is experiencing today in the history of human relations.

Believing I have clarified this point, I wish to conclude that, because of disagreement with the underlying principles, I shall never become devoted to the New Portuguese State.

Therefore, once the prison doors were opened for me, I dared to ask for a review of my case, with a view to rejoining my family, my friends and my fellow-countrymen.

If the Government continues to consider my presence there 'highly dangerous' because of the friendship that may be shown me, the affection my family should accord me and the solidarity my fellow countrymen should offer me, and if my return to Angola cannot be considered because of today's international and internal difficulties, I beg Your Excellency to grant me a passport for a foreign country — such as Argentina — where I can practise my profession with freedom and dignity, earning enough to sustain all of the members of my family.

Owing to my situation, my mother, some of my brothers and sisters and my mother-in-law, of Luanda and Lisbon respectively, live in precarious circumstances, suffering especially the anguish of separation from their children. The arrest of my brother Dionisio was a further cruel blow to my mother (how many Angolan mothers have not suffered similar blows in recent times).

On the other hand, the post of Deputy of Health on this island does not attract me and I am only discharging same out of sheer necessity. The living conditions granted me — low salary, impossibility of maintaining a private clinic, very high cost of living — do not guarantee me the minimum essential for the subsistence of myself and the members of my family. My wife, my mother-in-law and my son wish therefore to go to Luanda to join my mother.

I beg Your Excellency to consider the following petitions I hopefully submit:

(1) That I be permitted to return to Angola; or

(2) That I be granted a passport to go abroad — to Argentina, for example; or

(3) That passage be granted to my mother-in-law, Sra. Maria Amelia da Silva Salgueiro, residing at Rua de S. Joao da Praca No. 1, 2°, Lisbon, to move to Ponta do Sol;

(4) And, in this event, that my wife and mother-in-law then be granted passage to Luanda, where they will live with my mother.

Hoping my petition may be granted,
Very respectfully.

Ponto do Sol, 15 April 1961   Sgd.: Antonio Agostinho Neto

Third Petition
Excellency:

Although Your Excellency has not yet deemed it necessary to answer any of the letters and a petition sent by me, dwelling on my situation as a political exile, requesting issuance of a passport for Argentina or at least granting conditions allowing me to practise freely, again I appeal to Your Excelleny at a time when life in this city is becoming unbearable for me and my family.

I understand that the steadily worsening situation in Angola, which problem did not cease to grow worse since my arrest, in spite of the predictions of the PIDE, arouses the fear that if I were to go to Argentina, I would engage in political activities and have a political influence I do not now possess. The facts have shown that my separation from the Angolan people did not prevent armed clashes on an unexpected scale from starting there, as was to be foreseen. It is therefore to be concluded from these facts that my martyrdom, as well as that of thousands of other Angolans, some dead and others without air or light in the prisons of the PIDE, are not rescuing Angola from its political problems; rather, they may to some extent be worsening them, because of the anxiety and despair created in every phase of life in my country.

My establishment of residence in Ponta do Sol (without any official order published in the Diario do Governo) has been cloaked with a benevolence that is actually illusory. The post of Deputy of Health which I discharge is, in fact, the only means I have of practicing my profession and I have no alternative. Not one of my steps, my words, my acts fail to be duly weighed, interpreted and reported. The many secret orders that have arrived in connection with my case are generally known to almost everyone and even to me.

But the cynical thing about the situation consists of the attempt to isolate me and my family by means of pressures, threats and political sanctions against persons with whom it would be possible for us to associate. Some more faint-hearted individuals are afraid to be seen in our company or to come to our house. They become alarmed when they realize the inevitability of an encounter. My jailers in this prison have taken the trouble to terrorize directly or indirectly persons who would like to associate with us, telling them I know not what tales about my dark political past, of 'strict orders from above' and of the danger of sharing my thoughts in surroundings where everyone just has to do his duty and not think.

Thus, the 'benevolent' situation created for me and my family consists of incarcerating us in the residence of the Deputy of Health where I am *always* on duty at a ridiculous salary without the possibility of private practice and, by secret orders, limiting our social life through veiled threats against those who for one reason or another might like to associate with us. The fictitious freedom 'magnanimously' accorded consists of surrounding us with spies, from servants to patients. An inhuman situation this, in which not being in jail is considered great benevolence!

Despite all this, certain influential newspapers, like 'Arauto' of (Portuguese) Guinea, for example, openly announce such magnanimity.

The entire environment created around me by my zealous jailers prompts me once again to appeal to Your Excellency, pending the possibility of returning to Angola and now that the Portuguese political situation is tending to become more and more chaotic, to grant me a passport for Argentina.

Aside from the political effects, I believe this solution would be in accord with Your Excellency's conscience, for it would be one way of ceasing the oppression of a family that wishes to live a normal life.

I beg your Excellency to give this matter your attention.

Anxiously,
Agostinho Neto

Return to Angola
Agostinho Neto

> *Interview of Agostinho Neto, President of the MPLA, in Leopoldville, August 1962, made by members of the Portuguese opposition. Translated from Portuguese.*

In 1947, when I registered for the first time at the School of Medicine in Coimbra, the aspiration of the Angolan people for independence appeared to me as a necessity that demanded practical action. I started by giving my support to the students' associations and to the politico-literary meetings that sought at the time to clarify the bases of Angolan culture and to analyse our condition as a colonized people.

Afterwards, I took part in the activities of Portuguese youth organizations, with the intention of denouncing the true conditions of life of the people of Angola. In 1952, in Lisbon, I was arrested for the first time with two colleagues of mine, during a demonstration against the fascist politics of the government. I was imprisoned for 90 days.

When I was set free I adhered to the Youth Movement section of the Movement of Democratic Unity (MUD Juvenil), which led the fight for better conditions of life for youth, and against Fascism. In 1955, after having been elected as a member of the Central Committee of the MUD Juvenil, as a representative of the youth of the colonies, I was arrested for the second time, together with nearly 100 young Portuguese (students and workers), of whom 52 were brought to trial. I spent 28 months in prison until, in June 1957, I was set free after a trial that took six months. Meanwhile, the Court of the city of Porto which had been trying us in the most partial way only sentenced me to 18 months in a workcamp and this due to the intervention of literary and political personalities from different countries, and also due to the brilliant defense made by my lawyer and the ardent democrat, Dr. Antonio Macedo. Of the 52 on trial, six, all members of the Central Committee of the MUD Juvenil, continued to be kept in prison for 'security reasons' which, as we know, means that the defendant is kept in prison for periods from six months to three years, indefinitely renewable. The last of these comrades was set free only in June of 1962.

Towards the end of 1958 I received my degree in medicine, just when Angolan nationalism was taking on an organizational structure, which was a remarkable achievement, given the difficult underground conditions in which it had to operate. The Portuguese government set up at that time a branch of PIDE (the well known Gestapo of Salazar) in Angola and soon thereafter, several dozen nationalists were imprisoned, among them the leader Ilidio Machado who is at the moment in the concentration camp, along with some of his companions, of Chao Bom on the island of Santiago, in the Cape Verde Archipelago. We formed, separate from the Portuguese organizations, the Anti-Colonialist Movement (MAC) which was composed principally of Angolan political organizations located in Portugal. A few months later, MAC would take on a more marked Angolan flavor. Since approximately 1958, Mario de Andrade, Lucio Lara and Amilcar Cabral have become the pillars of the anti-colonialist fight abroad.

My internship in tropical medicine completed, I returned home and set up a private clinic in Luanda. The arrest by the Portuguese authorities of a messenger we had sent abroad, who received thereupon a cruel treatment that he was unable to endure, led to my arrest as well as to that of other nationalists. The people's action taken against this arbitrary policy caused a new flow of arrests and even more violent repression, such as the massacre of nationalists in Icolo and Bengo, my native village, who were demonstrating in favor of my liberation as well as that of my companions. Father Joaquim Pinto de Andrade, Chancellor of the Archdiocese of Luanda and a great Angolan patriot, was imprisoned at that time and later transferred to a monastery in the north of Portugal, in forced residence on the orders of PIDE. According to recent news we have received from Portugal, he has just been imprisoned once again.

The PIDE sent me under custody to Lisbon and later I was deported to Santo Antao Island, in the Cape Verde Archipelago. At that point, despite the vote by the UN General Assembly of the Declaration on the Granting of Independence to Colonial Peoples and Countries, the Portuguese government attempted to disguise the seriousness of the Angolan situation, and wished to make use of my name in its propaganda. Without my request, I was appointed Health Commissioner on Santo Antao Island. At the same time I was under pressure by the Portuguese authorities to take a position against the just struggle of the Angolan people.

In a moment of anger, and after realizing that the appointment had not converted me, the Governor of Cape Verde insolently let me know that the job had been given to me in an attempt to arouse in me a feeling of gratitude and loyalty towards the piratical policy of the colonial fascist government.

In retaliation, the PIDE decided to transfer me to an almost deserted island, to which I never got, since I was once again arrested, for the fourth time, in the city of Praia (Santiago Island) on the most frivolous pretext: possession of a photograph revealing the atrocities committed by the Portuguese colonialists in Angola.

The humiliation to which I was submitted was only bearable because of the presence of my wife who, you will permit me to say, has always accompanied me with great courage and combative spirit.

I should point out that during and after this last arrest, my family and myself received moral and material support from the anti-colonialists of various countries. This demonstration of solidarity was reinforced by a vigorous action which broke out all over the world and sought to force the Portuguese government to liberate me.

The People's Movement for the Liberation of Angola (MPLA), which organized my escape from Portugal with the aid of anti-colonialists from Portugal and other European countries, has accomplished great victories over the Portuguese colonial-fascist government, due to the great precision of the structures it has put in place. I will take advantage of this opportunity to express my gratitude to all those who, by risking their freedom and their life, have made great efforts to free me from the hands of the abominable PIDE.

To the countries which have received me, especially the African countries and to the Republic of the Congo [Leopoldville] in particular, I would like to express by these means my happiness for their demonstration of solidarity and understanding.

I share presently the fate of nearly 200,000 Angolan refugees in this Republic of Congo, having been expelled through the barbaric hatred of the Portuguese colonialists. In addition to this exiled group, there are thousands of Angolans who have taken refuge in the heart of Angola's jungles, where they are forced to lead a very precarious existence.

Guerrilla Warfare: Only Valid Form of Struggle
MPLA

Article in MPLA — Informations *(Algiers), March 1969.*

The entire world was shaken at the end of last year by the news that Marcello Caetano had been appointed to succed the old dictator Salazar at the head of the Portuguese government. A number of African political leaders immediately started to speculate about a change in the Portuguese attitude towards the colonies, since the reputation and ambiguous speeches of the new head of State had aroused the hope of 'liberalisation'.

Having intimate knowledge of Portuguese policy and the reactionary forces now in power, the MPLA always expressed its apprehension about these hopes, which were not founded on concrete facts.

Salazar was not a lone man in his country. He was the representative of Portuguese financial oligarchy, which is itself subordinate to international high finance. In governing, he was defending certain interests, those of exploiters.

These very same business circles chose Caetano to replace Salazar. The very same government team is in power. The fall of the dictator changes nothing in Portugal's fascist and colonialist policy. Changing one person, even if his name is Salazar, cannot change the Portuguese constitution, which designates the colonies as 'overseas provinces'.

In any case, neither the Portuguese government nor the settlers are prepared to yield their domination and influence in Angola and Mozambique to the political, economic and military expansionism of South Africa, which is highly industrialised and showing a tendency to interfere increasingly directly in the affairs of non-independent countries of Southern Africa.

For the time being, therefore, Portugal has to continue the war. Caetano has already confirmed this line in the speeches made some time after he came to power. He has shown himself to be clearly in favour of the continuation of colonial war.

He has sent already at least 7 battalions (3,500 soldiers) to Angola and Mozambique and he intends to increase troop effectives in Angola by 20,000 men. He reprimands those who speak against the war, notably young Portuguese Catholic circles who on 1st January, for example, demonstrated in favour of ending the war in a Lisbon church. These young people have been accused of treason.

It is the new Portguese government which is brandishing threats of reprisals against the Republic of Congo Brazzaville if it continues to aid MPLA.

At the present juncture it is therefore impossible that any substantial change might be effected in Portuguese colonial policy.

The MPLA has reached the conclusion that under the present conditions the only possible form of struggle in Angola is armed struggle, and to wage this hard and protracted struggle it is necessary for the whole of Africa to commit itself and sincerely to come to aid of the Angolan People through their organized representative and dynamic force, the MPLA.

Armed struggle is not simply a sacrifice to those who are fighting on the side of justice and against tyranny, to those who aspire to freedom. It is above a force. It is not simply a burial ground. It does not simply stain the battlefields with blood of the best sons and daughters of our peoples. It is also a school. It is also a means of ensuring that the people will continue that struggle in the future, after political independence, so as to be completely free: politically, economically and socially.

Colonization and Africa
UPA

Editorial in the founding issue of La Voix de la Nation
Angolaise, *edited by Holden Roberto for the UPA and issued
on 15 September 1960. Translated from French.*

The torrent of the African liberation movement is irresistible, and it can
neither be stopped nor channelled. Everything is happening very fast. The
revolutionary upsurge of the oppressed peoples blows up the straitjackets
of force instituted by the colonizers and their puppets. These truths carry in
themselves their logical consequences. It is in this way that today we witness
the birth of *The Voice of the Angolan Nation,* combative instrument of the
UPA, in this fraternal and independent land, where we enjoy most cordial
hospitality.

You may think, dear readers and fellow countrymen, that a critique of
the colonial system is today unnecessary. We who are colonized, speaking to
those who are or have been colonized, do not wish to show that the colonial
state is abnormal, inhuman and to be condemned. It would be grotesque on
our part to seek to convince you of the unacceptable character of colonial
oppression.

We wish simply to make a small point about what must be called the
regime established by force, since it is by force and against the will of the
people that colonialism has been implanted. Thus, a colonized people is
ideologically presented as being one whose evolution has been arrested,
impermeable to reason, incapable of conducting its own affairs, requiring the
permanent presence of a trustee or guide. The history of the colonized
peoples is transformed into meaningless agitation, and in fact we often have
the impression that for these peoples humanity began with the arrival of the
white colonists. Angola, a country with a population of 4,500,000 has lived
under Portuguese domination for the past five centuries, under a system of
settlement. In order to ensure White domination, the principle has thus been
adopted that no Black may be a landowner, whereas any Portuguese who sets
foot in Angola is immediately given a plot of land.

All the good land has progressively fallen into the hands of the Whites.
The second principle which was followed was that of forced labour. Any
settler whatsoever may requisition any African at any time and oblige him to
work fourteen hours a day.

Governing all of this is the third principle of the Portuguese province of
Angola, according to which a policy of national negation, of cultural persecution as well as of denial of the African personality is pursued with rare
ferocity. Here and there, a few Angolans 'pass' and are admitted to the dignity
of Portuguese citizenship, while the whole of the population lives in a
psychological and spiritual starvation, which poses precise questions to the
conscience of humanity.

To this question, the Angolan people have reacted for several years, but the colonial administration and the Portuguese colonists, jealous of their privileges, are set on keeping an iron-clad regime over the country, by multiplying the arrests, the torture, and the massacres, unworthy of a 'Christian' nation.

The Eternal in His plenitude, in His goodness and His mercy, has created man so that he may live freely. In the Bible there is no verse permitting the domination and the exploitation of man by man.

To the Portuguese People
FRELIMO

Resolution of First Congress of FRELIMO held in Dar es Salaam on 23-28 September 1962.

In these grave hours in the history of Mozambique, FRELIMO turns to you.

The Mozambican people, inspired by profoundly human sentiments of freedom, dignity, and justice, is firmly decided to struggle, if necessary with the holocaust of its own life, for the conquest of national independence. The Portuguese government, extending its tentacles, maintains a fierce oppression of the people of our country. Our people continue to be obliged to do forced labour. The fascist colonial government of Portugal pursues its policy of expropriating our lands and exploiting the labour of our people. The benefits of this exploitation go only to Portuguese colonialist circles.

To try to destroy our love of liberty, your government does not hesitate to massacre the Mozambican people: Mueda in June 1960 and Xinavane in February 1961 are deeds of barbaric reaction by the colonial fascist government to the legitimate aspirations of our people.

Nonetheless, not only Mozambique, but also Angola, Guinea, Cape Verde, S. Tome e Principe desire to be free and independent. It was to try to stifle the will of the Angolan people to be independent that the government led by Mr. Salazar launched a war in Angola. But the Angolan people did not succumb and will not succumb, nor will the Guinean people. On the contrary, colonialist repression leads only to an ever stronger reaction on the part of the collective peoples of Mozambique, Angola, 'Portuguese' Guinea, Cape Verde, and S. Tome e Principe.

On the other hand, the situation of the Portuguese government in the international arena is one of almost total isolation, supported totally only by the fascist governments of South Africa and Spain. In effect, a horrified world conscience is reacting against the barbaric actions perpetrated by the Portuguese in Angola and now in 'Portuguese' Guinea. FRELIMO declares today it will not be responsible for any loss of Portuguese life or property as a result of the potential conflict that the Portuguese government is creating between the African and Portuguese peoples in Mozambique.

The Mozambican people hope, therefore, that the Portuguese people will assume, in this conflict which opposes the Mozambican people and the fascist colonial Portuguese administration, a position worthy of its noble democratic traditions, and help to keep war from breaking out in Mozambique.

To the Mozambican People
FRELIMO

Proclamation of 25 September 1964.

Mozambican People
In September 1962 the Congress of the Mozambique Liberation Front (FRELIMO) affirmed unanimously the will and determination of the Mozambican people to fight by any and all means for the achievement of their National Independence.

During the past two years FRELIMO never ceased to work for the attainment of that goal.

FRELIMO tried, through peaceful means, to convince the colonial-fascist government of Portugal to give satisfaction to the fundamental political demands of the Mozambican people.

FRELIMO constantly made known to Pan-African, Afro-Asian and world organizations the situation in which the Mozambican people live, and denounced the crimes of colonialism in Mozambique.

As a result, not only the Mozambican people, but also the Organization of African Unity, the United Nations and, in general, world public opinion condemned the criminal policy of the Portuguese government.

In spite of this, Portuguese colonialism continues to dominate our country.

The richness of our country and the work of the Mozambican people continue to be exploited by the Portuguese colonialists and their imperialistic allies.

Our brothers are daily murdered for participating actively in the struggle for the liberation of our country. The prisons are full of patriots, and those who are still free live in uncertainty of what the next day will bring.

The PIDE increases the number of its agents, and perfects its methods of torture. The Portuguese army is being reinforced and constantly increases its potential in men and war material; and the 'Psycho-Social' continues its campaign of deceiving the Mozambican people.
Mozambican People
FRELIMO always carried on its work in order to assume completely its responsibilities as the leader of the revolution of the Mozambican people.

Therefore, concurrent with its peaceful efforts, FRELIMO prepared itself to face the eventuality of an armed struggle.

Today, faced with the constant refusal of the Portuguese government to recognize our right to independence, FRELIMO again declares that armed struggle is the only way for the Mozambican people to achieve their aspirations of Liberty, Justice and Social Well-Being.

Mozambican People — workers and peasants, workers on the plantations, in the timber mills and in the concessions, workers in the mines, on the railways, in the harbours and in the factories, intellectuals, civil servants, Mozambican soldiers in the Portuguese army, students, men, women and young people, patriots —

In The Name of All Of You

FRELIMO today solemnly proclaims the general armed insurrection of the Mozambican people against Portuguese colonialism for the attainment of the complete independence of Mozambique.

Our fight must not cease before the total liquidation of Portuguese colonialism.

Mozambican People

The Mozambican revolution, the work of the Mozambican people, is an integral part of the struggle of the peoples of Africa and of the whole world for the victory of the ideals of Liberty and Justice.

The armed struggle which we announce today, for the destruction of Portuguese colonialism and of imperialism, will allow us to install in our country a new and popular social order. The Mozambican people will thus be making a great historical contribution toward the total liberation of our Continent and the progress of Africa and of the world.

Mozambican People

In this decisive hour in the history of our country, in which we have unanimously decided to take up arms to confront Portuguese colonialism, FRELIMO is sure that each Mozambican will fulfil his duty.

We must continually reinforce our unity, the union of all Mozambicans, without any distinction, from Rovuma to Maputo.

We must consolidate more and more our Organization, we must always act in an organized way.

Everywhere FRELIMO will always be present and ready to direct the struggle.

We must be firm, decided and implacable with the Portuguese colonialists.

We must be firm, decided and implacable with those who collaborate with Portuguese colonialism, with the agents of the PIDE and with all traitors to our people and our country.

United, We Shall Win!
Independence or Death!
Mozambique Will Win!
Long Live FRELIMO!
Long Live Mozambique!
Long Live Africa!

3. National Movements and the Class Struggle: Theory

Editors' Introduction
One of the fundamental theoretical questions with which national liberation movements had to wrestle was the class struggle. It was not a new question. For liberation struggles have focused around both themes, nation and class, ever since at least the French Revolution. The two themes go together up to a point but then may become contradictory. The question of priorities when these contradictions emerge has no doubt been a major source of debate within liberation movements throughout the world.

We have already seen in Part I in the section on 'The Role of Various Classes and Groups in Colonial Society' how the movements in Portuguese and southern Africa perceived the class *structure* of their societies. We included then the important attempt at ideological clarification and resolution of the difficulty by Amilcar Cabral in his elaboration of the concept 'nation-class'.

But once a movement went beyond the stage of analysis of the existing society into the phase of action, it also had to theorize about the definition of the movement as a movement, in order that it might make practical decisions of how to conduct the struggle and with which groups to ally to defeat the enemy. Indeed, it comes back to the core question: who is the enemy?

As one reads the documents of the movements, one senses that their essential opinion on the priority to be accorded the class struggle is 'yes, but'. That is to say, virtually all the movements placed their struggle within the framework of a class struggle. They accepted the legitimacy of class analysis. *But* they were in fact engaged in a *national* struggle. They recognized the reality and political significance of internal stratification within their countries but they insisted that the essential contradiction was that between occupier and occupied, conqueror and conquered, foreign imperialist and *national*.

And yet, and yet! They also recognized that there were traitors to the national struggle, and that the origins of this treachery was class self-interest. So they called for unity, but not just any unity. It had to be, in Cabral's terms, a 'class-national' unity.

How then did they reconcile their position with that of workers and socialist movements in the rest of the world? First of all, they practised terminological abstinence. There are many socialist theories. There are even many versions of Marxism, or Marxism-Leninism, or scientific socialism. To use these terms was to risk grave confusion. To refuse these terms was to risk confusion as well. So they abstained.

But how could one 'abstain' between use and non-use? There was only one way – to use a code, which signals this 'abstinence'. This code word for the movements seemed to be 'ideology'. They spoke of the key importance of their having a clear 'ideological' base and commitment without specifying which of the existing words in the world this ideology was to be. The militants understood this code well. It referred to the class-national struggle, the class struggle in its 'yes, but' form.

Within the framework of this essentially common position, there were key stylistic differences between the three historically different situations of South Africa, Zimbabwe, and Portuguese Africa. In South Africa, there has existed for over half a century a South African Communist Party (SACP), composed disproportionately of Whites. The SACP has been in alliance with the ANC for most of the more recent period, and there exists the unusual phenomenon of a few persons who have simultaneously been active members of the ANC and the SACP.

Zimbabwe on the contrary had no local Communist Party, nor of course was the Communist Party a significant phenomenon in the mother country. Hence, Zimbabwe's political history was that of most British African colonies, one in which the leadership of the nationalist movements had primary contact with labour movements that were not Marxist in orientation.

The history of Portuguese Africa was different again. While no Communist parties existed in the African territories (with the possible exception of an ephemeral Angolan Communist Party, whose very existence is in doubt), there was of course an illegal, but intellectually significant, Communist Party in Portugal. And those of the CONCP leaders who went to the University of Lisbon were at least in contact with their clandestine organizations. However, in the late 1950s, these future leaders of the CONCP took the same kinds of distance from the Portuguese Communist Party, and for the same reasons, as did the French Africans and West Indians vis-a-vis the French Communist Party Aime Cesaire wrote his *Letter to Maurice Thorez* in 1956 rejecting the 'fraternalism' of the French Communist Party as he rejected the paternalism of French colonial authorities. In Portuguese Africa, the same kind of shock was felt when the Movimento Anti-Colonialista was founded in 1958. The very name reveals the game. For Portuguese Communists gave priority to the anti-*Fascist* struggle, whereas the African said the primary focus for them must be the anti-*colonial* struggle.

The evaluation of the ANC position can be seen by comparing the Freedom Charter of 1955 which they signed with other organizations including the Congress of Democrats, a White group in which the SACP was dominant, and the 'Strategy and Tactics of the ANC, adopted in 1969. Further clarification can be had by seeking the distinction the ANC draws between 'African socialism', a concept they rejected,and Tanzania's *ujamaa* as enunciated in the Arusha Declaration which they hailed. On the SACP itself, it is helpful to compare Nelson Mandela's statement to the Court on why he was *not* a

Communist with that of the Treasurer of ANC, Moses Kotane, on why he *was* a member of the SACP.

In the case of ZAPU, we give two texts of 1969. One said that 'Africans as a whole are neither capitalists nor communists'. The other analysed the danger of African 'capitalists' for the liberation struggle. By 1974, the statement of George Silundika showed a distinct evolution as a result of the experience of the struggle.

In the case of Angola, we may compare Neto's response to the question 'Does the MPLA have an ideology?' to Holden Roberto's rejection for the UPA of 'Marxist and Communist ideology' to Jonas Savimbi's definition for UNITA of what is an 'African Marxist'.

In the case of Mozambique, we present Joaquim Chissano's views on FRELIMO's ideology and Samora Machel's assertion that Mozambique was passing through a phase of 'sharpening of the internal class conflict' with the denial by the representative of COREMO, Artur Vilankulu, that there was 'Communist influence' in southern Africa.

For Guinea-Bissau, we compare Cabral's response to the question of the relevance of Marxism and Leninism with his eulogy of Nkrumah in which he linked the overthrow of Nkrumah to class struggle.

Lastly, we come to the question of the multiple Marxisms. On the one hand, Cabral in 1965 speaking to the CONCP referred to the 'solid allies' of the socialist camp. On the other hand he and other intellectuals of the PAIGC in 1966 agreed to attend a meeting in Peking only if it were guaranteed that they would not be embroiled in the 'ideological quarrels' that divided the Communist Party of the Soviet Union and the Chinese Communist Party. The closing phrase of this declaration underlined the overriding concern of the movements — the consequences of whatever they do or say for the national liberation movements themselves as movements.

The Freedom Charter
Congress of the People

> *Adopted at the Congress of the People at Kliptown, South Africa, on 26 June 1955 and endorsed by the ANC, South African Indian Congress, South African Coloured People's Organization, and the South African Congress of Democrats.*

We, the people of South Africa, declare for all our country and the world to know: that South Africa belongs to all who live in it, black and white, and that no government can justly claim authority unless it is based on the will of all the people; that our people have been robbed of their birthright to land, liberty and peace by a form of government founded on injustice and inequality; that our country will never be prosperous or free until all our people live in brotherhood, enjoying equal rights and opportunities; that only a democratic state, based on the will of all the people, can secure to all their birthrights without distinction of colour, race, sex or belief; and therefore, we the people of South Africa, black and white together – equals, countrymen, and brothers – adopt this Freedom Charter. And we pledge ourselves to strive together, sparing neither strength nor courage, until the democratic changes set out here have been won.

The People Shall Govern!
Every man and woman shall have the right to vote for and to stand as a candidate for all bodies which make laws. All people shall be entitled to take part in the administration of the country. The rights of the people shall be the same, regardless of race, colour or sex. All bodies of minority rule, advisory boards, councils and authorities shall be replaced by democratic organs of self-government.

All National Groups Shall Have Equal Rights!
There shall be equal status in the bodies of state, in the courts and in the schools for all national groups and races. All people shall have equal right to use their own languages, and to develop their own folk culture and customs. All national groups shall be protected by laws against insults to their race and national pride. The preaching and practice of national, racial or colour discrimination and contempt shall be a punishable crime. All apartheid laws and practices shall be set aside.

The People Shall Share in the Country's Wealth!
The national wealth of our country, the heritage of all South Africans, shall be restored to the people. The mineral wealth beneath the soil, the banks and monopoly industry shall be transferred to the ownership of the people as a whole. All other industry and trade shall be controlled to assist the well-being of the people. All people shall have equal rights to trade where they choose, to manufacture and to enter all trades, crafts and professions.

The Land Shall Be Shared Among Those Who Work It!
Restrictions of land ownership on a racial basis shall be ended, and all the land redivided among those who work it, to banish famine and land hunger. The state shall help the peasants with implements, seed, tractors and dams to save the soil and assist the tillers. Freedom of movement shall be guaranteed to all who work on the land. All shall have the right to occupy land wherever they choose. People shall not be robbed of their cattle, and forced labour and farm prisons shall be abolished.

All Shall Be Equal Before The Law!
No one shall be imprisoned, deported or restricted without a fair trial. No one shall be condemned by the order of any government official. The courts shall be representative of all the people. Imprisonment shall be only for serious

crimes against the people, and shall aim at re-education, not vengeance. The police force and army shall be open to all on an equal basis and shall be the helpers and protectors of the people. All laws which discriminate on grounds of race, colour or belief shall be repealed.

All Shall Enjoy Equal Human Rights!
The law shall guarantee to all their right to speak, to organize to meet together, to publish, to preach, to worship and to educate their children. The privacy of the house from police raids shall be protected by law. All shall be free to travel without restriction from countryside to town, from province to province and from South Africa abroad. Pass Laws, permits, and all other laws restricting these freedoms shall be abolished.

There Shall Be Work and Security!
All who work shall be free to form trade unions, to elect their officers and to make wage agreements with their employers. The state shall recognize the right and duty of all to work, and to draw full unemployment benefits. Men and women of all races shall receive equal pay for equal work. There shall be a forty-hour working week, a national minimum wage, paid annual leave, and sick leave for all workers, and maternity leave on full pay for all working mothers. Miners, domestic workers, farm workers, and civil servants shall have the same rights as all others who work. Child labour, compound labour, the tot system and contract labour shall be abolished.

The Doors of Learning and Culture Shall Be Opened!
The government shall discover, develop and encourage national talent for the enhancement of our cultural life. All the cultural treasures of mankind shall be open to all, by free exchange of books, ideas and contact with other lands. The aim of education shall be to teach the youth to love their people and their culture, to honour human brotherhood, liberty and peace. Education shall be free, compulsory, universal and equal for all children. Higher education and technical training shall be opened to all by means of state allowances and scholarships awarded on the basis of merit. Adult illiteracy shall be ended by a mass state education plan. Teachers shall have all the rights of other citizens. The colour bar in cultural life, in sport and in education shall be abolished.

There Shall Be Houses, Security and Comfort!
All people shall have the right to live where they choose, to be decently housed, and to bring up their families in comfort and security. Unused housing space to be made available to the people. Rent and prices shall be lowered, food plentiful and no one shall go hungry. A preventive health scheme shall be run by the state. Free medical care and hospitalization shall be provided for all, with special care for mothers and young children. Slums shall be demolished, and new suburbs built where all have transport, roads, lighting, playing fields, creches and social centres. The aged, orphans, the

disabled and the sick shall be cared for by the state. Rest, leisure and recreation shall be the right of all. Fenced locations and ghettos shall be abolished and laws which break up families shall be repealed.

There Shall Be Peace and Friendship!
South Africa shall be a fully independent state, which respects the rights and sovereignty of nations. South Africa shall strive to maintain world peace and the settlement of all international disputes by negotiation – not war. Peace and friendship amongst all our people shall be secured by upholding the equal rights, opportunities and status of all. The people of the protectorates – Basutoland (Lesotho), Bechuanaland (Botswana) and Swaziland – shall be free to decide for themselves their own future. The right of all the peoples of Africa to independence and self-government shall be recognized, and shall be the basis of close co-operation.

Let all who love their people and their country now say, as we say here: 'These freedoms we will fight for, side by side, throughout our lives until we have won our liberty.'

Who Are the Liberation Forces?
ANC

Excerpt from 'Strategy and Tactics of the ANC' adopted circa 1969.

So much for the enemy. What of the liberation forces? Here too we are called upon to examine the most fundamental features of our situation which serve to mould our revolutionary strategy and tactics. The main content of the present stage of the South African revolution is the national liberation of the largest and most oppressed group – the African people. This strategic aim must govern every aspect of the conduct of our struggle whether it be the formulation of policy or the creation of structures. Amongst other things, it demands in the first place the maximum mobilisation of the African people as a dispossessed and racially oppressed nation. This is the mainspring and it must not be weakened. It involves a stimulation and a deepening of national confidence, national pride and national assertiveness. Properly channelled and properly led, these qualities do not stand in conflict with the principles of internationalism. Indeed, they become the basis for more lasting and more meaningful co-operation; a co-operation which is self-imposed, equal and one which is neither based on dependence nor gives the appearance of being so.

The national character of the struggle must therefore dominate our approach. But it is a national struggle which is taking place in a different era and in a different context from those which characterised the early struggles against colonialism. It is happening in a new kind of world — a world which is no longer monopolised by the imperialist world system; a world in which the existence of the powerful socialist system and a significant sector of newly liberated areas has altered the balance of forces; a world in which the horizons liberated from foreign oppression extend beyond mere formal political control and encompass the element which makes such control meaningful — economic emancipation. It is also happening in a new kind of South Africa; a South Africa in which there is a large and well-developed working class whose class consciousness and in which the independent expressions of the working people — their political organs and trade unions — are very much part of the liberation front. Thus, our nationalism must not be confused with chauvinism or narrow nationalism of a previous epoch. It must not be confused with the classical drive by an elitist group among the oppressed people to gain ascendancy so that they can replace the oppressor in the exploitation of the mass.

But none of this detracts from the basically national context of our liberation drive. In the last resort it is only the success of the national democratic revolution which — by destroying the existing social and economic relationships — will bring with it a correction of the historical injustices perpetrated against the indigenous majority and thus lay the basis for a new — and deeper internationalist — approach. Until then, the national sense of grievance is the most potent revolutionary force which must be harnessed. To blunt it in the interests of abstract concepts of internationalism is, in the long run, doing neither a service to revolution nor to internationalism.

The Role of the Coloured and Indian People

The African, although subjected to the most intense racial oppression and exploitation, is not the only oppressed national group in South Africa. The two million strong Coloured Community and three-quarter million Indians suffer varying forms of national humiliation, discrimination and oppression. They are part of the non-White base upon which rests White privilege. As such they constitute an integral part of the social forces ranged against White supremacy. Despite deceptive and often meaningless concessions they share a common fate with their African brothers and their own liberation is in-extricably bound up with the liberation of the African people.

A unity in action between all the oppressed groups is fundamental to the advance of our liberation struggle. Without such a unity the enemy strength multiplies and the attainment of a people's victory is delayed. Historically both communities have played a most important part in the stimulation and intensification of the struggle for freedom. It is a matter of proud record that amongst the first and most gallant martyrs in the armed combat against the enemy was a Coloured Comrade, Basil February. The jails in South Africa are a witness to the large scale participation by Indian and Coloured comrades at every level of our revolutionary struggle. From the very inception of Umkhonto they were more than well represented in the first contingents who took life in hand to help lay the basis for this new phase in our struggle.

This mood was not only reflected in the deeds of its more advanced representatives. As communities too the Coloured and Indian people have often in the past, by their actions, shown that they form part of the broad sweep towards liberation. The first series of mass acts of deliberate defiance of the conqueror's law after the crushing of the Bambata rebellion, was the campaign led by that outstanding son of the Indian people — Mahatma Gandhi. Thereafter the Indian community and its leaders — particularly those who came to the fore in the 40s — played no small part in the injection of more radical and more militant mood into the liberation movement as a whole. The stirring demonstrations of the '50s from Defiance Campaign to the Congress of the People, the general strike, and the peasant revolts and mass demonstrations, saw many examples of united action by all the oppressed people. Indian workers responded in large numbers to almost every call for a general strike. Indian shopkeepers could always be relied upon to declare a day of Hartal in solidarity with any protest which was being organised. Memory is still fresh of the outstanding response by the Coloured workers of the Western Cape to the 1961 call by the ANC for a national general political strike.

The Alliance between the Congress organisations was a spur to the solidarity and reflected it. But events both before and after Rivonia put paid to the structures which had been created to express the Alliance. How can we strengthen and make effective the co-operation between the communities, and how can we integrate committed revolutionaries irrespective of their racial background?

Whatever instruments are created to give expression to the unity of the liberation drive, they must accommodate two fundamental propositions:

Firstly they must not be ambiguous on the question of the primary role of the most oppressed African mass and, secondly, those belonging to the other oppressed groups and those few White revolutionaries who show themselves ready to make common cause with our aspirations, must be fully integrated on the basis of individual equality.

Approached in the right spirit these two propositions do not stand in conflict but reinforce one another. Equality of participation in our national front does not mean a mechanical parity between the various national groups. Not only would this in practice amount to inequality (again at the expense of the majority) but it would lend flavour to the slander which our enemies are ever ready to spread of a multiracial alliance dominated by minority groups. This has never been so and will never be so. But the sluggish way in which the Movement inside the country responded to the new situation after 1960 in which co-operation between some organisations which were legal (e.g. SAIC, CPO, COD) and those that were illegal (e.g. ANC) sometimes led to the superficial impression that the legal organisations — because they could speak and operate more publicly and thus more noticeably — may have had more than their deserved place in the leadership of the Alliance.

Therefore, not only the substance but the form of our structural creations must, in a way which the people can see — give expression to the main emphasis of the present stage of our struggle. This approach is not a pandering to chauvinism, to racialism or other such backward attitudes. We are revolutionaries not narrow nationalists. Committed revolutionaries are our brothers to whatever group they belong. There can be no second class participants in our Movement. It is for the enemy we reserve our assertiveness and our justified sense of grievance.

The important task of mobilising and gaining the support of other oppressed non-White groups has already been referred to. Like every other oppressed group (including the Africans) we must not naively assume that mere awareness of oppression will by itself push the Indian and Coloured people in the direction of opposing the enemy and aligning themselves with the liberation movement. The potential is of course there, because in a very real sense the future of the Indian and Coloured people and their liberation as oppressed groups is intimately bound up with the liberation of the Africans. But active support and participation has to be fought for and won. Otherwise the enemy will succeed in its never-ending attempt to create a gap between these groups and the Africans and even recruit substantial numbers of them to actively collaborate with it. The bottom of the barrel will be scraped in the attempt to create confusion about the objectives of the liberation movement. More particularly, the enemy will feed on the insecurity and dependency which is often part of the thinking of minority oppressed groups. They will try to raise a doubt in their minds about whether there is a place for them in a future liberated South Africa. They have already spread the slander that at best for the Coloureds and Indians White domination will be replaced by Black domination.

It is therefore all the more important, consistent with our first principle, that the Coloured and Indian people should see themselves as an integral part of the liberation movement and not as mere auxiliaries.

Arusha, Africa and Socialism
ANC

Article in Sechaba *(ANC), I, 5, May 1967 reprinted from* Mayibuye, *organ of the ANC's Zambia office.*

The historic Arusha Declaration, made public by President Julius Nyerere on 5 February to a crowd of nearly 100,000, is a decisive document, not only for the socio-economic development of Tanzania but for the whole of Africa. It brings sharply into focus the real mass social base for economic advancement and draws the appropriate conclusions as to the nature and direction of this development.

Enemies and Carpers

It is understandable that such a vital step in the direction of Socialism will inevitably anger the imperialists who, we are sure, will do everything to sabotage the effective implementation of Socialism in Tanzania. The sneers are already there: one American weekly described it as 'tribal socialism'. Some so-called socialists, on reading of the nationalization of the banks in Tanzania, sneered: 'Hah, even the Labour Party in Britain nationalized industries. Was that socialism?' they ask. These gentlemen are the victims of their infantile brand of armchair pseudosocialism. We know them from South Africa. We remember how they used to brand leaders of the African Revolution, including Dr Nkrumah, President Nasser and others, as bourgeois aspirants, lackeys and agents of imperialism and so on !! These dogmatists overlook the fact that in Tanzania there are no big monopoly enterprises ready to take advantage of the cheap services of the nationalized sector, as in Britain.

'Socialism' — Use and Misuse

The term 'socialism' has been much misused and abused. But whatever the path taken towards genuine socialism, its basic tenets are unchangeable. In essence, socialism means the common ownership of the means of production, distribution and exchange, with scientific planning of the economy and with political power vested in the workers and peasants. The question was, and is, Can the African states embark on socialism under present circumstances? and not: Do the people of Africa want socialism? For there is no doubt that in the struggle against colonial oppression and for national liberation, the people recognised that imperialism was their main enemy and that socialism offered a chance to break away from the economic bonds of imperialism. This fact was so much a vital part of the masses in Africa that even anti-socialists had to hide their sinister plans under the guise of socialism.

The phrase 'African Socialism' has come much to the forefront since the wave of National Liberation first swept over Africa. Genuine socialists have accepted the phrase to mean that, while the basic tenets of socialism are unchangeable, conditions in Africa are different from those in other parts of the world, and the paths to socialism in Africa would, therefore, be different. However, reactionaries, imperialists and their apologists have grasped this term to suit their own purposes.

Thus, in the foreword to Father B. Onouha's book *The Elements of African Socialism,* Father John Maxwell, a Catholic priest, writes: 'Private enterprise can prosper and at the same time be socially responsible. By bold and scientific legislation, we can take the sting out of capitalism and render it harmless . . .' Father Onouha describes this as '. . . the capitalist monster subdued, purified and rendered marriageable to socialism . . .' This is a crude illustration to establish the point that socialism is accepted by the masses of Africa; that this fact is recognised by anti-socialists and that they will undertake all manner of contortions and distortions to confuse and mislead the masses. But leaving aside the imperialists and their apologists, the question of economic advancement seriously faced African leaders when their countries achieved political independence.

A long history of colonial plunder had left their countries poverty-stricken and backward, with the whole economy centred on one or two primary products which had to be exported to the industrialized metropolitan countries. In turn, Africa, lacking money and industries, had to import capital and manufactured goods from these very countries. The effects of this state of affairs are nothing short of devastating, for international monopoly, controlling world prices, can drive down the prices of these primary products and raise the price of its capital and manufactured goods.

The Secretary-General of the UN Trade and Development Conference in 1964 estimated that by 1970 the 77 developing countries would lose, in ONE year, £7,000 million to the developed countries of Western Europe and the U.S.A., as a result of the rise in the prices of capital and manufactured goods (Idris Cox, *Socialist Ideas in Africa*). The choice was therefore obvious at the time of the achievement of political independence. Either continue as in the colonial past and thus continue to suffer imperialist exploitation with its concomitants of poverty and backwardness, or break sharply from the past and take the path towards socialism. There was no third way: the development of capitalism was not possible, for the newly independent countries lacked the physical and economic resources, the financial reserves, the colonies and the armed might to foster and develop an indigenous capitalism against the expected and inevitable opposition of imperialism. In addition, the political climate was such that terms like 'imperialism' and 'capitalism' were hated by the masses, and their opposition could not be ignored.

On the other hand, the possibility of economic transformation through socialism was there. The mass social base at the time of independence comprised the workers and the peasants. The African bourgeoisie on the other hand was weak and small (less than 5%). The African past was rooted in tribalism with its tradition of communal living: so the psychological prerequisites were there. Further, the classical contradiction between co-operation in production on one side and private ownership on the other was sharply underlined by the fact that in most instances the latter was vested in foreigners. Also the struggle for national liberation had resulted in one single mass party, and the organizational framework was consequently there to carry the African Revolution through to socialism.

Several countries in Africa have already made their choice and have begun on the road to socialism. Ghana, at the time of the military coup, was in the process of carrying through its seven-year plan launched in 1963. Several overseas monopoly firms had been taken over, including shipping, cable and wireless, civil aviation, several diamond mines etc. The monopoly of the United Africa Company over cocoa had been broken and a Cocoa Farmers' Co-operative Society set up. Several new state enterprises were established with the aid of socialist countries. In agriculture by 1965 there were over 100 State farms and over 1,000 co-operative farms. Above all, there was the gigantic Volta Dam scheme with its potential for the transformation of the Ghanaian economy.

Similarly the Algerian Government after the victory over the French in 1961 had embarked on massive land reform and a radical change of the backward economy on the basis of socialism. Over half the agricultural land has been taken over already and more than 500 industrial enterprises nationalized. These are now managed by Workers' Councils. Egypt, having chosen the path of anti-imperialism and socialism, nationalized the banks and all major industries in 1963-65, and largescale land reform has been speeded up. The achievement of socialism is also the aim set by Guinea and Mali, and here too many French enterprises have been taken over, agrarian reform is on the way, and many co-operative farms are being developed.

Tanzania

The Arusha Declaration does not, thus, come in a vacuum. Socialism has been accepted and is being established in Africa. Tanzania has now openly and boldly chosen the road. However, it must not be thought that 5 Februrary brought about a sudden, dramatic revolutionary change in Tanzania – as though the past had been altogether different. President Nyerere and TANU have a long, principled and honourable record of being always on the side of Africa, on the side of progress and the future. Did not Tanzania break with Britain over the Rhodesian issue, despite the loss of much needed financial assistance? Did not President Nyerere have the courage to openly expose the weakness of the OAU? Did not Tanganyika unite with Zanzibar at a time when the leaders of the Zanzibar Revolution were being vilified on all sides?

The wheels of economic change had already been set in motion before the Arusha Declaration; thus, since independence in 1961, the number of co-operative societies has increased until today there are nearly one thousand and the Tanzania co-operative movement is one of the most highly developed in Africa. In 1963 these co-operatives handled goods to the value of over £14,000,000, and they have their own Co-operative Bank. 40% of investments in 1963 were in the public sector. The growth of State enterprises has long been encouraged. The need for the socialization of the means of production has been recognized. Thus President Nyerere stated in 1965: 'All countries calling themselves Socialist or Communist had one common aim, that is, the building of a society without classes. We have the same aim, but the methods to achieve it are different . . . Socialism means popular ownership of the means of production . . .'

So, on 5 February 1967, we had the Arusha Declaration, boldly proclaiming to the world that 'the policy of TANU is to build a Socialist state', and stating *inter alia* that 'all human beings are equal', that 'in order to ensure economic justice the State must have effective control over the principal means of production'. The Declaration is too lengthy to quote further here, but the most important features are:

(1) The stress on power and the control of the economy being vested in the workers and the peasants.

(2) The recognition of socialism as an ideology to be implemented by the people who believe in it and practise it.

(3) The effective control of all principal means of production, and the opening of the way for the collective ownership of the resources of the country.

(4) The need to eliminate exploitation.

(5) The need for vigilance in guarding against the temptations of feudalism and capitalism.

(6) The need for self-reliance and hard work.

(7) The need to work towards the liberation of all Africa.

(8) The need to co-operate with other States in Africa in bringing about African Unity.

In pursuance of the Arusha Declaration and the policy of socialism, the Tanzanian Government has already nationalized: ten banks, eleven export/ import and wholesale companies, eight major flour mills. The support of the masses for this policy was demonstrated by the joy of the thousands of marchers whom the President named the Green Guards.

The future will not be easy. Imperialism is watching, hawkeyed, over-ready to stifle all signs of progress. The series of counter-revolutions in Africa during 1966 were severe blows to the African Revolution. Democrats, progressives and socialists have to be doubly vigilant in protecting and advancing the Revolution. As the editorial in the Dar-es-Salaam 'Nationalist' on 6 February put it: 'The war is on. The war is on against the elements of capitalism, feudalism and servility in our society . . . The Arusha Declaration is a momentous blueprint in our history and gateway to the path to a democratic socialist society. Its full implementation will not be smooth. Indeed, we can anticipate that there will be those who will desire no alteration in the status quo, preferring the profits of the existing order. On them we have declared war. We intend to be vigilant.' Bravely spoken!

We in the ANC, struggling for a democratic non-racial South Africa, salute President Nyerere, the Government, the Party and the People of Tanzania on this historic advance in the realization of a world in which exploitation of man by man will forever be abolished.

I Am Not a Communist
Nelson Mandela

From speech in his defence at the Rivonia Trial while Secretary-General of the ANC, in June 1964. Speech is known by the title 'I Am Prepared to Die'.

Another of the allegations made by the State is that the aims and objects of the ANC and the Communist Party are the same. I wish to deal with this and with my own political position, because I must assume that the State may try to argue from certain exhibits that I tried to introduce Marxism into the ANC. The allegation as to the ANC is false. This is an old allegation which was disproved at the Treason Trial and which has again reared its head. But since the allegation has been made again, I shall deal with it as well as with the relationship between the ANC and the Communist Party and Umkonto and that Party.

The ideological creed of the ANC is, and always has been, the creed of African Nationalism. It is not the concept of African Nationalism expressed in the cry, 'Drive the White man into the sea'. The African Nationalism for which the ANC stands, is the concept of freedom and fulfilment for the African people in their own land. The most important political document ever adopted by the ANC is the 'Freedom Charter'. It is by no means a blueprint for a socialist State. It calls for redistribution, but not nationalisation, of land; it provides for nationalisation of mines, banks and monopoly industry, because big monopolies are owned by one race only, and without such nationalisation racial domination would be perpetuated despite the spread of political power. It would be a hollow gesture to repeal the Gold Law prohibitions against Africans when all gold mines are owned by European companies. In this respect the ANC's policy corresponds with the old policy of the present Nationalist Party which, for many years, had as part of its programme the nationalisation of the Gold Mines which, at that time, were controlled by foreign capital. Under the Freedom Charter nationalisation would take place in an economy based on private enterprise. The realisation of the Freedom Charter would open up fresh fields for a prosperous African population of all classes, including the middle class. The ANC has never at any period of its history advocated a revolutionary change in the economic structure of the country, nor has it, to the best of my recollection, ever condemned capitalist society.

As far as the Communist Party is concerned, and if I understand its policy correctly, it stands for the establishment of a State based on the principles of Marxism. Although it is prepared to work for the Freedom Charter, as a short-term solution to the problems created by White Supremacy, it regards the Freedom Charter as the beginning, and not the end of, its programme.

The ANC, unlike the Communist Party, admitted Africans only as members. Its chief goal was, and is, for the African people to win unity and full political rights. The Communist Party's main aim, on the other hand, was to remove the capitalists and to replace them with a working-class government. The Communist Party sought to emphasize class distinctions whilst the ANC seeks to harmonise them. This is a vital distinction.

It is true that there has often been close co-operation between the ANC and the Communist Party. But co-operation is merely proof of a common goal — in this case the removal of White Supremacy — and is not proof of a complete community of interests.

The history of the world is full of similar examples. Perhaps the most striking illustration is to be found in the co-operation between Great Britain, the United States of America and the Soviet Union in the fight against Hitler. Nobody but Hitler would have dared to suggest that such co-operation turned Churchill or Roosevelt into Communists or Communist tools, or that Britain and America were working to bring about a Communist world.

Another instance of such co-operation is to be found precisely in Umkonto. Shortly after MK was constituted, I was informed by some of its members that the Communist Party would support Umkonto, and this then occurred. At a later stage the support was made openly.

I believe that Communists have always played an active role in the fight by colonial countries for their freedom, because the short-term objects of Communism would always correspond with the long-term objects of freedom movements. Thus Communists have played an important role in the freedom struggles fought in countries such as Malaya, Algeria and Indonesia, yet none of these States today are Communist countries. Similarly in the underground resistance movements which sprung up in Europe during the last World War, Communists played an important role. Even General Chiang Kai Chek, today one of the bitterest enemies of Communism, fought together with the Communists against the ruling class in the struggle which led to his assumption of power in China in the 1930s.

This pattern of co-operation between Communists and non-Communists has been repeated in the National Liberation Movement of South Africa. Prior to the banning of the Communist Party, joint campaigns involving the Communist Party and the Congress Movements were accepted practice. African Communists could, and did, become members of the ANC, and some served on the National, Provincial and local committees. Amongst those who served on the National Executive are Albert Nzula, a former Secretary of the Communist Party, Moses Kotane, another former Secretary and J.B. Marks, a former member of the Central Committee.

I joined the ANC in 1944, and in my younger days I held the view that the policy of admitting Communists to the ANC, and the close co-operation which existed at times on specific issues between the ANC and the Communist Party, would lead to a watering down of the concept of African nationalism. At that stage I was a member of the African National Congress Youth League, and was one of a group which moved for the expulsion of Communists from the ANC. This proposal was heavily defeated. Amongst those who voted against the proposal were some of the most conservative sections of African political opinion. They defended the policy on the ground that from its inception the ANC was formed and built up, not as a political party with one school of political thought, but as a Parliament of the African people, accommodating people of various political convictions, all united by the common goal of national liberation. I was eventually won over to this point of view and I have upheld it ever since.

It is perhaps difficult for White South Africans, with an ingrained prejudice against Communism, to understand why experienced African politicians so readily accept Communists as their friends. But to us the reason is obvious. Theoretical differences amongst those fighting against oppression is a luxury we cannot afford at this stage. What is more, for many decades Communists were the only political group in South Africa who were prepared to treat Africans as human beings and their equals; who were prepared to eat with us, talk with us, live with us and work with us. They were the only political group which was prepared to work with the Africans for the attainment of political rights and a stake in society. Because of this, there are many Africans who, today, tend to equate freedom with Communism. They are supported in this belief by a legislature which brands all exponents of democratic government and African freedom as Communists and bans many of them (who are Communists) under the Suppression of Communism Act. Although I have never been a member of the Communist Party, I myself have been named under that pernicious Act because of the role I played in the Defiance Campaign. I have also been banned and imprisoned under that Act.

It is not only in internal politics that we count Communists as amongst those who support our cause. In the international field, Communist countries have always come to our aid. In the United Nations and other Councils of the world the Communist bloc has supported the Afro-Asian struggle against colonialism and often seems to be more sympathetic to our plight than some of the Western powers. Although there is a univeral condemnation of apartheid, the Communist bloc speaks out against it with a louder voice than most of the White world. In these circumstances, it would take a brash young politician, such as I was in 1949, to proclaim that the Communists are our enemies.

I turn now to my own position. I have denied that I am a Communist, and I think that in the circumstances I am obliged to state exactly what my political beliefs are.

I have always regarded myself, in the first place, as an African patriot. After all, I was born in Umtata, forty-six years ago. My guardian was my cousin, who was the acting paramount chief of Tembuland, and I am related to the present paramount chief of Tembuland, Sabata Dalinyebo, and to Kaizer Matanzima, the Chief Minister of the Transkei.

Today I am attracted by the idea of a classless society, an attraction which springs in part from Marxist reading and, in part, from my admiration of the structure and organization of early African societies in this country. The land, then the main means of production, belonged to the tribe. There were no rich or poor and there was no exploitation.

It is true, as I have already stated, that I have been influened by Marxist thought. But this is also true of many of the leaders of the new independent States. Such widely different persons as Gandhi, Nehru, Nkrumah and Nasser all acknowledge this fact. We all accept the need for some form of Socialism to enable our people to catch up with the advanced countries of this world and to overcome their legacy of extreme poverty. But this does not mean we are Marxists.

Indeed, for my own part, I believe that it is open to debate whether the Communist Party has any specific role to play at this particular stage of our political struggle. The basic task at the present moment is the removal of race discrimination and the attainment of democratic rights on the basis of the Freedom Charter. Insofar as that Party furthers this task, I welcome its assistance. I realize that it is one of the means by which people of all races can be drawn into our struggle.

From my reading of Marxist literature and from conversations with Marxists, I have gained the impression that Communists regard the parliamentary system of the West as undemocratic and reactionary. But, on the contrary, I am an admirer of such a system.

The Magna Carta, the Petition of Rights and the Bill of Rights, are documents which are held in veneration by democrats throughout the world.

I have great respect for British political institutions, and for the country's system of justice. I regard the British Parliament as the most democratic institution in the world, and the independence and impartiality of its judiciary never fail to arouse my admiration.

The American Congress, that country's doctrine of separation of powers, as well as the independence of its judiciary, arouse in me similar sentiments.

I have been influenced in my thinking by both West and East. All this has led me to feel that in my search for a political formula, I should be absolutely impartial and objective. I should tie myself to no particular system of society other than of socialism. I must leave myself free to borrow the best from the West and from the East.

The ANC and the CPSA
Moses Kotane

*Interview with the Treasurer-General of the ANC,
published in* Sechaba *(ANC), II, 8, August 1968.*

Sechaba: You are a well-known and prominent Communist. The ANC has been constantly attacked by sections of the Western press and governments as being a so-called 'Communist front organization'. What is your answer to such statements?

Kotane: Yes, I am a Communist and have never denied that I was. My membership of the former Communist Party of South Africa was never a secret to members of the African National Congress. I joined the Communist Party a year after I had joined the ANC. I was a member of both organizations from 1928 to 1950, when the CPSA was suppressed by the fascist government of South Africa. I was elected to the national executive of the ANC at a time when I was General Secretary of the CPSA. The reasons for this are the following: The ANC was and always has been a broad national organization and not a sectional or class party; The political demands and aims and objects of the ANC and the short-term or immediate of the CPSA were similar; I hope and believe that I am in the leadership of the ANC through merit and because of my past and present service to the organization.

The fact that I am a Communist has never changed or interfered with my representations on behalf of the ANC. When I have been charged with a mission by the ANC National Executive, I have protected and promoted the interests of the ANC and have never changed my mandate. Likewise when I have been charged with a mission by the Communist Party I have stuck to the terms of my mandate and defended the interests of the Party. In the formulation of policy I never think of two organizations. I look for a correct political stand and formulation for the organization concerned; The attacks on the ANC are either malicious or based on a misunderstanding of the character of our struggle. They are also largely due to the hoary old-wives-tale of a 'Communist conspiracy' everywhere and in everything.

Pet Ideas of Oppressors
ZAPU

Article in ZAPU's Zimbabwe Review *(Lusaka),*
25 January 1969.

Oppressors in Southern Africa have their pet ideas that freedom-fighters are instigated by Communists to wage wars against the settler unrepresentative regimes.

The settler dictatorships would like to convince everybody who is willing to swallow their trash that if it were not for the Eastern bloc, all would be quiet in Southern Africa.

This is such a stupid piece of propaganda that only the most naive people can believe it. It has been used in Asia, Latin America and in other parts of Africa which are now free.

Freedom-fighters are waging wars of liberation for their own lands and rights. They have to be armed if they are to win. It would be a very silly suggestion to say that the Western countries, most of which have big investments in Southern Africa, should arm the freedom-fighters.

If the West armed the freedom-fighters, they would be cutting their own throats in that the people who are looking after these investments are the same people the freedom-fighters are fighting because they are, again, the same people who oppress the majority.

It is the West which arms these oppressors against the freedom-fighters. It cannot, therefore, be expected to arm those who are opposing these regimes.

The most pertinent question to ask is: Do freedom-fighters support capitalism or communism? It is important to answer this question truthfully and succinctly.

Africans as a whole are neither capitalists nor Communists. They are basically communalists whose collective possession of land dates to times immemorial. But this does not mean to say they do not admire the good aspects of Communism or capitalism, if there are any.

Naturally, like anywhere else, there are now African capitalists just as there are African socialists. To pretend that all Africans belong to one ideological school of thought would be far from the truth. But to say that freedom-fighters are struggling because they are told to do so by people in the Eastern world is to assume very wrongly that the struggle began in Southern Africa after those participating in it actively had first gone to the East for indoctrination.

Without getting into unnecessary details about who is right or wrong between the East and the West, we must state quite categorically that in Southern Africa we are oppressed by and because of the West. We do not expect the West to support us against itself.

It is our right to be armed and to fight our oppressors. We never entertain the illusion that our oppressors have the right to question our right to get what weapons we can from anybody who appreciates and supports our cause.

If the oppressors on the whole think that by hammering on the bogey of Communism we will retreat, then they are living in a child's dream-land. If Communism means freedom, then we will fight for it. If capitalism means out continued suppression, then we will oppose it vehemently.

The Complex Enemy
ZAPU

Excerpt of article in ZAPU's Zimbabwe Review *(Lusaka),*
I, 4, October/November 1969.

The tendency of some elements within a struggling people to pursue wealth as against commitment to the struggle constitutes a problem. These elements move directly against the tide of liberation. They either have failed to find answers to the problems of an oppressed people beyond the status quo or are indeed of the types of the oppressors in their general motivations. They are pretenders to the privileges of the oppressors without the common sense of realising the injustice which brings it all about. The danger lies not so much in the economic strength they command — which in reality they do not — but in the acceptance of the system which has provoked the nation to revolt. No African in Zimbabwe, at the moment, runs a business or commands property worth mentioning as a factor in the conduct of modern economy. Wealth seekers are therefore just chasing an elusive hope which the controlling foreign capitalist will dangle for as long as there are resources for him to continue to exploit. The danger of these bourgeois-like elements is in that they are of the nature of capitalists and consciously or unconsciously work in the direction of entrenching the status quo. They are entry points to the real and destructive capitalists who stand to lose by the success of the liberation struggle. Tshombe's example is universally known to demonstrate and summarise the point. The advantage of the current liberation struggle is that the actual danger of these bourgeois elements in the society is more potential than real, as they do not as yet wield such economic force as to impose their line on the revolutionary struggle. The movement must, of course, always be watchful for elements that so often seek to bail themselves out of the struggle by their developing economic strength.

People struggling for liberation, like any other society, have within them all sorts of class tendencies which if not suppressed could overtake the struggle and ditch it. The quest for education is a tremendous force in Africa today. Education is naturally an element of social progress. It is part of colonialist education however to identify education with superiority over and not with service to the people. Since it is the colonialist who designs and dishes the education in colonial countries, he has used it as bait for building a 'species' contemptuous of the masses, called the 'elite'. In his conspiracy to grant independence, the colonialist has in some cases sought to create the petit bourgeoisie referred to above and the elite and then ceded power to them, which in fact is neo-colonial independence. These processes are manipulated in the course of the liberation struggle from among the oppressed in order to divert and defeat the objectives of the genuine struggle. This constitutes a problem to the liberation struggle. Whilst the colonialist must be blamed for promoting, and sometimes master-minding it, it must be acknowledged that the colonialist finds his material from among people struggling for liberation. Simple and straightforward acknowledgment of this fact is the first step towards honest and effective combating of the problem.

The endeavour towards education can constitute a problem to the liberation struggle not in a class sense but on the simple question of priorities. Perhaps the point is better put by saying it can be a problem for individuals in the struggle and not for the struggle as such. Even if it arises this way, it ultimately lands itself in the laps of the liberation movement. The mutual value of one carrying a gun at the fighting front and another studying to be a doctor at some university is not difficult to appreciate. The problem for the liberation movement is the mutual attitude between these two persons and the effect of this on the general internal state of the movement. Away from the clouds of general theories, these are basic questions which compel liberation movements towards precise definition of principles in a world full of all kinds of stresses.

The general principle is that education and the liberation struggle are not mutually exclusive providing the education undertaken is towards reinforcing the urgent requirements of the struggle and that the candidates understand it as clearly. In short the priority is the battlefield and any activity undertaken by an individual from struggling masses must be a contribution or commitment to the struggle. The fundamental problem to the liberation struggle, however, as pointed out earlier, is the design of a type of education, the promotion or acceptance of a nation of education which creates an 'elite' type regarding itself above and different from the society of which it is a part and unwittingly interpreting freedom as escape from the masses to a level in alliance with the oppressors and exploiters. This is not the elite that has come to be regarded historically in Europe as the leading exponent of the revolution. In fact the coloniser from Europe analysing the experience of his own situation has come to the clever conclusion that if you create and control an elite in a colonial country and thereafter control the whole range of information media, then you can carry out the economics of 'extraction' almost indefinitely. This point is worth stressing to enlighten those who conservatively and dogmatically apply the theory that the elite is the leader of the revolution without realising that the imperialists have already overtaken this development in their counter-revolutionary strategy.

ZAPU'S Ideological Position

George Silundika

Response to an interview question by Liberation Support
Movement by a leader of ZAPU, published in 1974.

We in ZAPU see the need to replace the oppressive economic system that now prevails in our country with a completely different system which will genuinely benefit the masses of people living under it. We proceed from analyzing the present conditions in Zimbabwe, conditions dominated by colonialism. Colonialism has developed from capitalism, and the lives of the Zimbabweans have been molded according to the demands of the capitalist and racist system. These demands, through which we have been exploited for generations, have oppressed and degraded us as human beings.

The racist regime has adopted policies to ensure privileges for a white minority under the capitalist system. And it is important to understand that capitalism in Zimbabwe benefits the entire white minority. The classical picture of the working class versus the bourgeoisie does not quite apply here because of the element of racism in our situation. An African worker and a white worker doing the same job belong objectively to different classes, even though they are both workers. Racism enters to create a privileged minority within the working class. This is an important feature of capitalism in southern Africa.

In our conception of the Zimbabwean revolution we recognize that the economic base must be changed in order to eliminate racism. In short, both capitalism and racism must be eliminated as we establish a socialist base in our country. In ZAPU we try to analyze our situation and conceive of socialism as it applies to us. We are conscious of the many problems that Zimbabwe's people will face on the road to constructing a new society — lack of capital, skilled manpower, education, etc., and we believe it essential that while these factors are being acquired our development must be based upon self-reliance, on our ability to produce for ourselves. Our people must attain full command over the development of a free Zimbabwe. Democracy should be exercised within the framework of socialism and for the well-being of the people.

MPLA's Ideology
Agostinho Neto

Interview with the President of MPLA by Sunday News *(Tanzania), 20 August 1972.*

Sunday News: Does MPLA have an ideology?
Neto: It depends on what you mean. There are schematic descriptions used to classify movements. . . communist, socialist and so on. But we consider that in our movement it is not possible at this stage to have this kind of classification. For a single party it is possible but when a movement consists of people who are different politically and ideologically it is not possible to say that this is, for example, a communist movement. Not all our people are communists, or socialists. But the movement has a political orientation. We have a precise target, we fight for a specific purpose, we must organise our resources in a particular way, we must organise our political life in a particular way.

Our movement has a programme not only for the present stage but also for after independence. In the present phase we say we must unite and fight the Portuguese and all those who are co-operating with them. After independence it will be necessary to organise a popular State. By popular, I mean democratic, where the people can participate fully, with assemblies and all the other organs that allow the people to express their opinions.

About the organisation of the economy we say that the Angolan people must have the riches of our country, we must give fair wages to avoid exploitation of the workers, and so on. This is what is normally called the socialist way. It is socialist because we don't intend to allow either Angolans or foreigners to exploit others in the country.

This is our orientation, our line. We think that ideologically we follow not necessarily the Communist or Marxist line but we follow the socialist line, with justice for everyone.

On Communism and Africa
Holden Roberto

*Two statements by the President of the FNLA. The first
appeared in an editorial of* La Voix de la Nation Angolaise,
*2, 15-30 September 1960. The second consists of answers
to interview questions by Germain M'ba, published in*
Le Progres *(Kinshasa), 76, 1-2 April 1967. Translated
from French.*

The colonialists try to demonstrate to the African peoples themselves that
both nationalism and the fight for dignity are identified with communism.
They have convinced a few Africans, who have been seduced by Marxist
and Communist ideology. Furthermore, many of these brothers say that it
is better to undergo anything rather than colonialism. These are Communists
of the worst kind. But the great majority of those who fight for the freedom
of their country have no other ideology than that of the dignity of man,
established by God himself.

It is quite well-known that Africa is attached to its religion, whichever it
may be. Its ideology is patriotism. This is what the Westerners call
nationalism.

All those who want to preserve their friendship with all the peoples of
Africa, with the Angolan people, should know that we have decided to be
nothing but Africans, masters of our destiny and our land, that we will not
be taken advantage of by any foreign propaganda. We are Africans, and will
fight to the death to remain Africans.

The colonialists may howl, but the caravan of freedom passes!

M'ba: Would you like to locate your revolution with regard to the two blocs,
the West and the East?
Roberto: This is obviously a question which interests many people. However,
in my opinion, to wish to locate our revolution in relation to the two blocs
is purely and simply a weakness. The Angolan revolution, being first of all an
Angolan affair and then an African one, has nothing to do with the ideological
conflicts which tear apart today's world. As I like to say, we are conducting
a war of liberation and not an ideological one. We accept help from anyone,
regardless of its origin, provided it has no strings.

M'ba: You often quote Fanon in your conversations. What does he represent
for you?
Roberto: Fanon was, in a way, my inspiration. Since our first encounter
in 1958, we were bound by friendship and fraternity. I was impressed by the
discernment and lucidity of his mind, and especially his profound knowledge
of African problems. All of Fanon's prophecies on Africa have come true. He
was a great man who, although a revolutionary, had the merit of approaching

problems realistically.

I still remember his last words when I was at his bedside in Bethesda Hospital in Washington, he spoke to me passionately of the independence of Angola which he took so much to heart, and which he regretted he would not see, since he knew he was dying of leukemia. It was then that he told Josie, his dear wife, to maintain the friendship they had for me until her death. It was the most moving moment of my life.

African Marxists
Jonas Savimbi

Interview with the President of UNITA, by Yvette Jarrico in August 1970, published as Document No. 1 of UNITA office in London.

Jarrico: Mr. President, mostly all the African states decry Marxism and profess the superiority of the socialist system. Do you think that Frantz Fanon was right when he said that the greatest enemy of Africa was a lack of an ideology? Do you agree with those who say that Africa has set off on the wrong foot? Or do you find that in the last two years the art of government in Africa has improved, and that what is most sincere and effective will soon follow such as class consciousness and revolutionary spirit?

Savimbi: Quite frankly, I think that's rather a long question, and my answer will be shorter. As to this business of talking about 'Marxism', 'efficiency', 'art of government' . . . what right does a European Marxist have to impose his own concepts on those Africans who call themselves Marxists? Marxism is a theory, a guide to action, a comprehensive science which must be applied according to the specific and concrete conditions in individual countries. So, why should a European Marxist today have any right to demand that African Marxists reply to this question? I am bound to doubt the sincerity of these European Marxists because they would like to see our political, economic and social views through the perspective of their own countries. I think that it is impossible to be a revolutionary, a true Marxist without having tested the effectiveness of the system in one's own country.

A Marxist prejudges neither a person nor an organization. Marxism is a theory. Oppressed people must fight for their freedom. If there must be a European, or an Asian guide to direct an African towards his own struggle for emancipation, then such Marxism is distorted and UNITA does not subscribe to it. To say that Africans claim to be Marxists in order to throw off Marxism, requires proof to be brought to us so that we can study this case. But to generalize, or to scold us is somewhat paternalistic (and imperialistic) I am afraid.

FRELIMO's Ideology
Joaquim Chissano

*Response to an interview question by a member of Central
Committee of FRELIMO, in Brussels, 27 November 1970.
Published in* Afrique Australe, *No. 2-3, 1971. Translated
from French.*

Afrique Australe: What is now the ideology on which is based the action of
FRELIMO?
Chissano: FRELIMO was created in order to fight Portuguese colonialism,
that is in order to fight a system of exploitation, a system of oppression,
an undemocratic system. This is why FRELIMO wants to create a united and
democratic Mozambique, that is one in which the people may choose its own
government, may participate and take part in the discussion of the country's
affairs.

On the other hand, FRELIMO wishes to create an economic system where
there will be no exploitation of man by man, an economic system in which
man works and benefits from his work, where men are united in a nation but
cooperate freely with other nations of their choice. We mean by freedom the
right to live, to work, to think, to speak, and above all the right to choose the
way in which we want to live, to choose our friends and to be part of Africa
and of the whole world. These are our politics and our external policies. I
may add that we support socialism as a means of development which brings
man towards dignity. We believe there is only one kind of socialism on this
basis, on this foundation. But we do not believe that the development of our
country, its independence and socialism, can be copied from other countries.
This is why we believe in the adaptation of these scientific ideas to local
conditions. I would like to make it clear that when we say that we support
socialism, it does not mean that we thereby lose our independence. Some
people think that since we receive help from socialist countries, we will
necessarily have to follow the policy of one or another socialist country. But
this is not correct, because since we fight for our independence (as we have
mentioned), we fight for the free choice of our way of life, of our relations,
and of our actions.

Sharpening of the Class Conflict

Samora Machel

Excerpt from speech given by the President of FRELIMO, at Symposium in Homage to Amilcar Cabral, Conakry, 31 January 1973.

Because the process of armed liberation struggle is not homogeneous in all parts of the national territory, it can happen that we experience different phases simultaneously in our countries. Whereas in one area the immediate task will be to launch armed struggle, in another the task will be to strike deeper roots, while in yet another the aim will be to establish the structures which make the liberation process irreversible. These heterogeneous situations demand of the leadership, of the militants who constitute the vanguard in the fight, an ideological clarity without which one runs the risk of misconstruing the struggle.

Knowing who should exercise power in a village and on behalf of which social group, deciding on the system of ownership, on how to organise trade — these are immediate and tangible questions which the whole people are capable of understanding and absorbing, so long as we do the necessary political work. In other words, it can be said that once the physical presence of the enemy has been destroyed, a new and more decisive conflict arises. The class struggle at an international level, between our people and the colonialist and imperialist enemy, is followed, at the internal level, by a class struggle against national forces with an exploitative bent.

It also means that the previous dividing line between colonisers and colonised has to be further completed by an even deeper dividing line between exploiter and exploited. This dividing line affects every field, and primarily the ideological and cultural fields. Ideas, values, habits, usages and customs, all the unconscious standards which regulate the everyday behaviour of the individual, are expressions of the ideology and culture of the existing society.

It so happens that we were all born into an exploitative society and have been profoundly imbued with its ideology and culture. This is why an internal fight against what we believe to constitue our moral framework is difficult and may at times seem impossible.

Divesting ourselves of the exploitative ideology and culture and adopting and living, in each detail of everyday life, the ideology required for the revolution is the essence of the fight to create the new man.

It is not the personal fight of one man wrapped up in himself. It is a mass struggle in which we accept criticism and do self-criticism, purifying ourselves in their fire, which makes us conscious of the path to be followed and fills us with hatred for the negative values of the old society.

When we launch this process, on the one hand the establishment of popular structures of political power and, on the other the fight to acquire a new mentality and behaviour, we are opening the doors to serious contradictions in our midst.

Discontent will arise. All those who were hoping to exploit the people, to step into the shoes of colonialism, will oppose us. Erstwhile companions of ours who initially accepted the popular aims of our struggle, but who in practice reject the internal struggle to change their values and customs, will move away from us to the extent of deserting or even betraying.

The successes achieved militarily, the feeling of the imminence of victory, will hasten the process of the discontentment of a handful of elements frustrated in their ambitions and corrupt tastes. In this way, a breach is made in our ranks through which the colonialist and imperialist enemy will penetrate.

The reactionary forces, the disgruntled elements, will see in an alliance with the enemy a way of safeguarding their petty and anti-popular interests, while the enemy will find in such an alliance a golden opportunity to strike a blow against the Revolution.

In the critical phase through which we are passing of the sharpening of the internal class conflict and the military and political defeat of the enemy, the protection of the Revolution and of its leaders, the survival of the revolutionary structures and of their cadres, depends now more than ever, on the masses.

No Communist Influence

Artur Vilankulu

> *Unpublished letter to* New York Times *replying to an article and sent on 6 April 1972 by the Representative to the US of the* Comite Revolucionario de Mocambique *(COREMO).*

To the Editor:

Without going into the East-West ideological squabble, let me say that it is a serious misconception to judge African nationalism as a result of either one's influence. Both the East and the West should have learned by now that Africans are neither pro-East nor pro-West, but pro-Africa. This thinking includes those of us in Southern Africa who are fighting for our freedom and independence.

Communism is a new concept in the world, but colonialism and imperialism are not. More than half the world population has suffered some kind of colonialism and that includes North America. One can say that North Americans were some of the first to fight against British imperialism, and certainly George Washington was not influenced by the 'Communists' to fight the unjust exploitation of man by man. Indeed he was influenced by the democratic spirit which allows people to choose their own form of government and decide their destiny without foreign influence. Likewise the people of Mozambique have been fighting Portuguese colonialism since the Portuguese arrived in our country.

After Vasco da Gama passed through Mozambique in 1498, the Portuguese sent an expedition under Pedro Alveres Cabral, who fought against the Arabs who were controlling the trade in Mombasa and Malindi. A second fleet was sent to Mozambique the following year under Commander Joao da Nova. In the process of carrying out their mission of exploring the new routes to the Eastern spice trade, the Portuguese 'discovered' not only new continents and people, but also a new and lucrative source of wealth, the slaves of West Africa, the ivory and gold of East Africa, and the tobacco and gold of the New World. Because the peoples of the nations in which these resources were found were not willing to hand over the wealth to the intruders, it became necessary for them to attack the indigenous people and destroy their political machinery before they could build the empire they meant to establish. In this connection it is interesting to note that for centuries the most common official term for the Portuguese overseas possessions was 'conquistas', meaning conquests.

The Portuguese have often said that the Africans are happy to be under the Portuguese flag. History, however, shows that the Africans resisted Portuguese control of their motherland since the time the Portuguese put foot in our country. They have never known peace in Mozambique from the fifteenth century until the present day. Major wars with Africans broke out in 1834, when the governor of Inhambane District, Candido da Costa Soares, moved against King Manukuse, who refused to pay vassalage to the Portuguese authorities. Again on August 25, 1843, the joint forces of Kings Magaya, Muwamba, and Manukuse attacked the fortress in Lourenco Marques.

It was in 1884-85 during the Berlin Conference which divided up the African 'pie' that Mozambique, Angola and Guinea Bissau were granted as colonies to Portugal, and it was at this time that Portugal desired to prove her 'effective occupation' of Mozambique. These provocations led to an open revolt in the southern part of Mozambique under the leadership of King Ngungunyane and his general, Magigwani, in 1885. Ngungunyane was captured and, according to the Portuguese, died in 1906, 'the man who led the important battles of Magul and Coolele'.

Also in 1867 there were five Portuguese expeditions against the Massangano people, who refused to pay vassalage to the authorities. Other resisters joined the Massangano, including the Baruwe King of Makonde in 1901. The Portuguese call this period the 'campanha e pacificacao de Barue', meaning the pacification of the Baruwe.

To say that the continuation of the Mozambican people's fight against colonialism is prompted by 'Communist influence' displays a lack of knowledge of African history and the nature of African nationalism. Today Africans in Mozambique have been forced to arm themselves and fight as our forefathers did. The Massacre of June 16, 1960, in Mueda, Cabo Delgado, where 500 Africans were slaughtered when they peacefully asked for higher wages, cannot be forgotten by any Mozambican. The Massacre of Mueda marked the end of a period when Africans strove through the United Nations and through appeals to world opinion and to the Portuguese government to attain a peaceful settlement. The only alternative left to us is to fight in the only language that our oppressors, the Portuguese, understand. We do not want to be made Portuguese citizens in our own land. We want to remain Africans and Mozambicans.

The fact that Portugal is a dictatorship is a matter for Portuguese to settle, but no decree passed by any body in Portugal will make Africa part of Europe. Portugal claims sovereignty over countries outside its boundaries through right of conquest, which is a violation, of the grossest kind, of international law.

Finally, the moral support that we receive from our brothers in Tanzania and Zambia and other freedom-loving people is welcomed, but we realize that no person, however sympathetic, can win our freedom for us. This we must do by our own hands and through our own sufferings. For this reason as much as any we do not believe that Chinese foreign aid to help Tanzania and Zambia build a railway will 'enable tens or hundreds of thousands of Chinese to come to Africa to strengthen their hold'. Similarly we do not believe that American aid now being given to build a highway from Dar es Salaam to Tunduru, will enable tens or hundreds of thousands of Americans to come to Africa to influence our thinking. We have been under Western colonial control for hundreds of years, and this had not turned us into capitalists. Certainly the five years of modest aid to Africa from China will not transform us into Communists.

'Communist influence in Southern Africa' does not exist. Jack Penn has a Communist phobia, just as we Mozambicans have a Portuguese colonialism phobia. No matter what labels are given to us, we will fight for our dignity.

Artur X.L. Vilankulu

The Relevance of Marxism-Leninism
Amilcar Cabral

Response to a question after speech in Central Hall, London on 26 October 1971, and published in 'Our People Are Our Mountains'.

Question: Besides nationalism, is your struggle founded on any ideological basis? To what extent has the ideology of Marxism and Leninism been relevant to the prosecution of the war in Guine-Bissau? What practical peculiarities, if any, have necessitated the modification of Marxism-Leninism?
Cabral: We believe that a struggle like ours is impossible without ideology. But what kind of ideology? I will perhaps disappoint many people here when I say that we do not think ideology is a religion. A religion tells one, for example, that Christ was born in Nazareth and performed this miracle and

that and so on and so on, and one believes it or one doesn't believe it, and one practises the religion or one doesn't. Moving from the realities of one's own country towards the creation of an ideology for one's struggle doesn't imply that one has pretensions to be a Marx or a Lenin or any other great ideologist, but is simply a necessary part of the struggle. I confess that we didn't know these great theorists terribly well when we began. We didn't know them half as well as we do now! We needed to know them, as I've said, in order to judge in what measure we could borrow from their experience to help our situation — but not necessarily to apply the ideology blindly just because it's a very good ideology. That is where we stand on this.

But ideology is important in Guinea. As I've said, never again do we want our people to be exploited. Our desire to develop our country with social justice and power in the hands of the people is our ideological basis. Never again do we want to see a group or a class of people exploiting or dominating the work of our people. That's our basis. If you want to call it Marxism, you may call it Marxism. That's your responsibility. A journalist once asked me: 'Mr. Cabral, are you a Marxist?' Is Marxism a religion? I am a freedom fighter in my country. You must judge from what I do in practice. If you decide that it's Marxism, tell everyone that it is Marxism. If you decide it's not Marxism, tell them it's not Marxism. But the labels are your affair; we don't like those kind of labels. People here are very preoccupied with the questions: are you Marxist or not Marxist? Are you Marxist-Leninist? Just ask me, please, whether we are doing well in the field. Are we really liberating our people, the human beings in our country from all forms of oppression? Ask me simply this, and draw your own conclusions.

We cannot, from our experience, claim that Marxism-Leninism must be modified — that would be presumptuous. What we must do is to modify, to radically transform, the political, economic, social and cultural conditions of our people. This doesn't mean that we have no respect for all that Marxism and Leninism have contributed to the transformation of struggles throughout the world and over the years. But we are absolutely sure that we have to create and develop in our particular situation the solution for our country. We believe that the laws governing the evolution of all human societies are the same. Our society is developing in the same way as other societies in the world, according to the historical process; but we must understand clearly what stage our society has reached. Marx, when he created Marxism, was not a member of a tribal society; I think there's no necessity for us to be more Marxist than Marx or more Leninist than Lenin in the application of their theories.

Homage to Nkrumah
Amilcar Cabral

Excerpt from speech delivered by the Secretary-General of PAIGC, at Symposium in Conakry on Kwame Nkrumah Day, 13 May 1972.

We must remind ourselves at this time that all the coins of life have two sides. All realities have two aspects; the positive and the negative. To positive action, negative action has been and will always be opposed and vice versa. President Nkrumah will remain part of the history of Africa and the world because the sum total of his positive action is more than positive: it is the expression of his outstanding achievements, of his creative and fruitful practice in the service of the people of Africa and of Mankind.

We must however learn the lessons which events teach us and, even in these painful moments ask ourselves a few questions so that our understanding of the past, our experience of the present and our preparation for the future may be improved. For instance, which economic and political factors made it possible for betrayal to succeed in Ghana in spite of the personality, inspite of the courage, in spite of the positive action of Nkrumah?

Yes, imperialism is criminal and ruthless but we must not place the whole burden of blame on its broad back. For as the African people are known to say: 'Rice only cooks inside the pot.'

To what extent was the success or betrayal in Ghana linked or not to problems of class struggle, to contradictions in the social structure, to the role of the Party and of other institutions including the armed forces – all in the context of a newly independent state? We must ask ourselves to what extent the success of betrayal in Ghana was linked or not to the search for a correct definition of those historical makers of history – the People – and to their daily actions in defence of their own conquests during independence? Or to what extent might not the success of betrayal in Ghana be linked to the fundamental problem of the choice of men in the Revolution?

Meditation over such questions may perhaps lead us to a better understanding of the magnitude of Nkrumah's work, as well as the complexity of the problems he had to confront, so often alone. These problems will also undoubtedly lead us to the conclusion that as long as imperialism exists, *an independent state in Africa must be a liberation movement in power – or else it will not be.*

Our Solidarities
Amilcar Cabral

Excerpt from interview at the Second Conference of the CONCP, 3-8 October 1965. Translated from French.

In international politics, the CONCP stands for a policy of non-alignment. This is the policy which is most compatible with the interests of our peoples in the present stage of our history. We are certain of it. But for us non-alignment does not mean turning our back on the fundamental problems concerning humanity and justice. For us, non-alignment means not to be drawn into blocs, not to follow the lines drawn by others. We reserve for ourselves the right to make our own decisions, and if by chance our options, or decisions, coincide with those of others, this is not our responsibility.

We support the policy of non-alignment but we also consider ourselves deeply committed to our people and to every just cause in the world. We consider ourselves as part of a broad front of struggle for the good of humanity. You will understand that we fight first of all for our peoples. This is our task in this common struggle. And that has implications in terms of solidarity. We in the CONCP are strongly committed to every just cause. This is why we from FRELIMO, MPLA, PAIGC, CLSTP, or from any mass movement affiliated to the CONCP, beat our hearts in unison with those of our brothers from Viet Nam who give us a unique example in fighting the most scandalous, the most unjustifiable imperialist aggression of the United States of America against the peaceful Vietnamese people. Our hearts beat also with those of our brothers from the Congo who, in the jungles of such a vast and rich country, seek to resolve their own problems but are faced with imperialist aggression and imperialist manoeuvres via puppets. Thus, we from the CONCP, loudly and strongly proclaim that we are against Tshombe, against all the Tshombes of Africa. Our hearts beat just as strongly with our brothers in Cuba who have also shown how a people, even surrounded by the sea can victoriously defend its fundamental interests with arms, and decide its own destiny. We are with the Blacks from America, we are with them in the streets of Los Angeles, and when they are denied any possibility of a decent life, we suffer with them.

We are with the refugees, the martyred refugees of Palestine who have been ridiculed, and expelled from their homeland by imperialist manoeuvres. We stand with the Palestinian refugees and we support everything that the children of Palestine do in order to free their country, and we support with all our might all that the Arab and African countries do to aid the Palestinian people to recover its dignity, its independence, and its right to life. We are also with the peoples of South Arabia, of so-called French Somaliland (Somali Coast), of so-called Spanish Guinea, and we side with understanding and sorrow with our brothers from South Africa who confront the most barbaric of racial discriminations. We are absolutely positive that the development of struggle in the Portuguese colonies and the victory which we are attaining every day against Portuguese colonialism is a significant contribution towards the liquidation of that shameful and vile regime of racial discrimination in South Africa, *apartheid.* We are also sure that peoples such as those of Angola, Mozambique, and we ourselves in Guinea and Cape Verde though distant from South Africa, will one day be able to play a very important role in the final liquidation of the last bastion of colonialism, imperialism and racism in Africa, which is South Africa.

Our solidarity goes to every just cause in the world, but we also derive strength from the solidarity of others. We have concrete help from many people, many friends, many brothers. I would only like to tell you that we, in the CONCP, have a fundamental principle which consists in counting above all on our own efforts, our own sacrifices. But, in the objective framework of Portuguese colonization, dear friends, we are also aware that our struggle is not solely ours in the present stage of man's history. It is one which comprises all of Africa, all of progressive humanity. This is why we from the CONCP, confronting the peculiar difficulties of our struggle, and in the context of current history, have realized the need for concrete help in what concerns Africa, of concrete help from every progressive force in the world. We accept all help, regardless of where it may come from, but we never ask for help just from anybody. We expect only that aid which each is able to offer to our struggle. This is our *ethic* of help.

We wish to tell you that it is a duty for us to say here clearly and loudly that we do have solid allies in the socialist countries. We all know that the African peoples are our brothers. Our struggle is theirs. Every drop of blood that we shed falls also from the body and heart of these African peoples, our African brothers. But we also know that since the Socialist Revolution and the events following World War II, the world has definitely changed. A socialist camp has emerged in the world. This has completely changed the balance of forces, and this socialist camp is today quite aware of its international duties, its historic moral duties, not moral ones because the peoples of the socialist countries have never exploited the colonial peoples. They have shown themselves to be conscious of their duty and it is for this reason that it is an honour to tell you here openly that we receive substantial effective aid from these countries, which reinforces that which we receive from our African friends. If there are people who will be unhappy to hear me say this, may they come also to help us in our struggle. But may they be sure that we are proud of our sovereignty.

We will maintain our position: we take help from anyone. And we will take help from the socialist countries because they show today the path which serves man, the path of justice. In this room there are representatives from socialist countries who have come here as friends. I would like to take advantage of this opportunity to tell the representatives of the Soviet Union and of China, those of Yugoslavia and of the German Democratic Republic, who are here as the representatives of the socialist countries, to please convey our gratitude for the concrete aid which their peoples give us in our struggle.

And those who do not like to hear us talk of the aid of socialist countries, what have they been helping us do? They aid Portugal, the fascist and colonialist government of Salazar. It is no longer a secret to anyone that Portugal, the Portuguese government, would not be able to lead a struggle against us if it did not or could not have access to the help from its allies in NATO.

Not Our Quarrel

Permanent Commission of Writers and Artists of Guine and Cape Verde

A Declaration signed on 26 July 1966 by five leaders of the PAIGC: Amilcar Cabral, Vasco R. Cabral, Dulce Almada, Jose Araujo, and Maria de Luz Andrade. Translated from French.

The Permanent Commission of Writers and Artists of so-called Portuguese Guinea and the Cape Verde Islands has given its assent to send a delegation from our country to the recent 'Extraordinary Assembly of Afro-Asian Writers ' (Peking, June 27 - July 9) under the following conditions:

(a) The 'Extraordinary Assembly' should limit its operations to the objectives listed in the agenda, specifically to a demonstration of the active solidarity of Afro-Asian writers for the heroic struggle of the Vietnamese people.

(b) Our delegation shall uphold, as firmly as possible, the political line established by our national Party (the PAIGC) in relation to ideological quarrels, which is that, as militants of a national liberation movement, we must never take part in such quarrels.

The first reports received from our delegation, which had remained loyal to our Party's line, unfortunately revealed that the 'Extraordinary Assembly' exceeded its legal authority, and went as far as to discuss the especially delicate problem of the exclusion of one of the members from the Afro-Asian Writers Organization.

Although our delegation indicated the juridical incompetence of the 'Extraordinary Assembly' in such a problem and indeed voted against the motion for the exclusion of a member presented by the delegation of Basutoland.

The Permanent Commission of Writers and Artists of Guinea and Cape Verde wishes to state the following:

(1) We entirely support the independent position which was adopted by our delegation during the 'Extraordinary Assembly' of Afro-Asian Writers held in Peking on June 27 to July 9th.

(2) We entirely support the claims of various delegations, particularly those from Guinea and Algeria, making public the fact that the motion for

exclusion formulated by the delegation from Basutoland was not adopted unanimously.

(3) We urge the Permanent Bureau of Afro-Asian Writers to include in its documentation our delegation's reservations, abstentions and votes.

(4) As writers and artists aware of the duties imposed upon us by the present phase of the history of our country, we thank all those who — particularly if they proclaim themselves as being friends of our people — do not attempt to involve us in ideological quarrels whose consequences have proved to be harmful to the national liberation movements.

4. National Movements and the Class Struggle: Practice

Editors' Introduction

The theories expounded by the movements in the last section found their moment of truth in the organizational practice of the movements. We present two case studies, each of which illustrates a different practical issue.

The first was the problem FRELIMO had to face in deciding, in the light of its general principles, what were the practical ideological bases of unity and of exclusion. At the beginning, the Mozambique national movement sought unity. Before FRELIMO was formed, the Uniao Democratico Nacional de Mocambique (UDENAMO) seemed the most promising core-group. It was a member of the CONCP from its creation in 1961. But soon thereafter, others in the CONCP became aware of things going wrong in UDENAMO — that it contained adventurers and perhaps Portuguese agents. We reproduce a document of the CONCP from June 1962 in which they tried to handle the situation.

When FRELIMO was formed in August 1962 from a merger of UDENAMO and two other groups, and under the leadership of Eduardo Mondlane, a more solid organization came into existence, one which launched the armed struggle in 1964. As the struggle intensified, FRELIMO began the slow transformation from a national front towards being a party with a clear ideology.

This was not without its problems. Mondlane discussed these problems in the context of the so-called 'tribal question'. He also discussed the desirability of moving towards a clear party structure in an interview given just before his assassination and heretofore unpublished.

His assassination was directly linked to the internal problems of the organization and crystallized the internal crisis. FRELIMO's Central Committee met it head on in a statement in 1969 recognizing the existence of two 'divergent groups' within the organization. They spoke of the dangers of men like Lazaro Nkavandame, who were in FRELIMO only because they wanted 'to substitute themselves for the Portuguese colonialists in exploiting (the) people'. Nkavandame was expelled, but the crisis was not over. A top leader, Uria T. Simango, attacked FRELIMO on ideological lines. (We reproduce this attack here.) He too was expelled. FRELIMO then regrouped under Samora Machel whose attack on the 'material, spiritual and ideological corruption' *within* FRELIMO we present.

The second case study is that of Namibia. Here the issue was how the movements view outside involvement with respect to questions of organizational disunity on ideological grounds. Shortly after the creation of the OAU in 1963, the African Liberation Committee began to put pressure on the two major existing groups at the time, SWAPO and SWANU, to unite. SWAPO resisted this pressure alleging that unity could not be achieved at just any price. On the other hand, when SWAPO saw an outside organization, the International Students Conference (ISC), explain this disunity in simplistic ideological terms, SWAPO wrote an angry open letter advising the ISC to keep out of Namibian internal affairs.

Eventually, SWAPO emerged as the only effective national liberation movement in Namibia. The African Liberation Committee then dropped all assistance to SWANU and all pressure on SWAPO for a merger. SWANU reacted by a bitter attack on the OAU, charging they were creating the situation (weakness of SWANU) to which they claimed they were reacting. The OAU and other African groups continued to feel nonetheless that SWAPO had come to incarnate the national liberation movement of Namibia.

To the Nationalists of Mozambique
CONCP

Statement issued by the Consultative Council of CONCP in Rabat (Morocco) on 13-15 June 1962 and reproduced in CONCP Bulletin, *4, 5 September 1962.*

The Consultative Council of the Conference of Nationalist Organizations from the Portuguese Colonies, meeting in extraordinary session from 13 to 15 June at Rabat, expresses its profound concern over the seriousness of the situation of the African People of Mozambique with regard to the real development of the national liberation struggle.

It is a fact that in Angola, in 'Portuguese' Guinea and even in the Cape Verde Islands, S. Tome and Principe, where geographical and political isolation have created difficulties for the Nationalists, nevertheless the struggle for National Liberation is developing rapidly in accordance with the concrete realities of these countries.

On the other hand, in Mozambique where six and a half million Africans continue to be subjected to all the crimes of the Portuguese colonial yoke, there is a clear lagging behind.

Such a state of affairs is serious indeed, not only because it augurs badly for the present and the future of the Mozambican people themselves, but also for the following reasons:

(a) As it is the most populous and one of the richest of the Portuguese colonies, Mozambique has grave responsibilities in the group of African countries dominated by Portugal, above all in connexion with the struggle for the urgent liquidation of Portuguese colonialism in these countries. Whatever delay occurs in the liberation struggle of the Mozambican people can only hamper the peoples of the other Portuguese colonies and be of advantage to Portuguese colonialism.

(b) The location of Mozambique in the vicinity of independent African countries or who are on the road to independence, its natural riches, and its relatively numerous population, create serious responsibilities for the Mozambican People in the framework of East, Central and Southern Africa. These responsibilities are the graver inasmuch as there are thousands of European settlers in Mozambique, the majority of whom not merely oppose the independence of African countries, but align themselves with the racist and colonialist forces of the Union of South Africa, the Rhodesias, Kenya and other neighbouring countries. The backwardness of the liberation struggle of the Mozambican people is contrary to the interests of these countries insofar as they concern liberation from the colonial yoke and the building of independence, sovereignty and the national security of countries already independent or so to be.

(c) Last, but not least, the backwardness of the liberation struggle of six and a half million Mozambican Africans gravely prejudices the general struggle of the peoples of Africa for the urgent and total liquidation of foreign domination on the African Continent.

World opinion, and in particular a number of African governments and organizations, is unable to conceal its astonishment and concern at the silence that reigns regarding the situation in Mozambique.

Although it is true that the names of two Mozambique nationalist organizations with delegations abroad — the UDENAMO (Democratic National Union of Mozambique) and MANU (Mozambique Africa National Union) — are well known, it must be recognized that news regarding the actual activities of the liberation struggle in the interior of Mozambique is few and far between or indeed practically non-existent. CONCP, by its structure, its objectives and its means of action, believes that the national liberation struggle, even though it requires support abroad, must be conducted inside each country by the people themselves.

Furthermore, the CONCP can under no circumstances ignore the responsibilities it bears in the struggle for the liberation of the Mozambican People, not only because it is a matter of one of the most important Portuguese colonies, but also because the UDENAMO, one of Mozambique's nationalist organizations, is affiliated to the CONCP.

The concern of the CONCP in this connexion, clearly expressed in the course of this meeting of the Consultative Council, is even more well-founded on account of the fact that its Permanent Secretariat has received no news whatever on the struggle in Mozambique from the leadership of UDENAMO. This renders it impossible for the CONCP properly to carry out its duties concerning the coordination of the struggle in the different colonies and hampers all chances of giving effective and permanent support to the Mozambican nationalists.

However, the situation is the more disturbing because in addition to his declarations and activities clearly contrary to the interests of all those who struggle against Portuguese colonialism, the leading officer of UDENAMO, Mr. Chitofo Gwambe, has latterly been the subject of severe criticism from many personalities, among whom are to be found members of the UDENAMO. These criticisms have been accompanied by the following grave charges:

(1) Of sabotaging the practical activity of the organization which he leads.

(2) Of having created great difficulties in the achievement of the unity of Mozambique nationalists.

(3) Of having eliminated very valuable nationalist elements, for fear of

their participation in the leadership of UDENAMO.

(4) Of having taken no effective measures at all towards providing possibilities for Mozambican nationalists of training and equipping themselves for the development of cadres both for the liberation struggle and for the building of progress in their country after independence.

(5) Of having converted to his own use material means accorded to the Mozambican People for the liberation struggle.

(6) Of making frequent false declarations and of being a personality with no prestige at all among nationalist circles inside Mozambique.

(7) Of collaborating with the Portuguese political police (the PIDE) against the interests of the Mozambican People.

(8) Of being responsible for the imprisonment of some members of UDENAMO by the colonialist authorities.

Although it reserves the right to proceed with the rigorous investigation required by such charges, the CONCP cannot fail to recognize that they come not only from organizations and leaders who are well known for the positive activity for the liberation of Africa, but also from an independent African State.

On account of such accusations the People of Mozambique have already been the victims of serious disadvantages, as for example the refusal of support and assistance on the part of personalities and organizations who refuse to collaborate with the leader of UDENAMO. For example:

(a) The Government of Tanganyika expelled this officer in July 1961, and up to the present has not granted him a residence permit.

(b) The PAFMECA (Pan-African Freedom Movement from East and Central Africa) refuses to grant membership to UDENAMO so long as this organization has such an officer at its head.

(c) Numerous African nationalist organizations, in particular those of the other Portuguese colonies, refuse to collaborate with this officer.

The recent disappearance of a member of UDENAMO, Mr Sigauke, who according to information received was kidnapped by the Portuguese police in Southern Rhodesia, has provoked profound disquiet among nationalist circles of the Portuguese colonies. The principal officer of UDENAMO, with whom Mr Sigauke was in complete disagreement, has been accused of being an accomplice in this disappearance.

Obviously all these matters could already have been clarified if Mr Chitofo Gwambe had agreed to participate in the Consultative Council. Although he was duly invited to this extraordinary session, the said officer did not believe it his duty to take part, which fact demonstrates his complete lack of interest, not only in the Consultative Council of which he is a member, but also in the sacred cause of the liberation of his people.

At this juncture, which is so serious and decisive for the Peoples of the Portuguese colonies, an attitude of this kind can only further strengthen the case for those who have made these most grave charges against the said officer.

The CONCP and its Consultative Council are firmly convinced that true Mozambican nationalists, who are to be found as much inside as outside

Mozambique, will know how to face up fully to their responsibilities and apply those measures necessary for the urgent clarification of the situation of the Mozambican People, for the solution of the problems of leadership of the UDENAMO, and for the development of the national liberation struggle in Mozambique.

The CONCP is firmly resolved to defend the sacred interests of the Mozambican People and to use all its endeavours towards the better service of the liberation struggle.

That is why, after having analysed the situation in Mozambique, the Consultative Council of the CONCP, meeting in extraordinary session from 13 to 15 June in Rabat:

Long live the united struggle for liberation of the Peoples of the Portuguese colonies!
Long live the struggle for national liberation of the People of Mozambique!
For a strong, conscious, honest and active leadership in all Fronts of the struggle!
Down with Portuguese colonialism and all its lackeys!

The Tribal Question in the Advanced Stage of the Struggle
Eduardo Mondlane

Response to an interview question by the President of FRELIMO. The interview was conducted in 1969 a week before his assassination, and was published in Tricontinental, *12, May-June 1969.*

Tricontinental: You said that the tribal question in the advanced stage of the struggle became a sort of problem. Was it at this stage?
Mondlane: Yes, the point at which tribalism arises, as does regionalism, is the point where psychological warfare comes into operation. When the Portuguese Army is being hurt by our forces, when the Portuguese become more and more aware that FRELIMO is a force to contend with, as it became in 1965-66, they begin to devise new means. Salazar launched propaganda which they were the only ones to believe: that there is no Mozambique without Portugal; that the Mozambique people are a motley of tribal groups who have never had any unity. According to the Portuguese, their presence in our country stopped the possibility of fratricidal fights and trouble from springing up among us. Well, there isn't such a thing. So how do you prove, how do you make happen, that which you wished for? They began to organize whatever ethnic or language differences existed among people in Mozambique and tried to foment them. Or, they tried to infiltrate into FRELIMO individuals who were from one region to create confusion among

the military by saying that 'you have been commanded by men from another region'. These attacks have all failed, but we are not fooling ourselves, as we sense even now that there is a constant pressure to make out of regionalism or tribalism a factor in every structure we create. We know that the enemy is still interested in fomenting these problems and we continue to fight against them.

Tricontinental: What has been the work carried out with the tribal chiefs?
Mondlane: What happens in every region where action is taking place is that any chief who is against the liberation struggle is sent away before military action takes place. But as soon as military action begins he either has to run over to the enemy or he is eliminated. Only those chiefs who have become part of FRELIMO, which means becoming chairmen, or secretaries of cells, sections, districts, or provinces of our work, can remain. And at that point they are one and the same with any one of us. So the functions they had before had an influence in their selection only because they had prestige and, therefore, they were elected chairmen, but, once the struggle begins, the whole thing is people of Mozambique together. And the paramount chief is unimportant as such in that stage.

Tricontinental: And how has armed struggle influenced the traditional political structure, habits, and so on?
Mondlane: The traditional political structure was really destroyed by the Portuguese. In some parts it took a longer period than in others. In the South, and in some parts of the West, it is only recent. But even then, for example, in my area, Limpopo Valley, in the southern part, the king of that area was captured and our army destroyed only in 1898, during my father's youth. The political structure is gone, practically. There isn't a traditional political structure, except the system of authority which is reflected by that administrative system which the Portuguese perpetuated. But even this is split into small units whose paramount chiefs are nothing but policemen. They have no value politically in the country. And most of them are so police-like that they are despised by the people. FRELIMO is organizing a new political structure out of a vacuum of no politics or no tradition, really, of politics. A system of authority did exist, and some people still cherish a tribal leader. But these tribal leaders possessing a real or spiritual influence have been emasculated by the eagerness of the Portuguese to destroy the tradition and create a new Portuguese administration. This is very favourable to FRELIMO now. In our economy we use the people to produce cotton, to produce sisal, to produce tea, and the other things that the Europeans want. People who are in the rural areas grow rice, cashew nuts, and so on for the European economic interests directly. We say: 'Look, you are being exploited.' And we can point to the paramount chief's excesses, the way he violates even the traditional system of work, because the administration of Portugal says he must, and when he does things that the administration doesn't want he is humiliated in public, beaten by the palmatoria, by the Portuguese.

This exemplifies the lack of power that we people suffer from in Mozambique. So the political structures of the past have gone, and have gone for good. FRELIMO must fill in the vacuum with new politics.

The Portuguese, because theirs is a fascist regime, in the last 40 years never encouraged any development of local traditional political structures the way the British have done in British Africa. Therefore, we are dealing with a fresh situation which is actually a challenge for us.

The Evolution of FRELIMO
Eduardo Mondlane

*Excerpt from a previously unpublished interview by
Aquino de Braganca, recorded in Algiers shortly after
the Second Congress in 1968.*

de Braganca: What would you say if it were asserted that FRELIMO began by being a front and has transformed itself into a political party?
Mondlane: Of course, of course. I agree that as a result of the experience of ten days of the [Second] Congress, FRELIMO has a political line that is much clearer than previously. In the first place because this line came to be seen as important in the conditions of our struggle, in part also because there were some elements within FRELIMO who brought these ideas with them to the struggle. A common base we all had when we formed FRELIMO was the hatred of colonialism, the necessity of destroying the colonial structure — but what type of social structure no-one knew. Some knew, had theoretical ideas, but even they were transformed by the struggle. There is a coalescence of thought that came about in these last few years that makes it possible for me to say, and I do believe it, that FRELIMO is now really far more socialist, revolutionary, and progressive than ever before, and now tends more and more in the direction of socialism of the Marxist-Leninist variety.

Because the conditions of life in Mozambique, the type of enemy we have, permit no other alternative. It is impossible to create a capitalist Mozambique. It would be ridiculous for the people to fight to destroy the enemy's economic structure and then reconstruct it for the enemy. It would be ridiculous, and I have said so several times. Now we're not going to do that. We are going to create a socialist system and there now exists a wealth of experiences of various socialist countries that we shall study carefully. So that it is in this way that the theory of Marxism-Leninism and the experience (including the errors) of the socialist countries that have been working and living a socialist experience since 1917 are very relevant for us.

The training of politico-military cadres includes instruction about socialism. So that those who came to the movement with a Catholic religious background continue to be Catholics but Marxist Catholics. It is possible!

Without compromising the Party which has not yet made an official declaration asserting it is Marxist-Leninist, I think FRELIMO can be said to be inclining more and more in this direction because the conditions under which we struggle and live require it.

Self-Criticism
FRELIMO

> *An editorial in* Mozambique Revolution *(FRELIMO)*, *38, March-April 1969, following the meeting of the Central Committee on 11-21 April.*

The Central Committee of FRELIMO met in ordinary session from 11 to 21 April. The agenda included the discussion of the main problems of our struggle. The work of the different Departments was analysed exhaustively, lines of orientation were drawn up for each one and their respective programmes of action were approved. So far, this meeting of the Central Committee was no different from any of the previous meetings.

But something completely new happened at this meeting, distinguishing it as an historical landmark in the development of FRELIMO: like a fresh wind there appeared a completely new element of criticism and self-criticism, resulting in the elimination of erroneous conceptions enabling us to lead some misguided comrades back to the correct revolutionary line, and to re-establish a sense of reciprocal confidence among us.

This confidence had been prejudiced by differences among the leadership. We were not very clear about where the basis of these differences lay, but we perceived that, when important decisions had to be taken there was a clash of standpoints, revealing the existence of two lines, each represented by a certain number of comrades, defending different positions.

All of us were conscious of this division — but, because we thought we would aggravate the situation if we brought the question into the open, because we were convinced that it was necessary and convenient to present at least an appearance of unity in the FRELIMO leadership, we never discussed the problem.

These divergences were manifested in many important instances. For example, in the definition of who is the enemy, in the question of deciding on the strategic line to take (a protracted people's war), on the importance to be given to the armed struggle in relation to the other forms of struggle, etc. This situation had become more evident since 1966, when we started having liberated zones in our country. Certain events had taken place since March, 1968, which seriously affected our organisation. We all felt that the origin of this situation was the division existing within FRELIMO — but we were unable to locate the roots of the contradictions and consequently, we were even less able to solve them.

On 3 February, 1969, Comrade Eduardo Mondlane, President of FRELIMO was murdered. The assassins used a bomb, hidden in a book sent to him through the post. It was not possible to discover the immediate agent of the crime: but the same preoccupation plagued us, might not this crime be related to the differences existing amongst us?

The Central Committee analysed this problem. For several days the items on the agenda concerning this matter were discussed. The ideological lines motivating the behaviour of the divergent groups was discovered. For example, one of the most active representatives of one group was Lazaro Nkavandame, Provincial Secretary of Cabo Delgado, Member of the Central Committee, responsible for the Commercial Section in that Province. His attitude and mentality are typical of the group to which he belonged. Lazaro was opposed to the strategy of a protracted war. According to him, we should concentrate all our forces in Cabo Delgado, drive out the Portuguese from the Province and proclaim the independence of Cabo Delgado. We thought at first that this position stemmed from ignorance, or from a distorted outlook of our real situation, confronted as we are with the enormous military power of the colonialists. But then we started receiving complaints from the people of Cabo Delgado. They complained that they were being exploited – the value of the goods they received from FRELIMO in exchange for their products was scandalously disproportional. These accusations were directed against Nkavandame who was in control of the commercial activities. Things then became clear. It was not ignorance. Nkavandame and his group had a precise objective when they demanded independence of Cabo Delgado alone. What they really wanted was to substitute themselves for the Portuguese colonialists in exploiting our people. Similarly, the preoccupation with a quick victory, before the people were politically mature: because then they would oppose resolutely any form of exploitation. The development of the struggle, the existence of liberated areas had thus made appear a specific category of persons – the exploiters of the people.

Certain other comrades opposed the correct solution because of their empirical conception of nationalism. This made it impossible for them to distinguish our friends from our enemies. For them, all Mozambicans of African origin were 'nationalists', and as such should be accepted in our movement, without any investigation of their political orientation, or of their possible connection with the enemy. Thus, when enemy agents like Mateus Gwenjere appeared in our midst perpetrating a series of actions aimed at destroying FRELIMO, these comrades opposed any action by FRELIMO against them, or at least abstained, alleging that 'they are also nationalists'. Thus, the enemy, taking advantage of our contradictions and erroneous conceptions, could strengthen its action against us.

Yet other comrades, by the bureaucratic nature of their functions coupled with their lack of a solid political base, were overtaken by the Revolution. Living outside, wrapped up in their small world of comfortable routine and papers, they lost contact with the reality of the war and became unable to distinguish the principal from the secondary, the immediate from the long-term tasks. So, they opposed measures aimed at the intensification of the war, at the subordination of all activities to the armed struggle.

Almost from the very beginning of FRELIMO there had been comrades with those erroneous conceptions. Some of them deserted in the course of the Revolution: they formed splinter organisations, through which they hoped to satisfy their personal interests; or, because they were weak, they surrendered to the Portuguese; or yet again, because their ambitions or greed for money could not be satisfied in the Revolution, they chose an easier way of life and sought employment in the neighbouring countries or gave themselves up to the Portuguese as did Lazaro Nkavandame. Gradually, therefore, it was seen that 'the Revolution itself ensures the rejection of the impure load it carries'. But other elements remained amongst us carrying their mistaken ideas. It was on the latter that the last meeting of the Central Committee had a decisive influence, bringing them back again to the Revolutionary path. This action was the work of a group of comrades who have always kept themselves faithful to the interests of the masses, respecting collective values and fighting individualism and personal ambition that foment opportunism, comrades linked with the concrete reality and immersed in the realisation of the principal tasks of the struggle.

Through criticism and self-criticism each one of us vowed to correct our conceptions and behaviour that do not conform to the exigencies of the Revolution. This is why we say that this meeting of the Central Committee had extremely important results, and has opened a new page in the history of our struggle for National Liberation.

Of course, we are aware of the difficulties that lie ahead of us. This unity we have now achieved will have to be implemented each day, with all its difficult implications. We shall need all our attention and all our strength. We shall have setbacks, but we shall know how to learn from them, how to improve ourselves and our work. We do not deceive ourselves with false hopes of an easy path: because it is not a mechanical process, it needs our complete and active engagement, our constant efforts. Our experience has shown us that it takes an endless process of criticism and self-criticism to eliminate the residue of the colonial system that still persists in us, for us to place ourselves decisively on the right side of history, for us to discover and implement the *necessity* of the Revolution.

While reaffirming our decision to fight with more determination, based on a new understanding of the situation and in the certainty of expressing more fully the will of the people, we wish to stress that all these innovations are in fact a continuation; and that all of them are linked with the policy of our late President, Comrade Eduardo Mondlane, whose work is not only being continued, but is being taken to greater heights by the Movement. The unity he came to represent has now reached a higher stage: it is unity at the service of the Revolution.

A luta continua

Gloomy Situation in FRELIMO
Uria T. Simango

*Excerpts from the paper issued on 30 November 1969
by Uria T. Simango, then a member of the
Presidential Council of FRELIMO.*

There are people in the organisation who tend to give/develop a theory that there are two groups in the organisation, one led by Dr. Mondlane and the other by Uria Simango. I refute this theory and say that there is one group, the first one. Events below described will prove this to be true. However it should be said that there are many people in the party who think that some of our policies are not correct. Such people do not constitute an organised group against anybody, but whenever they are informed of such bad policies they say their opinion. It is possible that they may be two or more who do not agree with certain decisions at the same time. Problems which divided the Central Committee are such as the Mozambique Institute which some maintained an opinion that it should be directed and controlled by FRELIMO and others sustained that it should be independent. Because the first group was right — the Institute was nationalised in 1968, when FRELIMO for the first time had the prerogative to appoint the Principal of the Secondary School. However there are distortions of decisions about the Mozambique Institute and there are certain things which still need to be settled. How finally these problems will be resolved is still a question mark.

There is a swing to say that we are divided on ideology. This can only mean difference on economic, religious, social policies (class), etc. I agree that ideology is very important but it should never be considered as a uniting or dividing factor of the nationalist liberation forces of Mozambique at this stage, if all agree and accept fundamental principles: a) liberate Mozambique from the Portuguese colonial domination and b) through the armed struggle. Our struggle today is not principally an ideological or class one; it is a struggle of masses of people against foreign domination, Portuguese colonialist, for freedom and independence of these masses. The question of scientific socialism and capitalism in Mozambique should not be allowed to divide us if it becomes a must, of course at a later stage of the struggle. This should not be interpreted to mean that we should allow or develop a bourgeois or capitalist oriented group in FRELIMO, for our objective is to emancipate our people completely . . . this is our commitment. Whether people with religious backgrounds should participate in the administration of the country is a problem that will be seen later too. It is wrong to say that we are implanting socialism in the country; to say so only reveals our ignorance of what socialism is. To say that we are not building socialism now does not mean that we may not in the future realise it. Therefore if there is an indigenous bourgeois class at the moment and if it is willing to contribute for the liberation of the country we must accept its cooperation because since our struggle is divided in various stages, the first stage is a liberation one by a national liberation movement by all the people without discrimination based on sex, creed, wealthy condition, etc. Fortunately enough there is no indigenous bourgeois class to contend with. On the other hand, we are not yet strong enough to fight the Portuguese and their allies and at the same time wage a war against a national bourgeois class. If they (the bourgeoisie) existed we would rally them to fight with us against the common enemy. Within the organisation, certainly we must fight all forms of corruption, reactionalism and bourgeoisie, using our machinery of political education. It therefore becomes ridiculous to waste our energy to a point of destroying our unity by fighting a pretended enemy, a bourgeois class, with an intention to impress somebody, if there is anybody who can be impressed. . . .

Towards the end of February and beginning of March this year, after the death of Dr. Mondlane, late President of FRELIMO, several people from the southern region of our country, amongst them Samora Moises Machel, Joaquim Chissano, Marcelino dos Santos, Armando Guebuza, Aurelio Manave, Josina Abiatar Muthemba, Eugenio Mondlane and Francisco Sumbane, held several meetings at Janet Rae Mondlane's house at Oyster Bay. She also took part in the meetings. They studied the circumstances surrounding Dr. Mondlane's death as a person from their tribe, as to who had killed him. Janet told the meeting that Filipe Magaia, Sansao Muthemba and Dr. Mondlane had been killed by the people of the north (from Beira to Ruyme river) because they are against us of the south. She was corrected by reference to the death of Magaia, being told that he was killed by a person from the south and not from the north. They also discussed how they could defend for and safeguard the interests of the people of the south,

The meetings concluded that Uria Simango, Silverio Mungu, Mariano Masinye and Samuel Dhlakama were their enemies, were responsible for Dr. Mondlane's death and should therefore be eliminated. This decision was criticised by two elderly men, Francisco Sumbane and Eugenio Mondlane, cousin of the deceased. They insisted that they should all cooperate and work with Simango; the contrary would be tribalism. Their advice was not given heed.

What happened in Mozambique is just a fulfilment of the plan drawn and decision taken at Janet's house at Oyster Bay by the clique of criminals in obedience to the imperialist plan, which they considered to be capable of satisfying their interest too. All those who participated in the meetings, are responsible for Mungu's cruel death, their hands are bloody, they are criminals. They are also responsible for many unnecessary executions of fighters and people. They must bear the responsibility for the most desertions and present situation of our movement.

We cannot say 'Let bygones be bygones'; those responsible for these crimes should bear the responsibility on their shoulders, the uncommitted to work for the imperialists must defend the lives of the fighters and of the people and their rights and interests.

As I have said above, personally I cannot agree to be part of crimes against our people. Only with radical and complete change of such a situation can I feel morally able to cooperate; otherwise it is an honour to dissociate myself from the actions of the criminals for you cannot trust them, they are vipers — tools of imperialism.

On Uria T. Simango
FRELIMO

> *Communique of the Executive Committee of FRELIMO, suspending Uria T. Simango from membership in the Council of Presidency of FRELIMO in response to his publication of 'The Gloomy Situation in FRELIMO'. Published in* Mozambique Revolution, *41, October - December 1969.*

The Mozambique Liberation Front (FRELIMO) informs us that, by decision of its Executive Committee, Comrade Uria T. Simango is suspended from membership of the Council of Presidency of FRELIMO until the next meeting of the Central Committee, to which his case will be referred for final consideration. The following is the text of the resolution of the Executive Committee:

'The Executive Committee of FRELIMO, meeting in Dar es Salaam on 8 November, 1969 in order to assess the situation created by the publication by comrade Uria T. Simango of a pamphlet entitled 'Gloomy Situation in FRELIMO':

(1) Deeply deplores that comrade Uria T. Simango, member of the Council of Presidency of FRELIMO, has refused to present his problems within the framework of the structures and institutions of FRELIMO, preferring to do this through the press.

(2) Condemns this attitude of comrade Uria T. Simango, which is extremely irresponsible, violates the principles and the rules of FRELIMO and constitutes a grave act of indiscipline.

(3) Notes with deep indignation that the contents of the pamphlet are a body of calumnious accusations, of insults and of falsities, aimed at denigrating the leaders of FRELIMO who are truly nationalists, patriots and revolutionaries. Indeed, the pamphlet constitutes an insult to the Mozambican people, to FRELIMO and to the revolutionary armed struggle of national liberation being waged in our country. It is inspired by the personal ambition of Comrade Uria T. Simango and serves only the interests of Portuguese colonialism and imperialism.

(4) Rejects categorically, formally and totally the contents of the pamphlet 'Gloomy Situation in FRELIMO', published by Comrade Uria T. Simango.

(5) Condemns Comrade Uria T. Simango for all the declarations contained in the pamphlet, which constitute an act against the unity of the Mozambican people, against FRELIMO and against the progress of the revolutionary armed

struggle in Mozambique, and consequently against the whole of Africa.

(6) Decides to suspend Comrade Uria T. Simango from membership of the Council of Presidency of FRELIMO until the next meeting of the Central Committee to which the case will be referred for final consideration.

(7) Reaffirms the unwavering determination of the Mozambican people, of the fighters and of the leadership of FRELIMO to continue relentlessly all efforts to preserve and consolidate the unity of FRELIMO and of the Mozambican people, to assure the continuation of the revolutionary armed struggle for national liberation, until final victory.

Internal Corruption
Samora Machel

Speech when member of the Presidential Commission of FRELIMO, in Bagamoyo (Tanzania) on 16 June 1969 and reproduced in Rasgando As Trevas, *I, 2, 30 June 1969. Translated from Portuguese.*

Today we commemorate, if I am not mistaken, the ninth anniversary of the Mueda massacre.

I believe that those who spoke before me have already mentioned its importance, and the important lesson which we have gained from it. For this reason, I will refrain from describing once again what happened on June 16, 1960, in the district of Mueda. The comrades all know that over six hundred Mozambicans, who were asking for freedom, who were asking for dialogue with the Portuguese, know what kind of answer they got because they were unarmed. We do not need to describe these events because you are all aware of them. What we shall try to see here, to understand here, is the lesson it teaches us, the lesson we have learned since June 16, 1960, when the Mozambicans started to understand the necessity of organization in order to be able to face in an efficient way the forces of repression, the Portuguese colonialist forces in Mozambique. . . .

You know that, ever since the beginning of the armed struggle, the Portuguese have intensified their attempts to keep the Mozambican people divided, using various manoeuvres, including the use of Mozambicans themselves. In the zones where we are fighting today, the first enemies which we encounter in the interior of the country are the Africans being used by the PIDE. This is possible because it is easy for an African to infiltrate himself among us, because they have the same face, they use the same expressions, the same language as we do, manifest the same wish for freedom. This is the present tactic, the fundamental weapon which the enemy uses and will continue to use . . . . Every time we attain a new stage of development, there is a necessity of clearly defining who are the enemies of the revolution, of FRELIMO, of independence, the enemies of the struggle for Mozambique.

It seems that the experience acquired in four years of war in Mozambique have already proved that we need to analyse, that we ourselves must attempt at organizing better, in order to confront the sly tactics which the enemy uses to disorient our peoples. That is what each of us must keep in mind, these manoeuvres which the enemy utilizes among us, inside our ranks, certain that he will thereby paralyse our war. He uses many methods; at this very moment he is using corruption. There is material corruption, there is spiritual corruption, there is ideological corruption. In the long run, ideological corruption is stronger than material corruption. We are familiar with the deserters from Mozambique who are to be found all over the place in Dar-es-Salaam, or near the borders, and who say, 'We do not want to fight because in Mozambique we are not fighting the Portuguese, but only each other'. Is it not what the deserters say?

This is the enemy's watchword. Recently they have been saying, 'The leaders of FRELIMO stay in Dar-es-Salaam, having comfortable life, a good life, while you who are here in the jungle eat rotting monkey meat'. And some accept this, and believe that the enemy is right. – 'Our leaders really do enjoy a comfortable life.' Some of us accept this theory of the enemy. To accept this idea of the enemy introduced amongst us is to accept corruption, to accept that we shall be corrupted. That our leaders lead a comfortable life, that they eat well, and dress well, these are the enemy's watchwords. These are words from the mouths of our enemies, or from those who want to cooperate with the enemy. What kind of life did we lead in Mozambique before we started the war? Did our enemy speak of what we had to suffer? Why does he say what he says today?

The enemy's tactics are clear enough. He wishes to destroy the nationalist spirit, the revolutionary spirit, because he is convinced that on the battlefront, in real combat, he is unable to defeat the organized force, the armed forces of FRELIMO. Thus today subversive methods are used by him more frequently in order to divide the Mozambican people, in order to weaken our struggle, since once this unity ceases to exist we will be easily defeated by the enemy. These watchwords are not only in the minds of those who are in the interior of the country, but also among those who are in the schools, right here in Bagamoyo, in the Mozambican Institute, in Tunduru, where the enemy knows FRELIMO is training its cadres to struggle and become leaders in the war, to know how to organize the people in a scientific way, to be able to instil in the people a revolutionary spirit. This is where the enemy is strongest – here, in Tunduru and in the Mozambican Institute, seeking to divide our people.

He was able to massacre our people in 1960, because our people were not armed, because we were not united. Because our people were divided, he was able to massacre over 600 people in less than half an hour. If we are still going to accept these watchwords today, such as that there are people who are living off the revolution, the enemy will easily defeat us again. But now it will not be a few people or a sector of the population, it will be the whole country, and we will never again be able to fight our war in Mozambique. We must take care to preserve this unity, a unity which unites us, directs us, which is an encouragement for each one of us here. It must be the daily preoccupation of each of the comrades here to defend our unity so that our struggle may live in the interior, for our basic weapon is *unity*.

This is why the enemy continues to try through subversive methods, mainly in the educational sectors, to corrupt us ideologically, to corrupt us materially, to corrupt our spirit. An individual without an ideology, an individual without a spirit, is nothing. He is like a rag, and has no strength to resist the enemy's tactics. The comrade who likes material wealth will be easily separated from the people and from its organization, FRELIMO, which defends the people's interests in Mozambique, from the Rovuma to the Maputo. This must become the current preoccupation of all of us here. And each one of us must realize and accept in his heart that wherever he may be, he is on a mission for FRELIMO. We are all on a mission for FRELIMO. We are on a mission for the people, a mission of the struggle. We are met here today, we are able to meet here today, because there is going on an armed struggle in Mozambique which defends the people's interests from the Rovuma to the Maputo. This is why the enemy finds himself impotent, unable to defeat FRELIMO on the front of battle, because we are united, because we are true defenders of the masses of Mozambique. Each one of the comrades here is on a mission for the party. This is all I have to say today on the importance of our unity, and on the lesson which we have drawn from the massacre of Mueda.

Long Live FRELIMO!

What Price Unity?
SWAPO

Editorial in SWAPO's South West Africa Today *(Dar es Salaam), June 1964.*

Unity is the great slogan in Africa today. It has given birth to the epoch Addis Ababa Conference which resulted in the Organisation of African Unity. Greater things are still to come. The remaining walls of white supremacy in Southern Africa will soon be smashed. And colonialism will be a thing of the ugly past.

It is small wonder, then, that there are strong urgings from many quarters that African freedom fighters, particularly those still in the thick of the struggle, must come together. This, without question, is essential. There is precious little time to lose. And to face formidable foes in the form of Verwoerd, Salazar and Smith, victory would be elusive if there are dissensions and eternal squabbling within the African front.

But one must draw a line. Unity must never be for the sake of the word. There must never be false fronts, shrouded in deceit and opportunism. Just imagine the course of Ghana, and Africa for that matter, if Kwame Nkrumah had made 'fronts' with those pseudo-intellectuals during Ghana's most trying days. But Dr Nkrumah was wise. He forged ahead against violent odds, and Ghana's victory became Africa's.

Zambia would still be in the revolting grip of Welensky's Federation if Kaunda and his men did not take their people out of the African National Congress morass. It would have been lunacy to form a united front with Nkumbula's despotism.

Roberto Holden has firmly resisted diluting the struggle of the Angolan people with dissenting rabble, consequently the revolutionary forces are moving from strength to strength,

Examples of this type are unending in the recent history of the African struggle, and we have drawn fruitful lessons from them.

We in SWAPO, after a long and careful assessment of the situation in our country, have come to the definite conclusion that all alternatives to an early liberation from the wretched South African administration are closed. We are now irrevocably committed to a course of armed revolution. And to a movement firmly dedicated to this path, a united front with tribal groupings, non-existent parties and collaborators could be nothing but sacrilege. We are determined to resist any blackmail or aid conditions which would make us succumb to a unity in pawn for what we hold dear.

Open Letter to the ISC
Emil Appolus

> *Reproduced in* Solidarity *(Cairo), IV, 2, April-May 1965.*
> *The letter was addressed to the International Students*
> *Conference and signed by the SWAPO Chief Publicity and*
> *Information Secretary.*

Thank you very much for the interest you have shown towards the situation in South West Africa. Your South West Africa Report submitted to the 11th International Conference, Christchurch, New Zealand, is another indication that this interest continues.

I must, however, draw your attention to one of the things that came to our notice when we read the mimeographed version of the above-mentioned Report. In the chapter dealing with political organizations the Report asserts that SWAPO accused SWANU of pro-Eastern tendencies.

But nowhere in any written or verbal statements made by SWAPO leadership at home or abroad can we find a record or trace of an 'accusation', even implied of this type. We therefore reached the conclusion that your contention that we have labelled SWANU as 'pro-Eastern' (we can only deduce that this phrase means 'pro-Communist') is decidedly false and misleading.

We shall be grateful if, then, for the sake of accuracy and principle, you produce concrete evidence that this particular assertion in your Report in fact emanated from SWAPO. Failing which, it then, in our view, would be your honourable duty to give this rebuttal the same wide public circulation and distribution the South West Africa Report of the ISC of June 22nd/July 1st, 1964, enjoys.

We must also, in very brief, set the record straight on 'bitter' relations between SWAPO and SWANU mentioned in the same Report. We in SWAPO recognise, without condoning, that in some instances of political awakening in any one people, the unfortunate tendencies of proliferation of 'parties' rears its head. Some of these 'parties' are still-born; some are unable to attain any significant mass-following. Others are only founded to further the narrow ambitions of their leaders. It cannot, however, be said that all of them are not well-intentioned for the furtherance of the independence cause.

In recent years we have witnessed the appearance of names like SWANIO, VOLKSWA, SWANU, UNIPP, NUDO, Chief Councils, Baster Road, etc., on the South West African political scene. But I must at once very categorically state that SWAPO harbours no bitterness towards any one of these minority groupings and factions. Our basic belief has been, and will always remain that of concentrating the entire energies at our command towards carrying our people out of the hideous morass of oppression. We cannot condemn innocent people for the sins of a handful of individuals who strut around abroad for their own selfish ends.

And as a national organization, we have made it our sacred duty to embrace all these diversified elements, irrespective of race or tribe into the fold of a struggle with a singular purpose. Already parties like the Caprivi African National Union (CANU) relinquished their independent status, dissolved, and joined SWAPO — rank and file. Progressive Chief Councils like the one of Chief Samuel Witbooi sought and received the close co-operation with SWAPO within the country.

The unity course is irrevocably set! Any one who now would attempt to diverse or reverse the direction and momentum of this trend will discover this to be a difficult task indeed. And it is quite easy to forsee that it is only a matter of time before the final confrontation between the forces of fascist oppressive regime and that of the oppressed African masses for the final liberation of South West Africa will be waged under the spearheading national umbrella of SWAPO.

> Yours faithfully,
> Emil Appolus
> SWAPO Chief Publicity and Information Secretary

Has SWANU Failed?

Festus U. Muundjua

Excerpt of an article in SWANU's South West Africa Review (Stockholm), II, 6, November/December 1970.

The enemies of SWANU — and why not also its friends — have for both good and bad reasons accused and criticised it that it is 'not serious' with the struggle of South West Africa. The Organization of African Unity (OAU), more particularly its Under Secretary-General, Mr. Muhammed Sahnoun, maintains that 'SWANU is not serious', 'it does not want freedom', 'its members or leaders are all in Europe and not in Africa', 'it has no military trained men', etc., etc.

Is all this true? It is absolutely not true; it is preposterous rubbish. That 'SWANU is not serious' is false, because SWANU was born out of seriousness — the seriousness of people who, unlike our critics, experienced perhaps the most ferocious and dehumanizing type of colonialization: the South African colonialization.

It is not SWANU that has 'failed' — if that is the word — it is those who are ignorant about the problems of our country who failed to understand

SWANU's problems, and because of their own misunderstanding and ignorance chose to victimise SWANU.

It is true, SWANU has not been able to do things as it ought to have done, and this is so, because of certain problems that some people do not understand — and, still worse, do not wish to understand. These problems are of two types: those that are created by the sophisticated (South African) colonial situation in which we, of South West Africa, find ourselves and those created by the misunderstanding of those who do not know our situation.

In my opinion, most of the problems that face SWANU (that is, its members abroad) come from the fact that 'SWANU is not recognised by the Organisation of African Unity', which is used as a pretext by those who actually oppose SWANU's ideological and political line and its fierce independence. In this regard, the question should be asked: 'Why is SWANU not recognised by the OAU?'

This question is not a new one. I asked it Mr. Muhammed Sahnoun, Deputy Secretary-General of the OAU. It was in New York City, April 18-19, 1967, during a Seminar on the Training and Utilization of the Southern African Refugees. He arrogantly replied:

> Because SWANU is not serious; it does not want freedom; its leaders and members are all in Europe and not in Africa; the leaders of other parties are in Africa, I see them; some are even in my own country (Algeria) in military training camps. Other parties like ANC, ZAPU, SWAPO are fighting a guerrilla warfare, and you are not. . . .

I have already touched on some of these absurd charges in my opening remarks and I do not have to burden you with a repetitious redundancy. However, on the issue of 'guerrilla warfare', many things had been said by many people, and, as such, I should, in addition to the well-known position of our Party on this issue, also have my say.

The position of SWANU on this very important issue is quite clear and simple. *We have not fought, and probably will not fight, a guerrilla warfare just so that we can be recognised by the OAU.* A guerrilla warfare is a people's war. This means that it must be carried out by and involve the greater number of the people, instead of just being a thing of only a handful of roving disorganised refugees, having their bases in far-away places like Cairo, Algeria, Dar es Salaam, etc., when the enemy and the battle field are in South West Africa.

A guerrilla warfare or a revolution without the support of the people *in locus* is no revolution at all, but shadow-boxing. A guerrilla war or revolution must take into account not only the people, but also the objective conditions as they obtain in one's own country. That is to say, conditions that will make the unleashing of such a revolution possible or impossible: i.e., things like one's own actual strength, the actual strength of one's own enemy, whether or not the topography of areas intended for operations is conducive, etc., to say nothing of the resources that one has to have to sustain such an onerous war, once it is begun.

Good organization and better preparation of the people are a *sine qua non* of a people's revolution, if at all it must succeed. This in itself calls into being a well-organised and disciplined party with a correct theory, knowledge of the country and her problems, the ability and capability to organise. Given things as they are in our country, such capability to organise effectively is almost impossible, owing to some of the problems that I mentioned earlier.

Therefore, to begin such a war without the right moment on your side, without the people and the resources, or, in the absence of all this, to try to import a phoney guerrilla warfare into South West Africa, is tantamount to trying to fly when you damn well know that you have no wings. This is exactly what SWAPO did, and what the OAU supported — or for which reason it recognised SWAPO.

Just as it will be in the end the people of South West Africa themselves who will have to bear the brunt of the actual fighting (as they did many times before), so must it be left solely to them to take the decision of when or when not to fight. To this end, I do not think that the OAU, or anyone for that matter, has any right to pass resolutions blackmailing us into suicidal so-called 'guerrilla warfares', the kinds of which were started by some other Southern African groups without better preparation of (or even contact with) their own people *inside* their own countries.

The failure and the atrocities experienced by some of these Southern African groups, like ANC, ZAPU, SWAPO, to name just a few, were caused partly, if not mainly, by the Liberation Committee of the OAU, because it was it that threatened these elements with *no funds* and *no recognition* unless they did something by way of taking arms against the minority, but well-armed, regimes of Southern Africa.

These were some of the basic things that we, in SWANU, took into consideration when we defied the threats and the blackmails of the OAU, and it was for this reason that the OAU stopped 'recognising' us. But what does this matter to SWANU? We knew, for instance, that *with* or *without* the OAU money and 'recognition' SWANU shall always exist and subsist, just as she did before the birth of the OAU. SWANU owes its existence and subsistence to the very existence of the people of South West Africa and the determination of its members to hold together, to share weal and woe in the defence of what we think is good for our country, and as long as our people will exist and our members hold on to the correct line SWANU shall continue to exist. After all, we in SWANU abroad do not beg and campaign for recognition and help but seek friendship and assistance from those who regard it as their internationalist duty to side with our people in their struggle for national liberation. That's all.

The decision that our National Union took NOT to throw its fighters into suicidal invasion shows, just for the sake of getting money and recognition, was not without seriousness. In fact, it was because of our seriousness and our understanding of the objective conditions of our country that we decided against jumping on the band-wagon of phoney and pseudo guerrilla warfares.

5. Racism and Anti-Racism

Editors' Introduction

Perhaps the single most contentious issue within the national liberation movements of Portuguese and southern Africa has been the stance these movements should take towards white persons who are sympathetic towards the goals of these movements.

There are two opposite positions that can be taken. One is to say that the white minority within the country is, alone or jointly with outside forces, the principal enemy of national liberation and that white 'liberals' or white 'radicals' are in reality part of this group and thus should be kept at arm's length. The opposite position is to say that the issue is fundamentally political or class-based and not racial, that the white man who supports the cause of African liberation is a welcome ally, the white resident who considers himself a part of the African 'nation' is simply one more member of the 'people'. And, of course, there are a number of possible nuances in between. This issue has been a factor in the splits in many countries. And even where the splits may have had other factors, this issue has often surfaced as a justification of the split.

As one might guess, it is in South Africa where the issue has been most ferociously debated since South Africa has had the longest historic tradition of a white left movement. The African National Congress has sought to achieve a multi-racial alliance for the achievement of national liberation. The 'Freedom Charter' was the product of four organizations, each representing one of the four 'official' racial groups of the country: Africans, Indians, Coloureds, and Whites. It was precisely this policy and this document which eventually led to the breakaway from the ANC of the Pan-Africanist Congress (PAC) in 1959. We start with a statement of the PAC's position against what they call the 'Luthulian approach'. And we add to it an attack by the PAC on the white 'friends of the revolution.'

In the course of the struggle, the position of the ANC has become clearer. They felt called upon to spell out in greater detail the role they felt the 'white group' might play in the struggle and what is meant by equal rights for all 'national groups'. They also felt called upon to comment upon the 'Black Consciousness' movement that emerged within South Africa, especially among students, in the late 1960s. The position was very nuanced. The ANC noted that Black Consciousness 'fills a temporary vacuum' but also 'smacks of pessimism'.

The PAC at this time revised its appreciation of the role of Coloureds (and to a lesser extent, Indians) and invited them to join as individual members. We reproduce the statement made by the Coloured People's Congress when it merged with the PAC in March 1966. By the 1970s, all elements seemed to agree that the 'official' racial categories were illegitimate, that the use of the negative term 'non-white' was harmful, and that the term 'Black' should be used to include Africans, Indians, and Coloureds simultaneously.

In this atmosphere, the leaders of the Indian and Coloured organizations allied to the ANC felt called upon to define once again the role they envisaged for their people. We include their statements. The Indian community also used the occasion of General Amin's expulsion of Asians in Uganda to draw the lesson for South Africa. And finally the South African Congress of Trade Unions, an organization sympathetic to the ANC, appealed to European white workers outside South Africa to show their solidarity by not migrating to South Africa.

In Namibia, this issue has been a far simpler one, and the position of SWAPO was made clear in a very brief comment of its President, Sam Nujoma. The movements in Zimbabwe all rejected the concept of 'multi-racialism'. The reason ZAPU gave was that multi-racialism in fact 'perpetuates racialism'. ZANU was even blunter. They agreed that 'white liberals' do not exist, at least in Zimbabwe, but asserted they were dedicated to building a 'non-racial society'.

In Portuguese Africa, the issue of whites has been less the issue than the issue of 'metis'. This was particularly acute in Angola where the UPA and its allies have often accused the MPLA of being dominated by persons of mixed blood. Also, as the war went on, the Portuguese movements were more and more involved both in encouraging Portuguese soldiers to desert and in co-operating with Portuguese underground opposition movements.

What distinguished the movements in the CONCP from rival groups in Portuguese Africa was their forthright 'anti-racist' position. Dr. Neto asserted clearly, 'we are not making a racial war'. At the beginning of the war, a group of white supporters of national liberation in Angola organized themselves as the Frente da Unidade Angolana (FUA). We include one of their statements. Later this group decided it was politically unsound to exist on a racial basis and dissolved itself. In 1968, the MPLA openly invited Angolan whites to join its ranks as individuals.

The dangers of racialism are quite clear in the case of Mozambique. We reproduce a document from an obscure group which had a brief life, the Uniao Nacional Africana de Rumbezia (UNAR), whose racially divisive tactics are quite clear from the document. It was against these and similar tactics that Samora Machel made his appeal to avoid confusion as to 'the identity of the enemy' — Portuguese colonialism, imperialism and the exploitation of man by man, but *not* 'white Mozambicans'.

In Guinea-Bissau, there were scarcely any whites. This did not keep the enemy from exploiting 'ethnic' divisions, or the role of the so-called 'Cape-Verdians'. How the PAIGC handled this problem is explained by Aristide Pereira and Amilcar Cabral.

The Luthulian Approach
PAC

From an article, 'The Struggle in South Africa: A Quest for Unity – Part I: The Dynamics of African Nationalism' in PAC's Pan-Africanist News and Views *(Lusaka), 1, November 1963.*

This intensive – ever so subtle – battle for colonisation of the mind might be said to have been won if half the leading Africans in South Africa were a party to a document known to its Black and other creators as a Freedom Charter, which declares in its preamble that 'South Africa belongs to all who live in it, black and white. . . .' But this charter is no less dangerous because supported by a comparative few. That, as a document intended to have a bearing on the present situation, it is supported at all by some leading Africans is a tragedy – and an eloquent reminder that if we are looking for fools, the place to find them is not among Imperialists. Didn't someone say that they will always find the negro to do the dirty work for them?

'South Africa belongs to all who live in it' is the platform of the sponsors of the charter, together with their handful of European allies. Nothing could be more calculated to dampen the fervour of the African Nationalist spirit, to smother the emotions and desires of the African people in a haze of confused goals, to blur their vision and blunt the revolutionary thrust of the struggle for national liberation. All this done in the name of multi-racialism! The enemy has chosen the battlefield for us, chosen the platform on which he wishes to fight: apartheid or racial segregation and discrimination. Many have readily obliged, consenting to be put on the defensive and protesting in a negative way against this or that piece of legislation because it discriminates against this or that group on racial grounds. Racialism, as an issue, has come to be accorded a place in the struggle which is out of all proportion to its importance in the altogether rotten social set-up, over-shadowing the fundamental issues which are inherent in imperialism and constitute a basic conflict between the interests of an alien group and those of the indigenous people. Starting off from this false premise, the premise that all our woes are anchored in racialism, we have come to think of the struggle purely in terms of race, seeing racialism even in the concept of Africa for the Africans.

In the process even history was falsified. The bloody battles which our forefathers had so gallantly fought for the retention of their land and its resources – these glorious battles which had lasted for more than a century and constitute part of our proud history and traditions — ceased to have a true political meaning or to be a source of inspiration in the struggle for liberation. The African Nationalist spirit was suffocated, suppressed and drowned in a pit of hollow multi-racialism and quasi-Christian polemics. Those who advocated a purely African Nationalist approach to the struggle were branded black racialists or chauvinists. Thus was created an ambivalence in the country in which the love-thy-enemy-as-thyself sermon was being ardently preached among the people.

A few quotations from typical speeches will illustrate this general theme in the South African struggle. In discussing the views of those from whose speeches and writings we quote, it is without any malicious intent to reflect on their personal integrity. Following is an extract from a speech made before his followers by Chief Albert Luthuli, President-General of the African National Congress, the main sponsor organisation of a public assembly that adopted the Freedom Charter. It is typical of the man who has since been awarded a Nobel Peace Prize:

> Hate the things he stands for, but it is wrong to hate the man himself. Whether he is willing to recognise it or not the white man is our brother. In the end in South Africa all the races will have to live together. Because our own people are in the vast majority, one day we shall be in power — then we must show that the black man knows how to use power fairly and with justice. When that day comes we must not be looking for revenge.

Safeguarding the Whites' Future

Whatever validity the Luthulian approach may have in the future (and one concedes it may well be necessary then to cool the embers of hate and revenge), it certainly doesn't fit in the revolutionary struggle of the present. Too many of the leaders are being unduly preoccupied with safeguarding the future position of the White aliens who, at present, are sitting on the necks of a groaning mass of Black humanity, and show no sign of willing to get off our backs without being rudely shaken off in an explosion of pent-up fury.

In the prevailing circumstances in South Africa, it is puerile to ask the African to 'hate the things he stands for' but not the White man himself. It is rather like asking a wounded human to swear at the gun and not the man who pulled the trigger. It is unearthly and unnatural to love the White man under present conditions, which is what we must do if we are to regard him as a brother. Since all these things cannot be done naturally, there can only be an unnatural response to the theme song that they have been made. In the struggle, that theme song has wreaked havoc with the Nationalist spirit in a nebulous mass of conflicting emotions and postures.

On the other hand, this kind of approach to the struggle was regarded as the height of statesmanship and earned our leaders accolades in the White settler press. The Chief, as Luthuli now came to be known, was showered with praises as South Africa's 'foremost African leader', 'a Christian gentleman' who eschewed violence in his fight for 'greater freedom' for his people. Latterly the accolades are pouring off the Western world's printing presses, with a Nobel Peace Prize to boot.

The White 'Left' at Work
PAC

From an article, 'Conflict of Values in South Africa',
published in PAC's Azania News *(Dar es Salaam),*
VII, 6, June 1972.

The crucial differences in the liberation movement of our country must be seen in their proper perspective. The people of our country are very clear about what is wrong in that society. Their differences arise over how to correct what is wrong. That is where the burden and predicament of material interest lies. Everyone is claiming his pound of flesh, like the old merchant of Venice, without the possible loss of a single drop of blood. To understand the matter correctly, we should remove some of the great misconceptions about the political situation in that country.

To begin with, apartheid or separate development, is not the exclusive policy of the present Nationalist regime under the leadership of Balthazar Johannes Vorster, or of the Boer (Afrikaner) section of the white community in that country. All sections of the 'Europeans' in South Africa, be they British, American, German, French, Japanese, Hungarian, Russian, Czech, Italian, Nordic or Lebanese, have contributed and continue to contribute their own share to the practice of oppression, exploitation, humiliation, persecution and the abomination that is apartheid in the life of the African people. These facts are fully well known and cannot be denied, but a considerable amount of propaganda has been mounted to divert attention from the real issues of the matter. This deception has even infiltrated the ranks of the liberation movement itself through the 'sympathetic' friends of the revolution and those in our ranks who champion their cause. . . .

We have warned over and over again that there are individuals and organisations who are seemingly in the forefront of the struggle of our people for national liberation and social emancipation, but whose identifiable activities are, to our mind, inimical to the best interests of that struggle. This is why our liberation movement speaks in a multiplicity of voices and has become a Tower of Babel. We isolated this point at the very foundation of our organisation. We warned that the days of the domination of Africa by Europeans were numbered and even in South Africa the writing was glaringly on the wall for those of our European rulers who had eyes to see and to decipher the message.

We pointed out that there was no room in any way and in any part of

Africa for those non-indigenous people who deny the indigenous population its fundamental right to shape its own material and spiritual interests effectively. We emphasised that South Africa, which is an integral part of the African Continent, is the inalienable heritage of the African people and its effective control is their undoubted and unquestionable birthright. . . . The implications are quite clear. We should therefore look closely into the case of the individuals who have taken it upon themselves to vilify the militant performances of our people and to cast aspersions upon their political motives. We must know what they stand for and their role in the national liberation movement of our country. It is not our intention to use this analysis as a criticism of the African National Congress. What we are showing is that the alleged ideological differences between the ANC and the PAC have always been contrived and intensified by the internal enemies of the African revolution, whose primary motive is to misdirect our struggle for their own purposes. In the main, the differences are mainly organisational. These are, to enlist Charles Dickens' support, the Bumbles and Fagins of the liberation movement. And there are gentlemen with white waistcoats also among them. Even the beadles are there . . . .

However, the so-called ideological differences between the PAC and the ANC are superficially manipulated. Then people who have contrived these differences, which have on occasion grown into rabid hostility, are the great enemies of our revolution by contrivance as well as by effect. We discovered and exposed these manoeuvres and contrivances almost twenty years ago, and were called all sorts of ugly and derogatory names for that. We pointed out that our people had always declared themselves for complete freedom; that they were unflinchingly determined to wrest the control of their country from alien hands; that they were determined to exercise that most fundamental of human rights, the inalienable right of indigenous peoples to shape and determine their own destiny as they wish, unmolested, unhampered and unrestricted.

The reaction of the enemies within our ranks, 'the Europeans who love us', are sharp and unmistakable. They raved and ranted. Fire spat out of their mouths rapidly and rabidly. In their panic and malice, they took the gloves off and fought with their bare knuckles. They raved mad over our 'racial hysterics'; branded us with the mantle of a 'menace to white society'; they failed to hide their bitter hatred of 'POQO's anarchistic murders', and 'the kind of terrorism we have always sought to prevent'. They even went out to Moscow in June 1969 and told the world that they had conclusive evidence to show that the PAC was formed with the assistance, and at the behest, of the United States Central Intelligence Agency. This insult to the PAC may be excused. The feelings of the African people who look up to it for leadership are unpredictable.

We pointed out unequivocally, and unambiguously, and emphatically, that because of the activities of a section of the leadership of the white ruling classes, 'the Europeans who love us', who had wormed their way into the ranks of the liberation movement, the broad masses of our people were in the extreme danger of being deceived into losing sight of the objectives of our struggle, and that a portion of the black 'leadership', which fought and brought division among us in the employ of these 'sympathetic friends' had completely abandoned the objective of freedom, and could no longer be regarded as being within the ranks of the liberation movement. It was our considered opinion that such black 'leadership' was incredibly naive and fantastically unrealistic to realise that the interests of the subject African peoples were in sharp conflict and pointed contradiction with those of the white ruling classes. That black 'leadership' accepted white domination, minus its frills and trappings, and called it multi-racialism.

The White Group in the South African Struggle for Liberation
ANC

From the 'Strategy and Tactics of the ANC', a document published circa 1969.

The above are only some of the important factors which have not always been studied and understood. It is necessary to stress these factors not only because they give balance to our efforts but because — properly assessed — they help destroy the myth of the enemy's invincibility.

But above all a scientific revolutionary strategy demands a correct appreciation of the political character of the forces which are ranged against one another in the South African struggle for liberation. Is the enemy a monolith and will he remain so until his final defeat? What is the main content of the struggle for liberation and, flowing from this, which is the main revolutionary force and who are its potential allies and supporters? These are questions of capital importance. They play a vital part in determining the tactics of the revolutionary struggle, the broad alliances for which we must strive, the organisational structures we create and many other fundamental approaches. They must be considered within the framework of the special feature of the objective situation which faces us. South Africa's social and economic structure and the relationships which it generates are perhaps unique. It is not a colony, yet it has, in regard to the overwhelming majority of its people, most of the features of the classical colonial structures. Conquest and domination by an alien people, a system of discrimination and exploitation based on race, technique and indirect rule; these and more are the traditional trappings of the classical colonial framework. Whilst at the one level it is an 'independent' national state, at another level is is a country subjugated by a minority race. What makes the structure unique and adds to its complexity is that the exploiting nation is not, as in the classical imperialist relationships, situated in a geographically distinct mother country, but is settled within the borders. What is more, the roots of the dominant nation have been embedded in our country by more than three centuries of presence.

It is thus an alien body only in the historical sense.

The material well-being of the White group and its political, social and
economic privileges are, we know, rooted in its racial domination of the
indigenous majority. It has resisted and will resist doggedly and passionately
any attempt to shift it from this position. Its theorists and leaders ceaselessly
play upon the theme of 'We have nowhere else to go'. They dishonestly ignore
and even twist the fact that the uncertainty about the future of the oppressor
in our land is an uncertainty born not of our racialism but of his. The spectre
is falsely raised of a threat to the White man's language and culture to
'justify' a policy of cultural discrimination and domination. By economic
bribes and legal artifices which preserve for him the top layers of skills and
wage income, the White worker is successfully mobilised as one of racialism's
most reliable contingents. In every walk of life White autocracy *creates*
privilege by the operation of the law and, where necessary, the gun and with
a primitive and twisted 'proof' of its own superiority.

Nevertheless, the defence of all-round economic, social and cultural
privileges combined with centuries of indoctrination and deeply felt theoretical rationalisation which centre on survival, will make the enemy we face a
ferocious and formidable foe. So long as the threat from the liberation
movement was not powerful enough to endanger the very existence of White
baaskap there was room for division – sometimes quite sharp in the White
political camp.

Its motivation amongst the ruling class was competition for the lion's share
of the spoils from the exploitation of the non-White people. It always centred
around the problem of the most effective way of 'keeping the native in his
place'. In such an atmosphere there were even moments when White workers
adopted militant class postures against the small group which owns South
Africa's wealth. But the changed world mood and international situation
inhibited these confrontations. The laagerminded White group as a whole
moves more and more in the direction of a common defence of what is
considered a common fate.

These monolithic tendencies are reinforced by a Hitlerlike feeling of
confidence that the fortress is impregnable and unassailable for all time. This
process of all White solidarity will only be arrested by the achievements of the
liberation movement. For the moment the reality is that apart from a small
group of revolutionary Whites, who have an honoured place as comrades in
the struggle, we face what is by and large a united and confident enemy
which acts in alliance with, and is strengthened by world imperialism. All
significant sections of the White political movement are in broad agreement
on the question of defeating our liberation struggle.

This confrontation on the lines of colour – at least in the early stages of
the conflict – is not of our choosing; it is of the enemy's making. It will not
be easy to eliminate some of its more tragic consequences. But it does not
follow that this will be so for all time. It is not altogether impossible that in
a different situation the White working class or a substantial section of it,
may come to see that their true long-term interest coincides with that of the

non-White workers. We must miss no opportunity either now or in the future to try and make them aware of this truth and to win over those who are ready to break with the policy of racial domination. Nor must we ever be slow to take advantage of differences and divisions which our successes will inevitably spark off to isolate the most vociferous, the most uncompromising and the most reactionary elements amongst the Whites. Our policy must continually stress in the future (as it has in the past) that there is room in South Africa for all who live in it but only on the basis of absolute democracy . . . .

In South Africa not only does the system at present enforce discrimination against individuals by reason of their colour or race but in addition some national groups are privileged, as such, over others. At the moment the Afrikaner national group is lording it over the rest of the population with the English group playing second fiddle to them. For all the non-White groups — the Africans, Indians and the Coloureds the situation is one of humiliation and oppression. As far as languages are concerned only Afrikaans and English have official status in the bodies of state such as Parliament or Provincial Councils; in the courts, schools and in the administration. The culture of the African, Indian and Coloured people is barely tolerated. In fact everything is done to smash and obliterate the genuine cultural heritage of our people. If there is reference to culture by the oppressors it is for the purpose of using it as an instrument to maintain our people in backwardness and ignorance.

Day in and day out White politicians and publicists are regaling the world with their theories of national, colour and racial discrimination and contempt for our people. Enshrined in the laws of South Africa are a host of insulting provisions directed at the dignity and humanity of the oppressed people.

A democratic government of the people shall ensure that all national groups have equal rights, as such, to achieve their destiny in a united South Africa.

There shall be equal status in the bodies of state, in the courts and in the schools for the African, Indian, Coloured and Whites as far as their national rights are concerned. All people shall have equal right to use their own languages, and to develop their own folk culture and customs; all national groups shall be protected by laws against insults to their race or national pride; the preaching and practice of national, racial or colour discrimination and contempt shall be a punishable crime; and all laws and practices based on apartheid or racial discrimination shall be set aside.

Black Awareness
ANC

*From an article, 'Coloured People in Renewed Rejection of
Apartheid' published in* Sechaba *(ANC), VI, 10, October 1972.*

According to a commentator writing from Cape Town: 'The use of the term
Black to describe Coloureds and Indians is by no means general yet, but until
a few years ago it was almost unheard of, for either of these two population
groups voluntarily to label themselves as Black. The use of the common term
Black implies they are all in the same boat.' According to the same commentator, 'The philosophy of "Black Consciousness' is that contact and co-operation with Whites, any Whites, blunts the edge of the Black struggle. One
manifestation of Black Consciousness was the formation of the Black People's
Convention in Natal. It will "operate outside the white Government-created
systems, structures and institutions' and preach, popularise and implement the
philosophy of Black Consciousness and Black Solidarity".'

Another writer says, 'Clearly a similar process of self-realisation is at present
at work in the African, Coloured and Indian communities in South Africa'.

'What we care about,' said the poet-philosopher Adam Small, a leading
coloured intellectual in Cape Town, 'is understanding ourselves and in the
course of this task helping Whites to understand themselves.'

The Johannesburg Sunday Times stated in April:

> The emergence of the Black Power movement among the Coloured
> people is threatening to destroy the inter-race academic movement
> started at the Grabouw conference last October by leading Afrikaner and
> Coloured businessmen . . . What is even more significant is that the
> Coloureds who participated in the original Grabouw venture have been
> forced to reconsider their own position in this Afrikaner-Coloured
> dialogue movement. At the Grabouw conference most of them
> disturbed many of the Afrikaners present with their bitterness, out-
> spokenness, uncompromising attitude and deep suspicion about the
> motives of the Nationalist Government and its policies. Nonetheless, in
> spite of their militant attitude, they have been branded by the majority
> of the Coloured elite in academic circles, the professions and in business
> as 'sell-outs' to the Whites. These Coloureds regard collaboration with
> Whites in any form as 'treason'. There is a growing feeling among them
> that co-operation with Whites is senseless, and that their future lies in
> themselves. They do not primarily think in terms of 'Brown Power' but
> align themselves with all 'non-Whites', who suffer from 'White suppress-
> ion'. . . . Since his return from the United States last year, Mr. Small
> previously an advocate of White-non-White contact has been a strong
> supporter of a 'Black Power Coloured movement' in close co-operation
> with the Blacks. He has now rejected any form of co-operation with
> Whites, and believes that the Coloured people must attain their goals

under their own steam. The serious aspect of this Black Power movement is that it is directed primarily against the Afrikaner, who symbolises the Government and its apartheid policies. Among the Coloured elite groups the use of Afrikaans is no longer tolerated. People who have grown up with Afrikaans as their mother tongue are now using English and sending their children to English schools — otherwise they will be completely ostracised by their own friends.

This report goes on to say that, 'this rapidly-growing movement among the Coloureds could have important political repercussions. There is no doubt that the leadership of both the Nationalist and United Parties are completely unaware of its extent. Their present outdated Coloured policies clearly reflect the shallowness of their political knowledge of the Coloured community. Furthermore, this development is bound to have a profound effect on the Coloured political parties themselves.'

It is not possible to judge this attitude among Coloured, African and Indian people without considering the background of increased arrogance on the part of the White racists, the widespread social and economic calamities caused by apartheid in all its forms, the 'helplessness' (as a SASO leader put it) of any White opponents of the system, as well as the difficulties of working effectively faced by the illegal underground Congress movement with their far more positive revolutionary programme.

The trend of 'Black Consciousness' fills a temporary vacuum left by the outlawing of the militant organisations, but what it claims to involve smacks of pessimism as well. It views South Africa only in terms of Blacks versus Whites in the Republic. Nowhere in the utterances of Black Consciousness does one find any view of the national liberation movement in terms of world-wide considerations, as an element of the world revolutionary process which must inevitably contribute to the situation in South Africa.

As the programme of the ANC says:

> The struggle of the oppressed people of South Africa is taking place within an international context of transition to the Socialist system, of the breakdown of the colonial system as the result of the national liberation and socialist revolutions, and the fight for social and economic progress by the people of the whole world.
>
> While the national character of our struggle dominates our approach, it is a national struggle which is taking place in a different era and in a different context from those which characterised the early struggles against colonialism. It is happening in a new kind of world — a world which is no longer monopolised by the imperialist system and a significant sector of newly liberated areas has altered the balance of forces. . . . Thus our nationalism must not be confused with the narrow nationalism or chauvinism of a previous epoch.
>
> We face what is by and large a united and confident enemy which acts in alliance with, and is strengthened by world imperialism. All

significant sections of the White political movement are in broad agreement on the question of defeating our liberation struggle. This confrontation on the lines of colour — at least in the early stages of the conflict — is not of our choosing; it is of the enemy's making . . .

Nevertheless says the ANC programme, 'Nor must we ever be slow to take advantage of differences and divisions which our successes will inevitably spark off to isolate the most vociferous, the most uncompromising and the most reactionary elements amongst the Whites. Our policy must continually stress in the future (as it has in the past) that there is room in South Africa for all who live in it but only on the basis of absolute democracy.' But, 'the national sense of grievance is the most potent revolutionary force which must be harnessed. To blunt it in the interests of abstract concepts of internationalism is, in the long run, doing neither a service to the revolution nor to internationalism. In the last resort it is only the success of the national democratic revolution which, by destroying the existing social and economic relationships, will bring with it a correction of the historical injustices perpetrated against the indigenous majority' and all oppressed people in South Africa.

Against Sectionalism

Cardiff Marney

*From an article by the President of the Coloured Peoples'
Congress, 'The Struggle for Unity in Azania (South
Africa)' published in the PAC pamphlet,* New Phase
in Azanian Struggle, *circa 1966.*

Sectionalism in South African liberation politics is the antithesis of unity. The sectionalist sees the needs, interests and aspirations of the people through the spectacles bequeathed by the white rulers. Seeing the destinies of the various sections as distinct from one another, it is his function to further the interests of racial groups or sections. Sectionalism therefore requires the separate organisation of each racial group and the propagation of the ideas and mythology of separatism and apartheid — with necessary acceptable embellishments.

By contrast, unity in the South African context demands the organisation of the working masses into unitary, non-racial bodies. As such, a unitary organisation brings to the people an awareness of their common nationhood and creates a common patriotism which challenges the validity of the current social arrangements and proposes an alternative. In this way the people are provided with the unifying ideas and political instruments required to overthrow white tyranny and exploitation.

Insofar as the multi-racial confederations called into question, even if only to a limited extent, the status quo, they cannot be charged with sectionalism. Similarly, those group organisations affiliated multi-racially to the extent that they were not consciously promoting antagonistic, divisive and group interests against the larger national interest, cannot be branded as racialistic. But the step from multi-racialism to sectionalism is a small one, and it is precisely in this that the danger of such organisations resides. They easily begin to accommodate themselves to the backwardness of the people. This is the slippery road down which the ANC skated, thereby becoming the most unashamedly sectional movement in the country . . . .

The danger of sectionalism is that it emphasises those things which divide the people and consign to limbo their common humanity and common national interests. In the ANC new heights of sectionalism were reached by way of the 'African Image'.

The emergence of independent African states and the oft-declared and genuinely felt sympathy and support of African statesmen for the struggle of the South African people had a considerable impact on South African thought. The disgust with which the PAC turned away from the ANC (whose concern for 'racial peace and harmony' had often bordered upon the studied neglect of the best interests of the oppressed) had to be given intellectual substance. And the disillusionment in ruling class philosophy and white pusillanimity required ideological content. Thus for the first time in South African politics the ideas of Pan-Africanism — bigger than nationalism but narrower than internationalism — were brought to the people. Under the influence of the newly-independent states PAC became the first to receive these ideas and bring them to the people — and became in turn the first to be received in the new states.

Nationally, PAC stole the thunder of the ANC by its militancy, by its utter rejection of white hegemony and by its complete confidence in the strength and revolutionary capacity of the black masses. Internationally, it won acclaim as the party of Robert Sobukwe, as the men and women shot down at Sharpeville, and as the darlings and representatives of new, emergent Africa. Great was the consternation in the ANC camp when its leaders saw their pre-eminence and influence challenged so mightily. This challenge they set out to meet by jettisoning the Congress Alliance allies, thus enabling them to inform the African masses that they were 'more African' than PAC and more truly representative of the African people of South Africa. In short, the ANC had to have an 'African Image' for international purposes.

Internally, the true extent to which the External Mission of the ANC went to present this African Image was not clear. South Africa is a big country and politicians are known to have said one thing in one place and the opposite a thousand miles away. Generally, however, while the intellectual climate was carefully prepared at home for the acceptance of the African Image, it would seem that the true nature of the activities of the ANC External Mission was not known inside the country.

What then in practical terms is the 'African Image'?

(1) To convince African statesmen of their 'pure' African nature, the ANC

had to take the people in South Africa backwards in time, destroying the measure of national and working class unity that had been achieved.

(2) To put across the illusion that a sectionalist organisation could consummate the revolution, groups like the Coloured and Indians had to be misrepresented internationally as unimportant, and expendable 'minorities'. Their organisations and political contributions had to be demeaned where they were not ignored.

(3) On the home front the retreat into unmitigated sectionalism had to be balanced by controls being exercised over the other organisations of the former Congress Alliance. Such controls had to be exerted through personal contacts and through members of the Communist Party, for publicly it had to appear that no relations existed with 'non-Africans'.

(4) Consistency required that, although overtures of non-racial unity had to be rejected, the CPC and the Indian Congress had to be prevented from becoming completely independent lest they should become uncontrollable and by their political intervention explode the myth that a sectional organisation can lead the whole people to freedom.

(5) The representatives of the Indian Congress abroad had to be rendered inactive and mute and the CPC had to be prevented from making itself internationally known. The treatment of Dr Yusuf Dadoo, the representative of the Indian Congress, who worked closely with the ANC External Mission, will remain one of the great scandals of ANC politics abroad.

(6) The youth who had been sent abroad for military training had all to be 'pure' Africans. Even a revolutionary 'non-African' youth, who made his way on his own to Dar-es-Salaam in order to secure military training, had to be sent back home to the waiting arms of Verwoerd's security police.

(7) Various outmoded tribal customs suddenly were now encouraged among African men and women — the women particularly appearing at political trials in tribal regalia, etc. — and the histories of various tribes and chiefs erupted into print.

Unquestionably, the practices and malpractices of the African Image have nothing to do with deepening the social crisis and developing the revolutionary capacities and instruments of the people. If they serve any purpose at all, they can only be that of side-tracking the people from their revolutionary objectives — a function we would expect from agents interested in furthering the counter-revolutionary objectives of imperialism, not from leaders of the people. Unhappily, not only is the ANC creating division and confusion among the oppressed and exploited people in South Africa, but even in its own ranks the tendency has developed for the tribal origins of men to be investigated! From racialism to multi-racialism, from multi-racialism to tribalism — this is the tragic pass to which things have come. But it is the logical outcome of sectionalism as it develops the machinery of racial classification, inspection and introspection.

The Role of the Indian People in the South African Revolution
Y.M. Dadoo

Response by the banned President of the South African Indian Congress, to questions by Sechaba *(ANC), published in a 'Special Edition', 1969.*

Sechaba: Dr Dadoo, you have just published a leaflet which is the first public call you have made to the Indian people since you left South Africa in 1960. Can you tell us what the background to this leaflet is, and why you have chosen to make your call at this time?

Dadoo: Today, history is witnessing a decisive turning point in the struggle for national liberation in South Africa. Armed struggle has begun. Under the leadership of the African National Congress in alliance with the Congress movement, the brave freedom-fighters of the Umkhonto we Sizwe are on the march. Already combat units of Umkhonto, together with contingents of the Zimbabwe African People's Union, are giving battle to the armed forces of Ian Smith and Vorster in Zimbabwe (Rhodesia). Reliable reports from the battle front, contrary to the whitewashing accounts put out by the South African press and radio, indicate that the freedom fighters are fighting with great daring and skill, and are inflicting heavy casualties on the enemy. Even the enemy has to admit that the freedom fighters, whom he calls 'terrorists', are not only well armed, but highly skilful in the use of their weapons. It is on the cards that soon there will be fighting on South African soil.

So, in this new period of armed struggle and developing revolutionary upheavals, it is necessary to make every section of the South African population, both white and non-white, aware of the changing situation and of the tasks and responsibilities that it is being called upon to fulfil. As a leader of the Indian people, it is my duty to ask them to respond unreservedly to the call made by the Acting President of the African National Congress, our comrade Oliver Tambo, in which he says: 'As our forces drive deeper into the South we have no doubt that they will be joined not by some, but by the whole African nation; by the oppressed minorities, the Indian and Coloured people; and by an increasing number of white democrats.'

Once this leaflet reaches the Indian people – and it is even now being distributed amongst them through the underground movement – I have no doubt that they will respond readily, and with the same spirit of self-sacrifice and determination that they have shown throughout their long and bitter struggles against segregation, and for human rights, ever since the days of Gandhijee [Mahatma Gandhi, who led the first Indian struggles in South Africa in the late 1800s and early 1900s – Editor] .

Sechaba: What precise role do you expect the Indian people to play, then, in this new phase of the struggle?

Dadoo: As an integral part of the South African population, the Indian community of half a million people has a very important role to play in the new form the struggle has taken. The militant Indian youth, who played not an insignificant part in the early struggles of Umkhonto since 1961 — several of them are serving long terms of imprisonment on Robben Island and in other South African jails together with their African, Coloured and White comrades-in-arms — have yet a larger role to play *in* the liberation army, and in mobilising the Indian people in town and country to support and help the freedom fighters in every possible way. The Indian people must and will, I am certain, help to make the path of freedom fighters easy. They must also mount ever-increasing resistance to every aspect of apartheid: the Group Areas Act must not be allowed to govern them; they must oppose and reject the regime's stooge body the South African Indian Council, which is being used by Vorster as an instrument to obtain the collaboration of the Indian people in the implementation of apartheid policies. Every form of opposition to apartheid is of help to the freedom fighters in the war against white supremacy.

Sechaba: The South African Indian Congress is still technically a legal organization. How legal is it in practice, and how is it functioning? And how will the publication of the leaflet, calling for support for the armed struggle, affect the organization?

Dadoo: The SAIC is a legal organization only in name. The terror let loose by the Government through its Special Branch has made the legal functioning of the SAIC and its constituent bodies, the Natal Indian Congress and the Transvaal Indian Congress, impossible. Every one of its office-bearers and committee members at national, provincial and branch level, has been banned, imprisoned or driven into exile. And this applies to the members appointed to replace those banned and imprisoned, and again to those appointed to replace *them.* The legal functioning of the organization is now impossible. But the new leaflet, and the fact that it is being distributed in spite of all the penalties, bears witness to the fact that the spirit of resistance for which the South African Indian Congress stands, lives on, and that no power on earth can crush it.

Sechaba: You spoke earlier of the Congress Movement. Can you tell us something of the background of the alliance between the South African Indian Congress, the African National Congress and the other organizations of the Congress Movement?

Dadoo: Freedom is indivisible. A section of the population cannot be free if the rest is in bondage. In the course of their struggle against unjust laws, and for the redress of their grievances, the Indian people began to realise that no fundamental changes were possible without unity of action between all the oppressed people. And it was this realization that made the younger members of the Indian Congress, in the late 30s and early 40s, set about trying to change the policies of the Congress, in order to seek co-operation in the common struggle with the premier national organization of the African people, the ANC, and with the national organization of the Coloured people.

A similar spirit also prevailed among the younger elements in the African political movement, and in the Coloured community. This led to the formation of united-front bodies to campaign to show the people that they must act unitedly, and to bring about changes in the national organization (and necessary changes of leadership) to follow the new policies of co-operation and united struggle. To bring about the changes in the Indian Congress, a vigorous campaign had to be conducted amongst the Indian people, and many bitter battles had to be fought against the 'moderate' leadership of the time. Members of the progressive groups were assaulted, sometimes brutally. In the Transvaal, a volunteer of the progressive group was actually killed. But with the crushing of the moderate leadership it was possible for the Indian people once again to conduct a militant campaign – the Passive Resistance Campaing against Smuts's 'Ghetto Act' in 1946. This was entirely a struggle of the Indian people, but a few African and Coloured volunteers participated as a gesture of solidarity.

Simultaneously there was a change in the leadership of the ANC, and this made possible co-operation between the Indian Congress and the African National Congress through a pact known as the Xuma-Naicker-Dadoo Pact of 1946. After that, many joint struggles were conducted, such as the stay-at-home on 26 June 1950 (the first South Africa Freedom Day), the stay-at-home on 1 May 1950, and the Defiance of Unjust Laws Campaign of 1952, in which over 8,000 volunteers of all races defied laws and went to prison. Under the leadership of the ANC in alliance with the organizations of the Indian and Coloured people, of the workers and of the progressive whites, the Congress of the People was held in 1955 – at which the Freedom Charter was adopted by over 3,000 delegates of all races. This Charter became the programme of all the organizations participating in the Congress Movement, and laid the basis for a united struggle for the transformation of South Africa. A Joint Consultative Council of all the organizations continued to operate until the premier organization, the ANC, was banned in 1960.

With the departure of Gandhijee from South Africa in 1914 and with the removal from the political scene of some of his staunchest lieutenants because of death or old age, the leadership of the Indian community fell into the hands of 'moderates' who believed in compromising with the Government on each and every legislative measure of racial discrimination against the Indian people. The Indian Congress was reduced to representing, by and large, the voice of the small Indian merchant class only.

The campaign for all-out resistance against all discriminatory legislation conducted by the younger progressive group among the Indian people culminated not only in ousting the moderate leadership but also in transforming the Indian Congress into a mass organization of the whole people.

The Indian Passive Resistance Campaign of 1946 against the Asiatic Land Tenure and Indian Representation Act enacted by the Smuts Government brought together in a united struggle all sections: the working people who constituted 80% of the Indian community, the professional class and traders. The unity it wrought was indeed so powerful that not a single Indian accepted even the limited franchise which the Act offered.

The Campaign of 1946, furthermore, laid a strong basis among the Indian people for the subsequent unity with the African National Congress and the other organizations of the Congress Movement in the struggle for liberation. The Campaign also made a significant impact internationally. It made the Indian community appreciate more fully the importance of international solidarity in the world-wide struggle against racialism, colonialism and imperialism. At the request of the SAIC, India demonstrated her solidarity by breaking off relations with South Africa and imposing economic sanctions. At its request India also took up the issue of the treatment of the South Africans of Indian and Pakistani origin at the United Nations. This was soon broadened to include the whole question of apartheid. Thus it is that the question of the apartheid policies of the fascist South African Government has been on the agenda of the United Nations Organization ever since its inception.

The Defiance of Unjust Laws Campaign, similarly, not only increased the attention of the world to the liberation struggles of the oppressed peoples, it also welded the masses of the African, Coloured and Indian peoples into a united force. Furthermore, it gave rise to the formation of the Congress of Democrats, a small but active group of white democrats, and the South African Congress of Trade Unions (Sactu), who later joined the united front, popularly known as the Congress Alliance.

Sechaba: How do you reconcile the tradition of passive resistance in the SAIC with your call for support for armed struggle?

Dadoo: Passive resistance was never the ideology of the organization, although it had been used as a method of struggle since it was introduced by Gandhijee in the early part of this century. The principles of Satyagraha as enunciated by Gandhi were never accepted as a *creed* by the Indian people. It is true that in the SAIC, as a national organization representing all interests and all viewpoints, there are some leaders – like Dr Naicker and Nana Sita – who implicitly believed in Gandhian principles and who have lived by them; and of course we honour their convictions and their sufferings for their convictions. But in this connection it is significant to note that when the ANC and the SAIC jointly embarked upon the Defiance Campaign of 1952, it was deliberately not called a passive resistance campaign. It was called a Defiance Campaign, although it was non-violent. It expressed a more militant outlook, because most of the leaders had realised that in the situation of South Africa, where violence was the normal instrument of Government policy, there could arise a situation where no alternative would be left to the people, if they were to continue to fight for their freedom, but to resort to violent methods. When Umkhonto we Sizwe (Spear of the Nation) was formed, Indian youth readily responded to its call, and participated in its activities.

Sechaba: The argument has often been put to the Indian people in South Africa that as a minority group they would be no better off under African rule than they are under White. In the light of what has happened in Kenya, for instance, what is your answer to this argument?

Dadoo: This is absolute nonsense — it is merely the tactics of divide and rule used by the authorities in order to maintain the divisions of the people, as they already do by law, keeping the national groups apart and preventing inter-communication. This is the argument of the South African Police who seek to intimidate the people from participating in the struggle; it is the argument of their agents provocateurs in our midst, who deliberately try to provoke hostility between African and Indian, African and Coloured, to convince each that their grievances are not the fault of an oppressive government, but of another oppressed group. They use this tactic precisely because it is our unity in the face of oppression that the oppressor most fears.

It must be understood that the fundamental of the liberation struggle is first and foremost the liberation of the majority of the population, the African people, and that it is unthinkable that there could be liberation without African majority rule. The position of the Indian minority in South Africa cannot, in any case, be compared with that of the Asian population in Kenya. We have no political or social rights and even the extremely limited economic opportunities we now possess are fast being whittled away through ruthless implementation of such laws as the Group Areas Act. The history of the two groups is different. Although the Indian community in Kenya suffered from certain aspects of segregation — for example, not being allowed to live in the Highlands — under British rule, they had greater opportunities for development than the Africans or the South African Indians: for example in questions of ownership of land and employment in the Civil Service. And because of this, they, except for a handful of brave Asian patriots, stood apart from the mainstream of the Kenyan liberation struggle. So when independence came, most of the Asians did not feel themselves a part of it, and they were encouraged in this by the withdrawing of the British authorities, who helped them to obtain British passports, making them feel that they had an alternative to identification with Kenya; so many of them did not become citizens. This is a situation where the imperialist policy of 'divide and rule' classically worked — and we are determined that it cannot work in South Africa. The lesson of this is that unless different sections of the population have a patriotic allegiance to a common cause, they can have no place in the new free societies now being built on the African continent. They must support local liberation struggles and most of all, be true Africans, just as the vast majority of the Indian people of South Africa are today.

Sechaba: How do you see the liberation struggle in South Africa developing, and how can a small minority group like the Indian community effectively participate?

Dadoo: The African people in the whole of Southern Africa, in the Portuguese colonial territories of Mozambique and Angola and Guinea-Bissau, in Rhodesia, and South Africa, are now engaged in a life and death struggle. This struggle may be long and protracted and bitter, and may call for tremendous sacrifices, but it will go on and on, until freedom is won. In this struggle all the oppressed people have a duty to play their part, and the small Indian community of South Africa has also a definite and significant role. Knowing the Indian people of South Africa as I do, I am quite convinced that they will not waver, that they will unflinchingly throw themselves into the struggle, wholeheartedly, not as a minority, but as South Africans.

The Role of the Coloured Community
Reg September

> *Response by the Secretary-General of the South African Coloured People's Congress, to questions by* Sechaba *(ANC), published in a 'Special Edition', 1969.*

Sechaba: Comrade September, the South African government has lately gone to a great deal of trouble to convince the Coloured people that their best interest lies in co-operating with apartheid. They have set up a Coloured Affairs Council in an effort to channel their political energy along apartheid lines. How successful would you say these efforts have been?
September: The Coloured community now totals approximately 1,800,000 the greatest majority of whom live in the South Western Cape with Cape Town as its centre. During the past 20 years of Nationalist rule, the position of semi-privilege which we occupied under previous white administration has virtually disappeared. Except for the obvious economic disparity, our position today closely approximates to that of the African people. The deliberate and systematic separation between White and Coloured has been one of the principle objectives of Nationalist rule, and today it is an accomplished fact. Only a few loose ends remain to be tied.

When we — my generation — were young, Cape Town was regarded (and quite rightly so) as the best South African city area for a non-white to live in. We counted ourselves fortunate. We travelled in the same train compartment or bus as the White man; we stood in the same Post Office queue; we went to the same beach; and there existed no legal barrier against our living in some of the more coveted parts of the Western Cape. We organized ourselves in trade unions together with white workers. The Cape was the only Province to send non-whites to the City and Provincial Councils. It was the only Province where the non-white could bargain through the ballot box. The Cape was the only province in which the white Parliamentarian, Provincial or City Councillor, sought our vote. Hence the position of semi-privilege. But the position of 'half-brother', in the relation between the white and the coloured man of the Cape, has been rejected by the white man in no uncertain terms during the course of the last twenty years. In its place the Nationalists have imposed on us a system of complete social, cultural, educational, residential and political segregation. We share in the full oppression of apartheid.

During the 'more liberal' Smuts era, the political organization of the community was in the hands of the African Peoples Organization (APO) led by Dr. A. Abdurahman. Within the status quo, the APO took up the cudgels on behalf of the community in whatever constitutional way it was possible at the time. However, our country and the Coloured community were no exceptions to the resurgence movement of the underdog during the post-war period. This was the period when the demand for full and equal rights for all took on a mass character. It was during this period that broad masses of the Coloured community saw their destinies as being more clearly linked with that of the African and Indian.

The Coloured Affairs Council to which you refer, is nothing but an imposed apartheid administrative machinery; and it is recognised as such by all elements in the community. This government has brought untold misery and hardship on the Coloured community and can never expect to get its willing co-operation.

Sechaba: What reaction has there been from the Coloured community to the Government's legislation banning racially mixed political parties; and the plan to end the system of Coloured representation through White members of the white Parliament?

September: The reaction of the Coloured community to the banning of mixed political parties can only be a negative one. The Liberal Party has never enjoyed any measure of mass support among the non-White people. However, even if it had, it is doubtful if there would have been any *public* outcry under the circumstances prevailing in South Africa today. The Progressive Party — which only in the very narrow white South African sense can be regarded as progressive — did poll a significant number of votes in separate Coloured elections, that is, from the limited percentage who were on the voters roll. This Party however is not regarded as a party which is likely to lead South Africa to any new horizon. But the plan of the government to do away with even this limited system of representation (i.e. Separate Coloured Representation) altogether, must, if anything, be regarded as a minor defeat for the government. It had gone to a great deal of trouble and political jerrymandering to establish the system of Separate Coloured Representation in Parliament, in the hope that they would be able to use it effectively in the process of the political enslavement of our people. Instead, they found that elections for Separate Representation were increasingly becoming a platform — however limited — of protest. Now, even these elected 'representatives' are found to be unacceptable to the government — despite their opposition to the CPC's policy. The government has now decided to do away with these 'representatives'. In their place the government now chooses to institute a system of so-called representation which it is in a better position to control — i.e. the Coloured Affairs Council. It must be remembered that any militant organization is today barred from functioning openly. The only organizations allowed to function are those which have the blessing of the government.

Sechaba: The Coloured People's Congress is still technically a legal organization. How legal is it in practice, and how is it functioning?

September: In practice, it is not legal. What has happened to all publicly known members of the similarly-placed South African Indian Congress — banning, imprisonment, forcing into exile — has also happened to members of the CPC. Our experience has shown that it was necessary to start afresh with completely new people whatever the difficulties. While organizationally we have suffered a severe setback at home, I am confident that time will prove our people to be competent to deal effectively with the immense problem of re-organization under these police state conditions.

Externally, we have no separate representation as the CPC. By arrangement in South Africa, when it was still possible for us to meet on a representative basis, it was decided that the ANC would officially bear the responsibility for representing the whole of the Congress Movement, that is, all its constituent organizations including the CPC. This position remains unchanged.

Sechaba: The CPC is a constituent of the Congress Movement. Can you tell us something about the background to this alliance?

September: The CPC was established in 1953. Many of us who founded the organization had enjoyed the closest working relationship with the ANC even before CPC was established. CPC commenced co-operation with the ANC and others, in preparation for the calling of the Congress of the People in 1955. The Freedom Charter which resulted from this historic Congress, was subsequently enshrined in our Constitution. Six months after the Congress of the People, 156 Congress members (including CPC members) stood trial for High Treason. Our Charter was on trial. In 1960 during the State of Emergency we again found ourselves in jail together with our comrades in the Congress Movement, after having been a part of the call to strike as a protest against the Sharpeville and Langa police killings. In 1961 again, we joined with Mandela and the ANC in calling for a three-day stoppage of work against the imposition of the Verwoerd Republic; again it was jail and court.

Our co-operation was and is, it can be seen, based on much more than a simple formal alliance. There is a common approach to problems, an almost indistinguishable similarity in the style of work developed during the course of years of closely coordinated struggles and common sacrifice. That is why we have come to be known as the Congress Movement. In the course of struggle tremendous strides have been made in building unity not only at the leadership level but also at the grass-roots level.

Sechaba: What is the attitude of your organization to the new stage — the stage of armed struggle, now reached by the liberation movement? Do you have plans to make a call on the Coloured people to respond to the call to revolution made by the Acting President of the ANC, Comrade Oliver Tambo, in January?

September: This is a matter that worried us for some considerable time. Members of our organization saw the correctness of this form of struggle some time ago. and some joined Umkhonto we Sizwe (Spear of the Nation) on an individual basis. However, in South Africa an illegal method of struggle could hardly be discussed by a legally functioning organization. This problem has now been overcome by virtue of the fact that all known members of the organization have now been immobilized in one way or another, and a new publicly unknown core has been built. I have no doubt that when the new organization inside the country sees fit, they will make their attitude known. You may rest assured that they are at one with Comrade Tambo.

Sechaba: What response would you expect to such a call?

September: Our community is a very heterogeneous one and we must expect the response to such a call to reflect this. The newly-formed groups will have to function illegally in a police state. They will be launching out after a long lapse of time. After all, the people have not heard from the CPC for some years now. During all this time, the only organizations which have functioned in the community are those which are today functioning with full government sanction. Intimidation by the government and its agents is rife, the system of spying and government age ̄ is part of the system of the South African government. The impression which is created is that the government is all-powerful. The community has been completely separated, from white *and* black. A small middle class of the community has been bought off by being granted favours or fringe benefits in 'their own areas'. However, the bulk of the people remain poor. They are faced with a rising cost of living, an inferior education, disgraceful conditions in the segregated or apartheid areas, and no real confidence in the future under this government. Resentment seethes under the surface of calm. The people await an alternative. Inside South Africa, our organization has the task of presenting this alternative, and working in the closest co-operation with the other member organizations of the militant united front of the Congress Alliance. This is being done right now.

Sechaba: From March this year, as reported in the S.A. press, all Coloured men aged 18 to 24 have had to register for compulsory training in labour camps. What are these youths being trained for? Will those who are trained be used as a counter-revolutionary force against the unfolding South African revolution?

September: This new Act is going to be used in order to regiment the young men of the community as the government sees fit. The South African economy is built on cheap, enforced and directed labour. In the same way that the African labourer has been shanghaied into specified jobs and areas, so the Coloured youth will now receive similar treatment. The fact that the government saw fit to drop threatening leaflets from the air recently, shows the extent to which the people are unwilling to co-operate in their own enslavement. It is a clear indication that they do not trust the government. Such a force, I believe, would prove to be most unreliable from the point of view of the government as a counter-revolutionary force.

Sechaba: What precise role do you expect the Coloured people to play, in the struggle that is to come?

September: Of the non-whites, our people are the most technically skilled, a process which was started when our forefathers (shoe-makers, tailors, builders, harness makers) were imported into the country from the East. Some sections are more fortunate economically, and have educated their children at tremendous sacrifice. I believe that they will prove to be valuable Freedom Fighters. The magnificent record of the Cape Corps in World Wars One and Two should be some guide.

However, it would be idle folly for us to boast of having a mass organization among the Coloured Community. While the roots of the ANC are deep among the Africans, ours have yet to be developed in our community. The community has fought many a valiant political battle in the past and I am certain that broad sections will respond now to the sterner battles which lie ahead.

As you know, we spring partly from the White man, and we share the same language and religion and have the same cultural background as the Afrikaner (Boer), while the Africans and Indians are not connected to the Whites in this way. Broadly speaking, it has been a peculiar relationship which has existed, and the position which we have occupied is, in many respects I suppose, similar to that of marginal groups in other parts of the world. Except, of course, our minority is relatively large.

Geographically, we occupy an important position, for the Western Cape just cannot be relied upon unless the Coloured Community can be contained. It can be likened to a second front. Psychologically, the white people of South Africa have yet to feel the backlash of their rejection of the man whom for so long they had taken for granted. I believe their morale is going to be seriously undermined when they are made to realise that they have lost the Coloured man. This, I believe to be inevitable.

Sechaba: The authorities often use the argument, when dealing with the oppressed minorities in South Africa, that they would be worse off under African rule than they are now. How would you answer this?

September: Under the present system of government we have no say. This is realised all too well by our people. The sort of South Africa for which we are struggling does not envisage an African overlord in the same way as we have a White overlord today. We envisage an African majority with all people having equal rights, irrespective of colour. We look forward to the time when our people will be full participants in the struggle for a new South Africa with the Freedom Charter as our goal. When once a people have fought for freedom, and won it, such a people cannot be enslaved. Such a people can only be respected.

Sechaba: How do you see the liberation struggle in Southern Africa, and what hopes have you, and your organization, for the future?

September: The guerilla struggle now unfolding in Southern Africa is being watched with keen anxiety by all responsible elements in the community. They hope that each battle will mean a shattering defeat for the forces of Smith and Vorster. They recognize this as the beginnings of the real struggle for freedom, and they are proud when they hear that young men from our community are also part of this force. The connection between Angola, Mozambique, Zimbabwe (Rhodesia), South West Africa and South Africa is clearly understood. I am certain that they will gain tremendous confidence as a result of the progress which the forces of liberation are making in the field of battle, and this must swell. It is this newly gained confidence which will spread and lead to a rising tide of struggle for change.

Within the Coloured community, drunkenness and crimes of violence — always a significant social problem — are increasing to a frightening degree. We know from experience that a more meaningful expression of the frustrations causing these phenomena is a complete disregard for the oppressive authority and all which their law represents. The fervent manner in which the people demonstrated against and smashed Stuttaford's Servitude Bill in the late 30s, and the manner in which they defended Elizabeth Mafeking's right to remain in Paarl, are but two cases in point [Elizabeth Mafeking was a representative of the Food and Canning Workers in Paarl in the Cape Province, deported to Lesotho in the late 50s — Editor]. One sees some resemblance between the Afro-American and the Coloured communities, in the similarity of many of the problems which they have had to face and their way of reacting to these problems.

The impending challenge to authority will take many forms, and demand many sacrifices, but I believe that the community will match its responsibility and play an extremely important role in the South Africa of the future.

They Preferred to be British
Searchlight

Analysis from a clandestine journal of the Indian community inside South Africa, Searchlight, *reprinted in the ANC's* Sechaba, *VII, 1, January 1973.*

The blatant hypocrisy of many of those now pointing the finger of accusation with horror at events in Uganda must be evident to all Indian South Africans. Those who are responsible for racialism in our own country are those loudest in their sympathy for the Ugandans. We have been the victims of and have lived amongst a racialism of the most vicious kind for over a century. To suggest therefore that Ugandan Asians might find sanctuary in South Africa is to ask them to jump from the frying pan into the fire.

Yet there are people in South Africa, and regrettably some Indians amongst them, who are deliberately exploiting the sufferings of the Ugandan Asians for their own purposes. They are using events there to try and instil fear in our minds, and by suggesting that this is somehow a 'natural' consequence of African majority rule are trying to alienate us from the African people. This is not a new tactic, but one used by oppressors everywhere. So fearful are our rulers of the united opposition of the black people, that they will use every single trick in the book, and a few outside also, in order to divide us and so perpetuate their rule.

It is nonetheless important for us to understand the truth of what has happened in Uganda and why — so that we may learn the correct lessons and draw the right conclusions.

First and foremost we must disabuse ourselves of any belief that the Ugandan expulsions are typical and an automatic consequence of black rule. It was Britain which, as the colonial ruling power, used the Ugandan Asians to help exploit the country's coffee, cotton and sugar for its own benefit and laid the foundations of the present problem. Regrettably, the Asians were so tempted by the privileges that they were given that they built further on these foundations.

As early as the 1940s some of our own leadership foresaw the inevitable consequences of such attitudes. They actively directed us in South Africa away from a similar position, and whenever occasion arose made their views known to the minorities in East Africa. In India Mahatma Gandhi and Pandit Nehru also repeatedly called upon Asians in Africa to identify with the African masses. In 1962 Yusuf Dadoo wrote:

> Whatever historical factors there may be for the position in which the Asian communities find themselves in East Africa today, the fact of the matter is that in the eyes of the African people they are looked upon as an immigrant class — a class of interlopers which is more of a hinderance than an ally in the national struggle for freedom and independence.
>
> Time is certainly running out, but it is yet not too late for them to meet the challenge of the times and fit into the new pattern of the African revolution. A new vision — a revolution in thinking and action — is what is required. A policy of appeasement will not work, an attitude of apathy will not do, a gesture of patronage and charity will not avail. What is required is to become true Africans in every sense of the word.
>
> The Asian people of Kenya and Uganda, and indeed, everywhere in Africa, have a responsible historical task to perform; that of being active participants in the struggle for national independence and freedom and in the achievement of the noble aim of building a mighty united democratic Africa.

But the attitudes of the majority of Asians in Uganda did not change. In the meanwhile the British, having used the Asians, discarded them and denied them the right to enter the country whose citizens they had become.

What has happened in Uganda is 'terrible, horrible, abominable and shameful'. These are not our words, but those of an African President who has done so much to help bring about freedom in our country and who was Chairman of the OAU — President Kaunda of Zambia. President Nyerere of Tanzania, referring to his own and African condemnation of apartheid, has said of Uganda: 'This is clearly racialism and representative of the same thing that Africans are deploring.' Vice-President Moi has assured Asians there that they are welcome to stay so long as they are loyal to Kenya. Unfortunately, these statements do not receive the same attention in the South African press as those of President Amin, yet they do put Uganda into its correct perspective — as the exception rather than the rule in East and Central Africa.

In common with the majority of South Africans, in their everyday life and experience our people know the meaning of deprivation. They know what it is to be moved around, to be thrown out of houses, schools, temples, mosques and land; to work in the cane plantations, in the mines and factories at wages that are so low that 70% of Indian South African families live at or near the breadline; to have limited opportunities for education and restrictions on the use of such skills and talents we do have.

Since arrival in South Africa we have been part of the oppressed majority in our suffering. In time we came to realise that we had also to be part of the majority in our resistance and our efforts to bring change. With the emergence in the forties of the Nationalist bloc in the Transvaal and the Anti-Segregation Council in Natal, various of our leaders have asked for and received support on the basis that we are part of South Africa and must participate fully in the struggle to remove apartheid.

Thus Indian South Africans have taken their place together with all the other Black people. Dadabhai, Saloojee and Timol are amongst those who have given their lives for their country; Kathrada, Nair, Naidoo and others have given their freedom and are on Robben Island and elsewhere with Mandela, Sisulu and thousands of our fellow South Africans. Today the NIC has once again forged links with representatives of other oppressed groups: the Black People's Convention speaks for African, Coloured and Indian South Africans and the students are united in their resistance to indoctrination, while the sportsmen are determined to play together. Our record hitherto can leave no doubt as to where we stand, and that is firmly on South African soil and steadfastly determined to free it from oppression and racialism.

In Uganda, by contrast, the Asians sought to be part of the ruling class. In colonial times they had economic privileges denied to the African majority, and they asked for a special say in ruling the country as 'Asians', not in common with all Ugandans. As a result they accepted privileged positions in administering colonial rule. They control nearly 50% of Ugandan industry and 80-90% of the commercial life of the country. 50% of the registered doctors are of Asian origin as are the lawyers. They are also the majority of the skilled workers and artisans in the country.

We have seen in our own midst individuals who have been prepared to collaborate, support and even advocate apartheid in order to preserve their economic interests and receive the 'honour' of talking with and being listened to by our rulers. In as much as the economic power of the Ugandan Asians was so much greater, so too was their collaboration and identification with the ruling colonial power. So convinced were they that they were part of the ruling colonial power that at independence the majority chose not to be Ugandan citizens, by which action they showed they had no confidence in a basically African Ugandan government. But as collaborators inevitably discover, they can never be part of the rulers but merely their tools. And so, having used the Asians and even given them citizenship in order to safeguard the white settlers, Britain rejected the Asians who chose to be her citizens and denied them the right to enter the U.K. In doing so she created a bottleneck and an artificial slowing down on a normal and natural process of citizens taking over jobs and opportunities in Uganda.

Democratic governments usually endeavour to ensure that foreigners do not take jobs and opportunities from their own citizens. Our own government, not being democratically elected, prefers to bring in foreign white workers as immigrants rather than allow the black people to take up the opportunities open. In India after independence citizens gradually took over jobs from the British. Similarly, in African countries after independence citizens took over and the foreigners of whatever colour returned to their own countries.

British discrimination against its Asian citizens, however, stopped this natural process and set up artificial tensions and pressures in Uganda, where even the Asian workers and less affluent were misguided enough to be drawn into a position where they saw the imperialist homeland as a sanctuary. Before the coup, President Obote, when asked about the Asians said quite categorically: 'Uganda has no Asian problem. There is a problem of 30,000 British citizens in my country.' It is this British racialism which must bear a heavy responsibility for the present situation.

For Indian South Africans the message from Uganda is quite clear: We must make sure that we do not in any way ally ourselves with the ruling minority. Those who collaborate with apartheid are endangering our future in a democratic South Africa and must not be allowed to do so. It is a message the whites would do well to heed.

Far from being depressed we can take heart from the principled stand of Presidents Nyerere and Kaunda and draw closer still to the African and coloured people. In a message to President Kaunda, Dr. Yusuf Dadoo has said: 'Your principled stand against racialism in Uganda and humanitarian concern for its victims has brought honour to our Continent and has given strength to the united voice of Africa against apartheid. South Africans of Indian origin who have been in Africa for over a century and who have long been united with our African brothers in a struggle to free our country, gather strength from your words and renew their pledge to continue the fight for a free and democratic South Africa.'

So let us respond as we have always done and associate ourselves firmly with the majority of South Africans. Just as we are part of the oppressed, we must more actively endeavour to be amongst those who fight against oppression, so that we will be an integral part of a free and democratic South Africa.

Stop Immigration to South Africa
SACTU

An appeal to European trade unions not to support apartheid, issued by the South African Congress of Trade Unions in October 1970.

Apartheid is known and reviled throughout the world as a system of ruthless racial discrimination. But it is more than that. Its basis and purpose is the perpetual exploitation of the African worker. The African worker is doubly oppressed: as an African he carries the hated 'Pass' and suffers all the indignities and persecution of white supremacy. As a worker he is exploited by the employers backed up by the State and its extensive armoury of anti-labour laws.

In this situation the African worker, backbone of the wealthiest economy in Africa is doubly in need of the support and solidarity of fellow workers. Yet he sees daily evidence of the readiness of other workers — white men from Europe — to benefit from his oppression. These are the immigrants who help the apartheid regime to maintain an industrial colour bar, who come from overseas to enjoy the fruits of apartheid. They come in their thousands, filling highly paid skilled jobs while African workers look on bitterly and struggle to survive on starvation wages. The white population of South Africa is 3½ million or 19% of the total. Of these, a quarter of a million are immigrants who have entered South Africa since 1961. More have come from Britain than from any other country — and the number is rising every year:

1966	13,130
1967	14,700
1968	16,000
1970	according to the South African Embassy, London, 100 applicants daily.

The apartheid regime insists on two criteria for these immigrants: they must be white, and they must be skilled. To ensure that they are white, the South African Immigration Department applies four tests, recently announced by the Deputy Minister Dr. Koornhof:

a) The prospective immigrant must state his race on his application form.

b) He must submit 'very clear photographs' of himself and his closest kin.

c) He must appear before South African officials 'with experience in recognising whether people are white'.

d) On arrival in South Africa he is carefully scrutinised by 'well-trained immigration officials'.

What comment is needed on these degrading racist practices?

Apartheid needs these pure-white workers. And it constantly seeks them out. In all the major West European countries the Vorster regime maintains permanent recruiting offices; there are eight in Britain alone. Agents move around, accompanying trade and propaganda missions, searching for areas and plants affected by redundancies — aircraft workers from Hawker Siddeley, boiler-makers from Cammell Laird, engineers and draughtsmen, fitters, electricians, pilots — anybody who is white, skilled, and willing to live with a fascist dictatorship.

South Africa has a dynamic economy. The Republic mines more than 50 minerals, and produces more than two-thirds of the world's gold (excluding the USSR). Gold holdings at the end of 1968 were R876.7 million (R1 equals 11.8). The growth rate has been 5-6% in recent years. The output of iron, steel and manufactured goods has been increasing, exports rising, and today South Africa is the industrial heart of Africa and the twelfth biggest trading country in the world.

None of this would be possible without African labour. Yet Africans reap none of the rewards. For them, as for Coloured and Indian workers, there are low wages, insecurity, sickness and starvation, poverty in a land of natural wealth. An African miner might earn 8.10d a shift in cash and kind. His white boss gets £6.16.6d for the same day's work. In the building industry a white worker can earn £138 in a month, an African only £24. The same discrimination applies in housing, education, social services, health, etc. In 1968 a record number of cases of tuberculosis was recorded — over 70,000 new cases. Over 60,000 of these were African, representing a 4.3% increase over the previous year. Figures for the other races went down in the same period. For the black man, these are the fruits of apartheid.

Why not make skilled jobs and training facilities available to Africans? The Vorster regime refuses to consider this obvious solution to the country's alleged 'manpower shortage'. In August 1968, the Minister of Immigration, Dr. C.P. Mulder and his Deputy Koornhof told a Nationalist Party Conference that *'without the annual immigration intake of between 28,000 and 30,000, South Africa would not be able to maintain the normal 5½% economic growth rate set out by her planners'*. The delegates to the Conference had expressed some misgivings about the Government's immigration policy, and to intimidate and brace them to submission Dr. Mulder bluntly told the Congress that South Africa could do any one of three things:

1) She could slow down her economic growth rate, thereby reducing the number of skilled workers needed by the economy. But this would bring dangers of recession and depression and the Government rejected this course of action.

2) The required number of between 12,000 and 13,000 skilled-worker vacancies could be filled by non-whites. The Government also rejected this. (This statement dispels forever the myth that non-whites are incapable of doing skilled work.)

3) She could meet the economy's needs by maintaining her current intake of carefully selected and educated immigrants. He further told the delegates that the best possible means of maintaining white numbers was still immigration and that the white birthrate was low and immigrants had to be brought in to make up the shortfall.

On 2 August 1968, the Deputy Minister of Immigration said in Johannesburg that 'South Africa was *the only country in the world which took only skilled immigrants'*. Let me repeat Dr. Mulder's remark quoted above that between 12,000 and 13,000 skilled worker vacancies could be filled by non-whites, but *'The Government rejects the idea'*. This is the kernel of the issue. Through Job Reservation, the prohibitions on vocational and artisan training for non-whites, the criminal sanctions imposed on Africans who take strike action or go-slows; through the refusal to permit African workers to form recognised trade unions which have status as negotiating bodies; by the pass laws and the use of migrant labour on the mines and on the farms; by the recent laws which deprive Africans of any residence rights in cities; by such means the Government maintains the 15 million non-whites as a vast reservoir of unskilled, cheap labour. It is on this exploited labour that the whole apartheid economy is built.

Although African trade unions have never been allowed recognition and bargaining status, African workers have organised to defend their interests. The Government's reply was ruthless. Hundreds of active trade unionists were arrested, many were banned or driven into exile, some were executed. This onslaught on the workers' organisations has left them vulnerable to the collaboration of white workers and employers. Typical of this collaboration was the shocking agreement in the engineering industry described by the Johannesburg *Star* (30 March 1968) as follows:

> The recently concluded agreement in the engineering and metal industry is a 'sell-out' of more than 150,000 African workers, many of whom will be getting near-starvation wages for the next two years. *The Agreement was reached after eight months of tough bargaining by the representatives of the eight registered trade unions and of the Steel and Engineering Industries Federation* . . . the agreement brings about job fragmentation, by means of which African workers will do aspects of journeymen's work at wages correspondingly much lower than paid to skilled workers'. (Our italics).

In other words, when Africans are permitted to do skilled or semi-skilled work, their jobs are downgraded. Management and representatives of the registered trade unions get together and simply write in starvation wages for African workers into the agreement for the industry. No African workers are represented at these negotiations. British immigrants, through their registered unions, will become party to such shameful proceedings as these. Every skilled worker who migrates to South Africa is not only taking a job that rightfully belongs to the people of the country and could thus be regarded as a scab or a blackleg. It is more serious than this. Every British worker who emigrates to South Africa chooses to support white fascism against the African and other non-white people. Every able-bodied white man from the age of 16 to 65 is on call-up and lives under a legal obligation to defend the regime when required. The children of immigrants receive military training — there are no exemptions.

Apartheid demands the ultimate sacrifice from its supporters.

Our people have declared war on apartheid. This decision was never a light one. Nelson Mandela, leader of the African National Congress and now imprisoned on Robben Island said at his trial in 1964: 'It was only when all else had failed, when all channels of peaceful protest had been barred to us, that the decision was made to embark on violent forms of political struggle and to form Umkonto We Sizwe (Spear of the Nation). We did so not because we desired such a course, but solely because the Government had left us with no other choice.'

In August 1967, the armed guerillas of the African National Congress, in alliance with ZAPU (the Zimbabwe African People's Union), emerged in open conflict with the Smith regime in Rhodesia, aided by troops and police rushed in from South Africa. Today a war of liberation is spreading over Southern Africa. It brings the hope of freedom daily closer to millions of oppressed African workers and peasants. There can be no middle way. Brothers! Have you forgotten your own struggles for trade union and political rights?

Don't be a party to the oppression of the non-white of South Africa. Don't emigrate to South Africa and assist in the oppression of the non-white workers.

Stop the selling of arms to South Africa!
Overseas investments support apartheid.
Show your solidarity with our people in the struggle for freedom and
    democracy! Support the South African Congress of Trade Unions in the
    struggle for Trade Union rights!

Alliances with Whites

Sam Nujoma

> *Response by the President of SWAPO to interview question*
> *by Doc. Curtis Powell, member of the International*
> *Committee of the Black Panther Party, published in*
> Right On! *I, 10, 19-31 December 1971.*

Doc: You know there have been some organizations in America that have made alliances with some white organizations like Gay Liberation Front, Women's Liberation Front, petty bourgeois white organizations. Do you have any opinions on this type of coalition?

Sam: Well, I'm not really quite familiar with some of the organizations involved. But we in SWAPO do not very much count on color. If a white person joins our forces he would be welcome on condition that he or she went in the framework of the SWAPO policy. We accept no white domination, we accept no white advisers, but she or he would have to work within that framework, entirely controlled by SWAPO. Allow nobody to control your movement, otherwise you will be misled and you will be sabotaged from within, so be careful about this point.

ZAPU and Racialism
ZAPU

Article in Zimbabwe Review *(Lusaka), 9 April 1966.*

Many times Rhodesian white settlers have tried to denigrate the Zimbabwe African People's Union by calling its officials and members black racialists. This has been done both in the minority House of Assembly and at public meetings of the racist Rhodesian Front.

Of course the allegation is as untrue as it is weird because ZAPU does not believe in any form of racialism. ZAPU is anti-racialist. It is precisely because of this strong belief that ZAPU exists and is fighting tooth and nail to establish a fair social, political and economic situation in Zimbabwe.

ZAPU does not and will never believe in what is often termed multi-racialism because this is but a myth meant to cover up blatant racialism practised by Rhodesia's white minority settlers.

Lord Malvern and his political son, Roy Welensky, tried their best during their era to preach this myth under various names. They called it partnership at one time and multi-racialism at another but the myth was exploded once and for all by Malvern himself when he tried to define partnership in their now dead Federation as like that which exists between a rider and his horse.

Multi-racialism is nothing other than multiplied racialism. It is some artificial catchword aimed at enticing and capturing political opportunists and believers in political gradualism.

ZAPU's attitude towards individuals is not coloured by any form of racialism (either multi-racialism or anything else) but is based on the natural fact that a human being is a human being whether he is white, black or yellow and must have his full rights as a human being irrespective of his colour.

But this myth frequently called multi-racialism perpetuates racialism by making certain privileges for a certain race or races under various guises.

If equality of human beings is to be realised, then, it is high time it was realised that people are not better people just because they are white, brown or black. The only qualification for a creature to be called a human being is for it to be human and no more.

It is on this basis that ZAPU is prosecuting the struggle against British racialism in Southern Rhodesia.

The national leader of Zimbabwe, Mr. Joshua Nkomo, has said many times that the Rhodesian whites are an indivisible part of the community of our country and must realise that they cannot succeed in creating an artificial community of their own by claiming racial superiority based on the colour of their skin.

No sane person can expect to forge a nation out of people some of whom are striving to create political, social and economic barriers against others just because they have a different skin-colour from their own.

A *sine qua non* political, economic and social set-up can be created only when everyone is granted his inalienable right to choose his or her own representative or representatives anywhere but not where oppression is adored.

No White Liberals
ZANU

Article in ZANU's Zimbabwe Today *(Cairo), I,*
15, 14 July 1967.

In politics a liberal can be defined as a broad-minded politician who is opposed to privileges and who favours democratic reforms. For this reason the liberal can be regarded as being comparatively closer to the masses than the conservative who stands for class privileges.

There is not a single politician of this description in the settler community of Zimbabwe. The white community consists of ultra-conservative elements who, to a man, have thrown in their lot with the band of white fascists calling themselves the Rhodesian Front. Every white settler in Zimbabwe is entitled to some of the rarest privileges in the world. None of them finds anything wrong with this sort of racist monopoly of privileges. Everyone of them exercises his colonial right to humiliate the African for no other reason than that he is black. This should be noted because there are a good number of settlers who pose as liberals in the outside world and who in misleading many people about the political situation in Zimbabwe. There are two distinct groups of settlers who pose as liberals in Zimbabwe: missionaries with apparently no axe to grind regarding political issues facing the country and politicians who pretend to be opposed to Smith's fascism. Both of these groups in fact support fascism spear-headed by the Rhodesian Front to the hilt. Both groups are scared of a Zimbabwe without land and African labour for nothing. What is worse, both are used by the colonial enemy for hoodwinking the African masses and the outside world.

By virtue of their role as 'innocent' spreaders of the gospel, missionaries work among Africans whom they try to win both for God and for the Rhodesian Front.

They also serve as informers for the fascist rebel government and are directly responsible for some of the arbitrary imprisonment and detention of innocent Africans. Because of their political sins they live in mortal fear of

African nationalists and try to make Africans regard their political leaders as uncivilised monsters. Some of them have even tried to set themselves up as substitutes for African nationalist leaders.

The group of liberal impostors who go in for open politics are no less dangerous to the cause of justice and democracy in Zimbabwe. These are the Todds, the Barons, the Welenskys, the Gibbses, the Whiteheads, the Malverns etc. Like the missionary, all of this group are one with faith in their demand for minority rule until they are dead. They differ with Smiths, the Lardner Burkes and Harpers in that whereas the Smith clique say so openly, this wily group would rather keep their fascist demands to themselves until such time as they think they are out of woods. Accordingly they are cautious in the choice of their words in support of fascism. For example rather than say openly that there would be no majority rule until they are dead (i.e. forever), they prefer to say that the reins of government should remain in civilised (i.e. white) hands for a long time to come.

They try to hide the same evil intentions not only with high-sounding words, but with a veneer of liberalism. For example when in power they backed their talk of 'partnership' with limited desegregation of public facilities solely in order to get independence from Britain in exchange for promises of extending more liberal reforms to Africans. Lest they should be misunderstood by their fascist followers their one-time god-father Welensky told white settlers that the partnership they meant was nothing to be frightened of because it would be the same as between the horse and the rider, with the white settler as the rider and the African as a horse. Though they have been ousted from power they still think that their methods can produce better results than the Smith clique's antics. And not without reason. It is an open secret that if the settlers stopped backing the Smith clique and started backing those impostors Wilson would call off his largely abortive selective mandatory sanctions and grant formal independence to the settlers through the front door. And we would have been sold down Limpopo River much more openly than is the case at present. It is not without significance that Britain has not intervened militarily to restore legality in Zimbabwe because Gibbs threatened to resign if she did. And for his sham anti-Smith noises Whitehead is now running the Commonwealth Affairs Office of the British government. We would not be surprised if the Wilson government took Leo Baron on as its legal adviser on Rhodesian affairs. But this so-called liberal told African detainees at Gonakudzingwa before he left that they had better apply to Smith for pardon and go into private life rather than rot in detention because Smith would rule in 'Rhodesia' for the next twenty years. And several pseudo-nationalists have followed his advice.

From the foregoing we see that the sham liberalism of settler politicians in Zimbabwe has benefited fascism in one vital respect. It has made Britain regard the political deadlock in Zimbabwe as composed of a conflict between the Smith clique and the sham liberals to the exclusion of the four million owners of Zimbabwe. Wilson's sanctions are aimed at making the settlers choose endless minority rule under sham liberals rather than make them reconcile themselves to majority rule.

The Future of White Settlers
Herbert Chitepo

Response to an interview question by the Chairman of ZANU,
published in Zimbabwe Today *(Cairo), I, 21, 28 October 1967.*

Zimbabwe Today: What is the future of white settlers if they continue with their present attitude?
Chitepo: We have said this not once, not twice, not thrice but many many times, that what we are seeking in Rhodesia is not a racialist state. We are seeking a state based on political justice. This is why we have stuck to our idea of one man one vote. All that means equal dignity for all men. This is what we have stuck to. This has no reference to white people at all. Had the white people been able to accept this, there need not have been what is taking place. It is quite clear that it is the white people who are determined to keep political rights restricted to themselves in order to enjoy all other rights that flow from the possession of political power for themselves alone. This is what they are trying to get. Obviously a polarisation takes place when you get a situation of this kind. And as far as I can see the longer the struggle between us and the white people goes on, the less likely it will be possible for us to maintain a strictly non-racial society in Zimbabwe. I think a great deal of anger of feeling and ill-will against white people as such as having been the cause of that which we are suffering through now, will have stayed and may take a long time to eradicate. I regret it. But the ball is not in my court.

Not an Isolated Struggle
Agostinho Neto

From a message by the President of MPLA, broadcast on
6 June 1968 on the 'Voice of the Angolan Freedom-
Fighter' on Radio Tanzania.

One of the more debated of problems in recent times is the presence in our territories of Portuguese, or the descendants of Portuguese, whose ideas coincide with ours, whose lives have been dedicated to the struggle against fascism in Portugal, and who understand and accept the right of the peoples of the Portuguese colonies to regain their Independence and self-government, like any other sovereign people.

On this point we have sometimes observed negative reactions on the part of some of our combatants and of our friends. It is those negative attitudes that can prejudice and deter the success of our struggle for freedom. I speak of the problem of racialism.

In our countries we are not making a racial war. Our objective is not to fight against the white man solely because he is white. It is that we fight those who support the colonial regime. All those in our territories who show raised unarmed hands, or who show themselves willing to give their collaboration to the guerrillas, providing them with foodstuffs and products that are unavailable in the forests; all those who in any manner show their desire not to cooperate with the colonial regime must not be despised or treated as enemies. They constitute a force that operates in our favor, in the same way as on the international plane. There we do not seek support only in the countries of Africa south of the Sahara, called Black Africa, where the skin of the inhabitants is darker; but we also go to look for the aid of countries of North Africa, where the people have a light skin. We go even further to Europe to look for political, diplomatic and material help from countries where the majority of the population have white colour, and in other continents where the racial differences are even more evident. If, on account of racial differences, we despise that formidable force that is represented by progressives of the whole world, and by the underdeveloped countries, we will only be digging our own grave . . .

Therefore, we invite the Portuguese, the sons of Portuguese people, who are in uniform and armed in Angola, Mozambique and Guinea Bissau, to desert the ranks of the colonialist army and not to soil their hands with the blood of innocent men, women and children whose only objective is to be free — acting in the same manner as did the heroic Portuguese themselves during the Arab occupation of Spain. Instead of assassinating defenceless people, they must raise their arms in surrender when confronted by the guerrillas of MPLA, FRELIMO or PAIGC. They will be received as men and will be given the choice of a destination in those countries that accept political refugees. Or better still, we make an appeal to the Portuguese to desert with their arms and cross to the side of the nationalists, avoiding the shame of participating in an unjust war that is as dirty as the war in Vietnam.

During the course of the war in Angola, MPLA have had occasion to admit to neighbouring countries some Portuguese who had deserted. And there, in various countries, some of them are actively engaged in struggle against the Salazar regime, while others go about their work so that they and their families may live in peace.

Therefore, if there exists in some of our combatants the idea of a war against the white man, it is necessary that it be immediately substituted by the idea of a war against colonialism and against imperialism; a war against oppression, for the liberty and for the dignity of all men in the world. This idea will fortify our struggle. It will offer more guarantees and new prospectives that open up a brilliant future for all men. In a time of hatred we will have fraternity and understanding.

The White Community in the Struggle for Angolan Independence
FUA

Article in Kovaso, *the journal of the Frente da Unidade*
Angolana, 2, March/April 1963. Translated from Portuguese,

The independence of Angola is a historical fact that nothing and no one will stop. It cannot be stopped because the rights of the people are inalienable. They may be crushed, or insulted for a more or less long period of time, but the human grouping which constitutes a people will eventually free itself and conquer the right to live. This is the experience all peoples have lived, some more harshly than others.

The struggle which the Angolan people carries out in the fight for its country's independence, in the desire to build its happiness, is an absolutely just one. This struggle is imposed by Portuguese colonialism!

And what is Portuguese colonialism? Is it fair to consider the white community of Angola and Portuguese colonialism one and the same thing? Is it correct to confuse the Portuguese people with Portuguese colonialism?

Each Angolan must ask himself these questions, and must try to answer them, for in so doing, he will feel certain he is contributing in a most positive form to the struggle for independence in which we are all involved. This struggle will only become valid once we accord it its real context. Otherwise we do it at the mercy and profit of what there is plenty of around us: the opportunist!

Portugal is a semi-colony. A great part of both its economic and human riches are exploited in the interest of international trusts. This means that Portuguese colonialism is nothing but one of the varieties of imperialism. The Portuguese colonial empire exists today because of guarantees given to England in the Treaty of Methuen (1703) led England to defend Portugal. It will continue to exist, in large part due to the support which the powers interested in exploiting its wealth still accord to the colonialist government of Salazar. The realization of this truth allows us to conclude that it is not correct to confuse the Portuguese people with Portuguese colonialism. The condemnation of this colonialism which was made by the Frente Patriotica de Libertacao Nacional, which comprises all currents of the Portuguese opposition, thus representing nearly all the Portuguese people, is the most valid proof that the Portuguese people reject colonialism. The Portuguese people are also victims of imperialism.

This same distinction was emphasized at the National Conference of the MPLA.

In view of the fact that Portuguese colonialism established itself in reality in the colonial territories via colonists who were sent there, and who constitute today, with their descendants, the white communities of such territories, are they to be considered the strength of Portuguese colonialism? We have already analyzed this situation (in the first issue of our paper) and argued that the Africanized white population rejects colonialism.

But insofar as the army and the colonial repressive forces, reinforced by collaborating civilians, are white, then the fight for independence displays racial characteristics. These characteristics were cleverly and criminally imposed upon by the colonists themselves, as we have shown in our work. These characteristics are maintained for several reasons, two of which will be emphasized. One is the fact that Portuguese colonialism provokes it as the last weapon in its defence, by presenting it on the one hand as a proof of the incompetence of the Black race to govern itself, and on the other by keeping the white population under a state of racist terror, and so to use it as its ally. The other reason consists in the fact that the white population, which is actually anti-colonialist, has a passive attitude, which in the present moment signifies connivance at colonialism.

All these factors of the dirty and criminal policy of Portuguese colonialists are being taken advantage of by many opportunists on all sides. They are the ones who defend and promote a racist campaign on both the colonialist and nationalist sides. They are the ones — and unfortunately there appear among all people such types — who live at the expense of the thousands of dead who died gloriously and nobly fell for a just cause.

But insofar as this racism is a product of the white race, it is mainly up to whites to struggle against its continuity. The FUA which fights against racism and for the edification of Angola as an independent nation, free from the colonialist evils, appeals to the white community to feel the need to combat racism and to take an active part in the struggle against colonialism.

Rumbezia, Not Mozambique
UNAR

> *A document issued by the Uniao Nacional Africana de Rumbezia in Limbe (Malawi) in 1968. Translated from Portuguese.*

After a long and careful study of the situation in Mozambique today taken in relation to that of international opinion, the Rumbezians have concluded that it is necessary to form a national political organization solely for the people north of the Zambezi river, a region which comprises provinces of Tete, Zambezia, Mozambique, Cabo Delgado, and Niassa. This region will be known as Rumbezia, a name derived from both of its great rivers the Rovuma and the Zambezi. Rumbezia is thus the entire area generally contained between the Rovuma and Zambezi rivers. (Also included in Rumbezia is the area belonging to the province of Tete, south of the Zambezi river.) The name of our national political organization is 'Uniao Nacional Africana de Rumbezia' (UNAR), since all the inhabitants of the above-mentioned five provinces are Rumbezian.

When FRELIMO was established in 1962 in Dar-es-Salaam (United Republic of Tanzania), Dr. Eduardo Mondlane was elected President of this political organization by the Mozambicans. The constitution and the programme of FRELIMO were to unite all the people of Mozambique, to organize them politically and to prepare them militarily in order to fight against the Portuguese government. The presumably revolutionary plan of the President of FRELIMO was to send all the young men north of the Zambezi river for military training, whereas those who came from the south of the river were, and still are, sent to institutions of higher learning. No sooner said than done; only the man from the North is forced to fight rather than to acquire an intellectual preparation?! Dr. Mondlane, in order to accomplish a programme harmful to the Rumbezian people, shrewdly allowed the people from the South to occupy more important positions in FRELIMO, whereas the people from the North became merely militants without any responsibility or voice in that organization. It was for this reason and for several others that in September 1964, six members of FRELIMO's Central Committee broke away from this political party, upset by the tribalistic activities of Dr. Eduardo Mondlane.

From the year 1964, when the first guerilla group was sent to the interior of the country, until today, only the northern people are called upon to fight against the Portuguese. There has not been elaborated a revolutionary program for the southern part of the Zambezi river, not even a political organization.

In short, the northern people are blindly fighting under the direction of southern chiefs. These so-called revolutionary leaders, who are very cunning, do not wish to introduce such armed struggle in their own provinces, from which they originated. Why? Because Dr. Eduardo Mondlane and his group know very well that the armed struggle which goes on in Mozambique under their direction will never have satisfactory results for the Mozambican people.

Dr. Mondlane and all his brothers from the South, realizing the impossibility of eliminating the Portuguese in our country by means of an armed struggle led by FRELIMO or COREMO, sought not to provoke the enemy in the region south of the Zambezi river where they themselves came from, in order to keep their families from suffering.

Why is it that only the people from one part of this country has to fight while the other is spared without justifiable reason?! ... Is it the case that this people deliberately wishes to save itself, while preparing to dominate the people who are presently fighting?! ... Brothers, brothers, let us carefully study this problem, which seems to be hard to resolve but isn't.

Thousands of Rumbezians have taken refuge in Tanzania, Malawi and Zambia, and there is nothing to indicate that they will one day return to their home.

We therefore conclude with certainty:

(a) The brothers from the South are not prepared to fight the Portuguese, because they do not wish to do so.

(b) They want to achieve the independence of Mozambique through an armed struggle effectuated by northern people.

(c)   Dr. Mondlane is thus the initiator of tribalism in Mozambique's revolutionary movement.

(d)   The existing unity between our brothers of the South and those of the North cannot but be fatal to the latter.

The Rumbezians must thus repeatedly study these conclusions so that they may discover the danger of such apparent unity with our brothers from the South and each Rumbezian must thus be able to shake off **FRELIMO's** policy and programme, as well as that of **COREMO**, which will never really help the liberation of Rumbezia.

Now every Rumbezian is called to participate in UNAR, to become valid members of this new organization and to work with perseverance

Both Mondlane and Gumane, in exchange for money sent to them by their bosses, Russia and Communist China, treat like slaves their brothers who fight, so that they may fill their pockets. Why do not Mondlane, Uria, Marcelino, Gumane and Gwambe fight in the jungle with their soldiers?

They are the peddlers of Mozambique. The facts speak for themselves: they want to sustain a war from which they profit. Meanwhile, our brothers who are forced to fight are dying by the dozen.

Just as the seed which sprouts, grows and becomes an adult plant, and only then blooms and gives fruit, so will our people grow in the Christian faith and culture, and one day will produce ripe fruit. Only then will it be an adult, respected and accredited nation.

We must first prepare ourselves to become self-sufficient, which means we do not need help from Russia or China, who only wish to exploit our land and enslave us with their government. Let us look at those who surround us!

All our land must be cultivated and the wilderness sown. We must do it ourselves. And if each one of us gives of his best, our land will prosper.

The agents of Mondlane and Gumane who infest the land of Rumbezia must be eliminated. And since the word is our weapon, the only way to fight them is by unmasking them!

Your small bit, plus our brothers' small bit . . . will add up to much and will be enough to support UNAR and its service which is to work for a greater Rumbezia!

Long live the unity of the Rumbezian People!
Long live the courage of the Rumbezian People!
Long live UNAR!
Rumbezia and Unity!

White Mozambicans

Samora Machel

From a message by the President of FRELIMO, on the
day of the Mozambican Revolution, 25 August 1971.

Our war is a war of national liberation against Portuguese colonialism, against
imperialism and against the exploitation of man by man. The colonialists want
our war to cease being a struggle against the exploiters and to be transformed
into a war against the Portuguese people, to stop being against imperialism
and to become a war between the black people of Mozambique and the white
population in Mozambique, a racist war. In order to achieve this objective,
Portugal is systematically driving the African people from their fertile lands
and settling European people there.

When the Portuguese government drives Mozambicans from their land in
order to put settlers there, their prime aim is to force the emergence of contradictions between the Mozambican and Portuguese peoples. In so doing,
colonialism will tell the white farmers that they must defend their land against
the Africans, at the same time creating in the African population a feeling of
hatred for those who have occupied their land. Transforming the nature of
our war and making us become confused as to the identity of the enemy,
would be to create confusion as to who should be the target of our bullets.

A very great responsibility faces FRELIMO and the Mozambican people in
avoiding any perversion of the content of our struggle, making the masses ever
more deeply aware of the identity of the enemy and making the Portuguese
and white Mozambicans understand that our struggle is not directed against
them, that they have only to gain from the defeat of colonialism and
Portuguese fascism.

On the Chiefs in Gabu

Aristides Pereira

Response to an interview question by the then Administrative
Secretary of the PAIGC, published in Revolution Africaine
(Alger), No. 99, 19 December 1964. Translated from French.

Revolution Africaine: Thus you are optimistic. Do you envisage the end of
the colonial era in Guinea, in the near future?
Pereira: Yes, indeed. The end is near. We have our difficulties. Certain ethnic
groups have not totally accepted our ideas on unity. We have problems concerning the chiefs but we are seeing to resolve them.

In the Gabu area, a fief of certain traditional chiefs still favourable to the
colonists, there has recently taken place an important meeting of political and

military leaders. Amilcar Cabral, our party's General Secretary, presided over the meeting. As a result we have established new guerilla bases in this region.

The Tactic of Division
Amilcar Cabral

Excerpt from a message in September 1970, on the occasion of the 14th Anniversary of the founding of the PAIGC. Translated from French.

Lately the Portuguese colonialist criminals have resorted to another tactic in order to attempt to end our struggle: divide our people and get Africans to fight Africans. This is an old and widely-used tactic, both by colonialists and in colonial imperialist wars, but we must denounce it and combat it vigorously, so that this new and criminal initiative taken by the enemy shall suffer a great defeat. The colonialists have now invented what they call the 'ethnic congresses' in our country. Their aim is to coopt some of our brothers with high positions and honours, and even more to destroy the awareness and the national unity which both our party and the struggle have already achieved. By holding these so-called congresses and promising each ethnic group its own leader, the colonialists hope to revive the tribal tendencies which we have already extinguished, and to sabotage from the beginning the possibilities of a harmonious national existence for our people in the independence which — they know it well enough — we will certainly conquer. By pretending to want to create a political authority for those populations in the form of chiefs that they can still control, they really wish to prepare the field for new conflicts among the ethnic groups, so that the Balantes may not be able to relate to the Mandjaques nor the Fulas with the Pepels, in order that confusion be established among us, thus rendering impossible the life of the African nation which we are building. The colonialists, with all their congresses, their activities bring obvious harm to our people. But they will not succeed, because our party exists, because our people is increasingly more aware of its rights and duties as an African people, because no manoeuvre will be able to block the victorious march of our armed struggle for liberation. And those who, either by ambition or opportunism, allow themselves to be deceived by the lies of congresses will waste their time and will be marked as deliberate traitors to the interests of our people and of those of Africa.

Always seeking to divide our people, the Portuguese colonialist criminals have been developing a great campaign against the Cape Verdians on their radio, especially in the vernacular languages of Guinea. In this campaign, as well as in a certain number of letters sent to leaders of our party, with promises of honours and riches, they claim that they will expel all Cape Verdians who serve colonialism in Guinea, and that they will offer the positions which the latter now occupy to what they name 'the real children of Guinea'. The colonialists know that the political, moral and fighting unity of our people in Guinea and the Cape Verde Islands is the main strength of our party and of our struggle. They also wish to destroy it, by attempting to create hate where it has never existed, to diffuse lies, to stir up lust and to awaken a sense of ambition and opportunism among those who, even if they are not participating in our struggle, are nevertheless nationalists who wish the independence of our country. But even there they have completely failed. Firstly, since the real nationalists from Guinea are neither racist nor opportunist, and they know who are their leaders and which is the value of a unity of the people of Guinea and the Cape Verde Islands. Secondly, because the colonialists are lying when they say that they are going to expel the Cape Verdians. They will not be able to do so, because they need the Cape Verdians and the Guineans who are in their service. And the colonialists are well aware of the service which they would render our Party if they really did expel the Cape Verdians from Guinea. But they have already rendered us this service, because they have clearly shown to all the children of Cape Verde who serve the colonialists in Guinea that we are right: the colonialists use them while at the same time having no consideration whatsoever for them. They must thus, together with the best children of our country — of Guinea and Cape Verde — become aware of their situation and support our Party and our struggle, with a view to the total liberation of our African nation. The colonialists have already failed, since their propaganda has not until now found an echo other than from those individuals who are socially declasse, drunkards, robbers, even criminals, integrated in a so-called 'Committee for a Better Guinea'. But these traitors, who have not the least respect for our people, are aware of one thing: they must enjoy the privileges of colonialism while it lasts, because it will be the real children of Guinea and Cape Verde, who are militants and fighters from our party, who will condemn them and punish them for being in the service of the enemy of both our country and of Africa.

6. African Churches and the Movements

Editors' Introduction

The challenge to world Christianity implicit in the analyses of the movements of the historic role of the Christian churches in the colonial situation has been taken and furthered by African Christians — both Protestant and Catholic — who have actively identified themselves with the national liberation movements.

One of the first to do so was Rev. Fr. Joaquim Pinto de Andrade, one-time Chancellor of the Diocese of Luanda (Angola). First interrogated by the secret police (PIDE) in 1960, he spent the years since then either in prison or in restricted residence in Portugal. Brother of Mario de Andrade, he was made in 1962 symbolically the Honorary President of the MPLA. We include two of his statements: his deposition to the PIDE in 1960 and his statement to the court in 1971, his testimony of a decade of moral and physical torture.

In South Africa, many white Christian clerics have been considered 'liberals' on racial issues. Some have been exiled or expelled. Yet as a whole, M.B. Yengwa felt 'the South African Church has failed'. He called for them to support wholeheartedly the World Council of Churches' campaign to isolate South Africa and aid the liberation movements. Similarly, five African Catholic priests condemned the 'pretence' of the Church that it opposes apartheid, and called on the Church 'to expedite Africanization.'

In Namibia, the African leaders of two of the principal churches sent two messages in 1971 — one to the Prime Minister of South Africa and a second to their congregations — asserting their determination to support change and the respect of human rights, and their opposition to the 'Homelands Policy', that is, the creation of Bantustans in Namibia.

The Necessity of Dialogue
Joaquim da Rocha Pinto de Andrade

Complete deposition of Rev. Fr. Joaquim da Rocha Pinto de Andrade before officers of the PIDE (security police) in Luanda, 30 June 1960. Translated from French.

Without having formally adhered to any political movement or party, I have never ceased to take an active interest, as far as my character and my priestly activities permitted me to, in the aspirations and problems which concern Angolan political organizations.

I believe that the aspiration to independence is a just and reasonable sentiment, in the line of the great philosophical and theological thinkers, and following from the great Christian tradition and the teachings of recent popes (notably Leo XIII and John XXIII). As the bishops of Upper Volta have recently declared in a collective pastoral letter: 'Independence is to the people what freedom is to the individual.'

It goes without saying that because of my temperament, my education, and my religious background, I am against violence and fraudulent methods. I believe that men were given a tongue so that they could understand one another, and that all differences should be resolved through pacifist and democratic methods, and negotiations.

In the capacity of a priest, an African, and a native of this country, I share the problems which preoccupy this people, a direct and everyday knowledge, one derived from experience, and I live these problems with the particularly sharpened sensitivity of a man who feels a solidarity towards them through blood ties and historical attachments. These problems are those of teaching and culture, of work and salary, of racial discrimination, of access to citizenship, of participation in governmental affairs, and so on.

The delays in the resolution of such problems cause preoccupation and discontent among us. The younger and more enlightened ones among us tell us with bitterness that legal and constitutional means are in practice denied to them. So in desperation they have begun a clandestine struggle. Now, as Pope Pius XII once stated in one of his memorable Christmas messages: 'Although the paths which one sometimes takes may be in error, what man and especially what Christian and what priest can remain deaf to the cries rising from the depths, and which implore justice and fraternity in a world of a just God?'

It is evident that a priest due to his character and duties must serve as a moderating and enlightening element. But this should not be interpreted as being indifference.

It was also Pius XII who said that one must fight in order to destroy the fashionable mentality of today which wishes to confine the action of the Church to the four cold walls of the sacristy.

In conclusion, I believe that I may define my position in terms of the past and future as follows:

I am not, have never been, a member of any political party, either legal or clandestine, and I do not intend to become one.

As a priest, and I am honored to be one, politics neither interest me as such nor concern me. Nonetheless, I shall continue to be attentive and sensitive to all the preoccupations of men whoever they may be. And whenever I think it necessary, useful, and expedient I will not hesitate to present those claims which I consider just to appropriate higher authorities, either ecclesiastical or civil.

I am deeply convinced that in the relationships between individuals and peoples, monologues cannot but be prejudicial, and that a need for dialogue becomes more pressing each day. This is called collaboration. Quoting from Saint-Exupery: 'They only are my brothers who collaborate.'

Apologia and Accusation
Joaquim da Rocha de Andrade

> *A statement to the Special Tribunal by Rev. Fr. Pinto de Andrade, on trial with nine others for 'subversive activities' written in Caxias prison on 9 January 1971 and smuggled out for publication in* Algerie-Actualite, *21-27 February 1971. Translated from French.*

Upon my return in 1953 from Rome where I have received a Doctorate in Philosophy and Theology from the Gregorian University, I was named professor in the Seminary of Luanda and in a secondary school, whilst also serving in a priestly capacity in several churches in the capital of Angola.

In 1958 and 1959 I held simultaneously the positions of Chancellor of the Archdiocese, Professor in the Seminary, Secretary of the Ecclesiastical Chamber, chaplain of a convent, and director of an experimental parish in a suburban area (Samba) inhabited by 25,000 people (mostly housedwellers and fishermen), and finally Ecclesiastical Assistant of the Catholic University League, exclusively comprised of Europeans.

In 1959 the first massive arrests of Angolan nationalists (the famous 1959 trial) took place in Luanda. The PIDE did all it could in order to incriminate me, going as far as attempting to get confessions from the prisoners by means of torture. This tactic failed.

However, the families of the prisoners, suddenly poverty-stricken, never ceased to ask of me both material and moral aid. I tried to satisfy them to the degree that I could. I often went to the prisons, having received permission from my Bishop and the police, to bring the prisoners some spiritual and material comfort.

A spontaneous solidarity movement arose in the city towards the prisoners and their families, and thus the people decided to centralize the financial aid, food and clothing, in the hands of someone whose personality and moral prestige were of a nature to inspire confidence and offer assurance that the money and other services would be equitably and honestly distributed. Everyone agreed that I was the right person for this task. I believed that it was my duty to accept it, because it concerned a cause of Christian charity and human solidarity. I did nevertheless ask advice from my Bishop who not only accorded me his moral support but even offered a financial contribution.

My moral prestige and popularity had increased in the city, undoubtedly due to my cultural level, my integrity and the simplicity of my relationships with the people, but especially with the poorest sections of the population, because of my uncompromising position regarding truth and justice, my denunciation of racism and economic exploitation, my courageous defence of the oppressed.

The meaning of my sermons in the Cathedral and Carmo Church was often distorted by ill-intentioned people who spread accusations against me to the Bishop. I had a habit of writing everything I said in public, and then of learning it by heart. I was thus able to show the text of my sermons whenever I was the object of slander. The Bishop never ceased to encourage me: 'Keep preaching in the same vein.' The Governor of Angola himself, Lieutenant-Colonel Sa Viana Rebelo (today General and Minister of Defense) often came to hear me, sometimes ostentatiously sitting in the first row, sometimes mixing with the parishioners who filled the Cathedral or who had to hear me outside the Church by means of loudspeakers.

I began therefore to read the texts of my sermons in order to avoid intrigue. But this was in vain since I was pursued constantly. Tired of this situation and in order to avoid other calumnies, I decided not to preach for a while. The Bishop indicated his disagreement, telling me that my absence in Sunday mass could be interpreted as being caused by his disapproval, when he in fact supported me. Given my determination to confine myself to total silence, the Bishop replaced me for Sunday mass. It was he now who preached. 'I will thereby demonstrate,' he claimed, 'that I entirely approve of you and that my sermons are in the same line as yours.'

In charge of the experimental parish of the lower-class district of Samba (Museke), I was continuously faced by the arbitrary measures of the administrative authorities. The children in the missionary school which functioned in the chapel were often arrested, on the pretext that they were loitering, and were then taken as servants in the houses of the Whites. The policemen went abruptly to their straw huts at dawn and shot at them in their straw beds.

All this, despite the fact that these children had possession of identification documents with their pictures and the Bishop's seal over my signature, identifying them as pupils of the missionary establishment. On these identification documents the teacher marked their attendance at class. The policemen took the documents from them and tore them up. They were children from ages 7 to 14. And even the tiny ones aged 4 to 6 who went to a modest kindergarten were torn from their toys and forced to work as servant-companions to poor Whites.

I rarely left my house (in the upper part of the city, near Government House) without being stopped by two or three people who were waiting for me, invariably to complain that some member of their family had been arbitrarily arrested. I had to go to the administrative office to see about the liberation of the unfortunate individual. In the end it was no longer solely the people from my region, towards whom I had pastoral obligations, who required my intervention to help liberate someone from their family, but it was also people from other working class districts.

In view of the increasing repression and the arbitrary methods which spared neither schoolchildren nor even tiny ones, I often discussed this problem with the Bishop and informed him of my intention to expose it in a document to be presented to official authorities, and to ask for a hearing with the General Governor. The Archbishop invariably answered: 'You are right, my son, but it is I who should do so. Being Bishop and White, nothing will happen to me. Besides I am old. But keep in mind that you are Angolan and Black; your protest will be interpreted as being a subversive and racist act.'

On 25 June 1960 around 1.00 pm, I was arrested by the PIDE, when leaving work at the Chancellery of the Archdiocese. After a week of interrogations on my alleged subversive activities, the Director of PIDE, Inspector Anibal de S. Jose Lopez told me: 'I have brought your declarations to the Governor-General Silva Tavares at the time. We have arrived at the conclusion that there is no reason for your being kept in prison. You could be immediately released. However, your presence in this city has become dangerous. There are some hotheads who want to organize demonstrations to release you, and you would then be received as a hero or a martyr. Now, we do not wish to make either heroes or martyrs. We have thus decided that you will leave immediately on a military plane to Lisbon, where you will remain as a free man for three or four months, the time necessary to calm down the flow of indignation which your arrest has aroused. Then you will be able to return to Luanda.'

It was in this way that I was brought to Lisbon *manu militari*. But instead of the promised freedom, I was brought to the Aljube prison by a PIDE brigade chief, where I was kept in solitary confinement for over four months. I had to go on a hunger strike for six days to obtain an improvement in my prison conditions which were terrible. During this time I was not interrogated by any agent or inspector of PIDE. The letter of protest which I sent to the director of this organization received no answer.

In November 1960 I was thrown on a Campanhia Uniao Fabril cargo ship, accompanied by a PIDE agent. We travelled for 20 days and no one told me where we were going. I was forced to disembark on Principe Island and taken to the local PIDE post. Agent Moreira said I was under probation in forced residence on the island and must present myself every day at the police office. All my letters were censored. To my question, where was I going to be able to find a place to stay in a totally unknown country, without money, the PIDE agent said: 'That's your problem.' I asked the local Catholic Mission for shelter, where I stayed for the next five months.

On 25 April 1961, at 3 am, I was pulled out of bed by two PIDE agents who pushed me, without explanation, into a military plane where I was kept under guard by a soldier with a machine-gun in his hands, his angry eyes staring at me.

Once in Lisbon, I was again locked up in the Aljube prison, where I was to be kept for four months, no accusation being formulated against me. I was submitted to a single period of questioning, during which I was asked which had been my subversive actions in Principe Island, and what my relationships with the liberation movements in Angola were. I obviously answered negatively to both questions. That was all. In spite of this, I was still kept in solitary confinement for four months.

I went on a hunger strike once again for a period of four days in order to obtain better prison conditions.

Finally on 19 August 1961, two PIDE agents brought me to Singeverga Monastery (Roriz-Negrelos) in Minho province, where I was forbidden to leave the premises, to preach, or to hear confession.

Then followed another eleven months of confinement.

On 12 July 1962, I was once again arrested at the Singeverga Monastery and taken to a prison in Porto without any accusation or explanation. I was asked who were my visitors, my correspondents, and the nature of the subversive activities I had led, without however indicating or suggesting any to me.

A month later, I was thrown in a cell in Aljube, which was extremely narrow (one metre in width by two in length) where both the air and the light which were filtered by two iron doors passed through a crack no larger than 15 to 20 cm, and which was invariably blocked up. On the board which served as a bed, there was a straw mattress as hard as rock, full of knots which hurt me and so dirty that in order to avoid its repugnant touch I was forced to sleep curled up in a towel. It was forbidden to have sheets. When I sat on the bed my knees touched the wall. I had no place to move. My eyes wore themselves out in this dungeon worthy of Papa Doc's cages. I had to satisfy all my physiological needs including defecation, with the toilet door open, under the vigilant look of the jailer, and only after the guard had slowly and crossly deigned to permit me to do so.

In 1963 I had a conversation in Caxias with Lord Russell of Liverpool, former judge at the Nuremberg Trial, when he was visiting the prisons of this country at the invitation of the Portuguese government. I then described to him, in front of Inspector Gomes da Silva and Senior Inspector Barbieri Cardoso the atrocious conditions in which we 'lived' in the Aljube *curros.*

Lord Russell then proceeded to praise, *ad usum Delphini,* the Portuguese penitentiary regime. Despite this he at least had the honesty to write at a later date to the Portuguese government in Lisbon (and this, after visiting at my explicit request cell no. 2 in Aljube) saying that such a prison should be closed down, and that the cells of the *curros* (notably the one in which Rev. Fr. Pinto de Andrade had been caged) were unfit for even dogs.

It was there, nonetheless, Your Honor, in such an ignoble, ignominious and filthy cell no.2 of the miserably famous *curros* of Aljube that I was obliged to 'live' (if so it can be called) for 86 days without any indictment.

On 5 June 1963, I had completed 177 days of preventive imprisonment without indictment. There were three days left before reaching the maximum punishment allowed by the law. I was released but . . . immediately arrested at the door of Aljube prison and transferred to Caxias!

On 8 January of the same year, having been taken to PIDE headquarters, I was told that I had been freed three days earlier and once against arrested at the door . . . for new subversive activities. But where had I managed to lead such activities, inside the prison or at its door? To this question I got only curses and insults as an answer.

I was not interrogated, and no explanation was to be given to me. Thus did my fourth detention drag on, and having passed the maximum allowed by law was prolonged for another six months. After 180 days I had however sent a letter of protest to the Director of PIDE, with copies to the Ministries of Internal Affairs and Justice. No answer.

My lawyer, Antonio Alcada Baptista, thereupon sought 'Habeas Corpus'.

On 14 August 1963 (that is, after 221 days of preventive imprisonment, or rather 396 days of uninterrupted custody without indictment) I was released (?) with forced residence in Ponte do Sor, district of Portalegre.

I was under the watch of the GNR (National Republican Guard). Armed guards in plain clothes watched over the door of the inn where I was housed day and night, and followed me at a distance of 10 metres whenever I travelled in this village which I was not allowed to leave. Every four hours, the guards were relieved and had to present a report on my activities during those hours to the GNR lieutenant. This latter sent a weekly report to the PIDE director, the GNR General commanding officer, and the Minister of Internal Affairs.

I was unable to communicate with the Papal Nuncio, since my correspondence and telephone were censored. My rare visitors had to go through an indentification checking. I could not use any means of locomotion (other than my legs), not even a bicycle. I was also forbidden to preach, or to hear confession at the risk of prison.

On 24 January 1964, I was again arrested when taking my lunch at the inn.

Taken to Lisbon, I was immediately enclosed in the dungeons of Aljube for ten days, without any interrogation or indictment. Once in the PIDE headquarters, Inspector Sachetti wanted to force me to write and to sign a declaration in which I was to accept a new residence, 'under the pain of suspension of holy orders, being forbidden to say mass, in accordance with the agreement made between the Overseas Ministry and the Apostolic Nunciature in Lisbon'.

I refused to write such a declaration whose terms I could not accept. Inspector Sacchetti then threatened to keep me in prison indefinitely. I maintained my refusal and even went as far as to doubt the existence of such an agreement. In view of the stubborn attitude of the inspector I insisted on seeing the Apostolic Nuncio or a secretary of the Nunciature. When the latter (Monseigneur Rotuno) arrived at the PIDE headquarters, Sacchetti asked me not to speak of such an agreement. But I raised this question and Monseigneur Rotuno did assure me, in the presence of the PIDE inspector, that the so-called protocol of agreement had never existed!

On 3 February 1964 I was released (?) and taken to Vilar do Paraiso (district of Vila Nova de Gaia), where my residence was to be the Boa Nova Seminary, led by the Priests of the Overseas Missions. In Gaia, my movements were controlled, the telephone and correspondence were checked, and visits were limited. PIDE agents and informers patrolled day and night the exits of the seminary and followed me everywhere.

It was in such conditions that I resided in Vilar do Paraiso for three years (1964-1967).

Pope Paul VI, at the time of his pilgrimage to Fatima (on 13 May 1967) intervened personally with the President of the Republic, and I was consequently allowed to circulate freely within Portugal. I was still forbidden to return to my country or to go abroad.

On 7 April 1970 I was arrested for the sixth time, on the street, when leaving my house, in the extravagant circumstances peculiar to kidnapping in Latin America: I was violently thrown in the back of a 'Volkswagen', to the stupefaction of many people who rushed to watch such an edifying scene. . .

The South African Church Has Failed
M.B. Yengwa

Article in Sechaba *(ANC), V, 4, April 1971.*

During the past year world Church and religious leaders have moved significantly in their opposition to apartheid and they have taken some far-reaching decisions to assist those who struggle against it. Strong resolutions condemning racism taken at the international level have been followed up by action to help eliminate it, representing a welcome change from the traditional pious condemnation and learned sermonizing of the past.

Of special importance is the decision of the World Council of Churches Central Committee last September to allocate grants to liberation movements including the African National Congress. This step triggered off a world-wide debate on the morality of the use of violence to resist race oppression. The discussion rages yet, and Archbishop Ramsey, who ought to have learnt better on his South African tour has now come out in opposition to the WCC decision. Others have shown a similar faintheartedness, but the WCC has stood firm and we have no doubt that its position will come to be accepted in time by most of its affiliates. There were no hesitations in the ranks of the liberation movements or among the racially oppressed peoples who congratulated the WCC on this courageous, Christian act. It has been doubly welcomed since it is based on a realization that 'it is not enough for churches and groups to condemn the sin of racial arrogance and oppression. The struggle for radical change in structures will inevitably bring suffering and will demand costly and bitter engagement.'

In its efforts to combat racism the leaders of the Church have said that religion will come up against powerful, entrenched forces which have helped to sustain racism, and which derive special economic, political and social benefits from it. It will first have to contend with the member churches themselves, who have branches and institutions in racist regimes of Southern Africa and whose white members help to keep the Church rich and powerful. They have no desire to abdicate their position of power and superiority attained purely on the basis of their colour.

The churches in South Africa have already condemned the decision of the World Council of Churches on the ground that it implies support for organizations whose purpose it is to change the social order in South Africa by the use of force. The Church in South Africa suffers from the fact that it identifies itself with white South Africans, in many ways it is itself a white institution deriving its power and influence from a white government. Its effective leaders are white even where the majority of its followers are black. The fault there is therefore not with the World Council of Churches but with the Church in South Africa that has identified itself with a Government which resists social change (i.e. racial equality) by the use of force.

The Church in South Africa has failed to disassociate itself from the actions of a Government which claims to be Christian but practises the most un-Christian policy of racial and social repression since Adolf Hitler. It is the Church in South Africa which has given implied support for the equipping of the South African armed forces budget with the taxpayer's (Christian and non-Christian) money amounting to over R 271,000,000. This army's task is to defend the status quo in South Africa — the perpetuation of a racist, fascist dictatorship. This same army has previously been used to crush unarmed non-violent demonstrators protesting against racial oppression.

The South African churches have also done nothing to protest against the supply of arms by Britain and France. They have not opposed the collection of monies for the relief of Portuguese soldiers in Mozambique and Angola. Nor have they acted with any seriousness against the Government's continuing violent suppression of our own freedom struggle. On the contrary their own discriminatory policies in the Church have led to numerous protest actions led by Black clergy who are heartily sick of the hypocritical condescension offered them. There has yet to be seen any deepgoing reassessment of Church practice in South Africa such as would lead to its dissociation from the discriminatory institutions of the system as a whole.

Objections by the South African Churches to the WCC grants have been equalled by the Government which reacted quickly and predictably against the WCC. They said, 'This was the work of communists and those for whom the downfall of South Africa is more important than the Word of God.' If the subtle psychological play on words, to mean the exact opposite, were not so successful, we would find some amusement in these jokes. But this is no joke at all. Mr. Vorster and his followers do indeed seem to believe that 'Communism and the downfall of South Africa' are more important than the Word of God. Such is the ignorance that is begotten by stupid prejudice and isolation.

Apart from the WCC other religionists are also reexamining the old and outmoded positions they adopted in colonialist days and they are increasinlgy challenging the holy citadels in Canterbury and Cape Town.

In a conference of religious leaders from all over the world — held in Kyoto, Japan, in October, last year — a resolution was unanimously passed condemning racism and urging support for those engaged in the struggle against racism.

> The World Conference on Religion and Peace bringing together in Kyoto men and women of religious faith from the ends of the earth has concerned itself with the urgency of the explosive situation in Southern Africa. It is our judgement that the brutality of apartheid in Southern Rhodesia, South Africa and Namibia, and the repressive colonialist exploitation in Angola and Mozambique represents a situation of racial war against the African people with all the consequent destruction of human life typical of other wars raging in today's world. Therefore, as men and women of religious faith:
>
> (1) We repent our own share — directly or indirectly — in the perpetuation of structures that entrench racial discrimination in Southern Africa.
>
> (2) We condemn the involvement of our religions and other nations in this system of violence to man's humanity based on racism.
>
> (3) We call upon all governments to implement the measures they have already adopted in the United Nations, and to support further mandatory sanctions aimed at creating conditions conducive to justice, liberation and peace in Southern Africa.
>
> (4) We plead especially for the fullest implementation of sanctions against Rhodesia and for the extension of mandatory economic sanctions against South Africa.
>
> (5) We plead with the allies of Portugal — especially NATO allies to terminate immediately all forms of military assistance that enables Portugal to wage war in her African colonies.
>
> (6) We demand an immediate end to all types of military assistance to South Africa, including the sale of arms and condemn all such assistance and collaboration with evil as abhorrent to all the values cherished by humanity.
>
> (7) We urge the full support by our religions for the victims of racism and colonialism and for those involved in the struggle to bring justice, liberation and peace in Southern Africa.
>
> (8) We address this resolution to the Secretary General of the United Nations Organisation and urge him to transmit its contents to the

member States of that organisation.

Addressing the Kyoto conference Dr. Blake, General Secretary of the World Council of Churches, had an answer to those who hid behind the status quo and law and order. He declared that:

> An unjust social system on national or international levels, however peaceful and orderly it might appear on the surface, is potentially and actually a war situation. Wherever and whenever a group or a nation dominates and exploits other groups or nations, a neatly camouflaged state of war actually exists which may erupt into open war at any time. The exploiting groups or nations maintain the status quo, using either brute force or some subtle means of psychological violence. In the name of law and order they often try by force to prevent the oppressed groups from challenging their position of privilege. Those who are committed to a dynamic peace recognise the hypocrisy of such a stance. In such situations certain disruptions of superficial calm and peace are inevitable and even necessary in order to establish true and lasting peace. Stable and lasting peace can only be built on social justice.

Another speaker at this conference Archbishop Helder Camara of Brazil said: 'The plight of the millions of people in Africa, Asia and Latin America is as much the result of built-in injustice in the international framework of our present-day world as of the built-in injustice in their own societies.'

Soon after the Kyoto conference there was a conference in London of Pax Christi, a Catholic organisation committed to world peace which had delegates from most of the countries of Western Europe. Like the Kyoto conference — the London Pax Christi conference passed a resolution on Southern Africa which condemned racism and pledged support for the organisations fighting against racial oppression. At about the same time the Pope received in audience leaders of the liberation movements in the three Portuguese colonies in Africa, after the conclusion of the successful Rome solidarity conference.

The gestures by church leaders throughout the world in support of the just cause of liberation from social oppression have met with violent opposition from vested interests in church circles in South Africa. In opposing the decision of the WCC the South African Council of Churches has stated that its reason is that the decision implies support for violence. The South African Church is the last organisation that should complain of implied support for violence. They are wholly culpable themselves. Have they not been bolstering a regime of violence and thriving on their share of the proceeds?

It is unlikely that the WCC will be put off by such spurious opposition. The requests made by the ANC to the WCC were modest enough. We asked for and obtained commitments of support for social welfare, health, educational and legal aid programmes. The requests were not for military aid. Even then the requests must be seen in the context of the present situation. Violence in South Africa is not of the choosing of the African National Congress and other liberation movements, it has been brought about by a system that denies human beings political and economic rights solely on the grounds of their colour and keeps them in subjection by sheer force. The world has come to recognise this and has expressed its recognition of the justness of our cause in many ways.

In the present case, the WCC grants to the liberation movements are only a small part of its programme to combat racism throughout the world and White racism in Southern Africa in particular. It is to be hoped that nothing will deter the WCC from its planned activities.

The Church must play its part in a major offensive for the isolation of South Africa. It must influence its membership to take part in a world wide campaign to press Governments and individual firms to stop all arms sales to South Africa, to withdraw investments there, to break off diplomatic relations, and sever all trade, sport and other relations.

The Church can undoubtedly play a major part in bringing an end to all international collaboration with racist South Africa. By turning to this task with energy it will not only contribute to the success of the UN-sponsored 1971 International Year Against Racism, but it will also contribute magnificently to the downfall of a regime which daily violates the principles of justice and human dignity.

Church Pretence

Mangaliso Mkha Tsha et al.

> *Document written by five African priests of the*
> *Roman Catholic Church in South Africa, the Rev. Fr. P.*
> *Mangaliso Mkha Tshwa, the Rev. Fr. D. Moetatele, the Rev.*
> *Fr. J.L. Louwfant, the Rev. Fr. C. Mokoka and the Rev.*
> *Fr. A. Mabona. It was published first in the* Rand Daily
> Mail *(Johannesburg) and republished in* Sechaba *(ANC),*
> *IV, 4, April 1970.*

Ingane engakhali ifela embelekweni – a Zulu proverb meaning that when someone fails to voice his grievances in time, he has only himself to blame if this results in tragedy.

There was a time when most people believed that Africans had infinite patience. Their mental inertia and natural laziness were partly responsible for this. Be that as it may, we want to state that the African is capable of an agonising *'Enough! enough!'* In spite of our ordination to the priesthood, we have been treated like glorified altar-boys.

We kept quiet even when it was our duty to speak up. We were afraid that our White colleagues would misunderstand our stand. Consequently the bad situation became worse.

After a long prayerful self-examination we resolved to ventilate our grievances and take the public into our confidence. For one thing, Church politics are hidden from the rank and file; for another, our fellow-men have the right to know the truth about their priests. We are primarily concerned with the well-being of our Church. How long must we plead for its Africanisation in Southern Africa?

The Catholics pretend to condemn apartheid. And yet in practice they cherish it. The Church practised segregation in her seminaries, convents, hospitals, schools, monasteries, associations and churcles long before the present Government legislated against social integration. The bishops, priests and religious bodies are divided on the question of apartheid.

The statement of one late Metropolitan is still fresh in our minds. Bishop G. Van Velsen made a public defence of apartheid when he was interviewed by the *Sunday Tribune* in March last year.

We know from reliable sources that a number of bishops and priests are sympathetic towards the police. Quite rightly, of course, they condemn some aspects of its implementation, particularly those which bring suffering and injustices.

If we understand the philosophers of separate development correctly, they argue that 'as long as the Blacks are in our midst, their position will always be precarious and uncertain. Racial frictions will be inevitable. The Whites do not want to mix socially with Black people. They believe in preserving their identity as a White nation. So why encourage, let alone, foist integration on them? It won't work.' Let's be honest. The Whites would never accept a Black or multiracial government. Whites in South Africa are not prepared to serve under Africans in any capacity. Socially, culturally and intellectually the Whites consider themselves quite different from the Blacks. The obvious conclusion is that most Whites have opted out of the concept of integration.

Among other things they feel that one can't break down traditions which are more than three centuries old, by the stroke of the pen.

As Christians we believe in a multiracial society. We feel this is the only way in which real Christianity can be practised. Unfortunately we haven't a free choice. Segregation, apartheid, is imposed on us and living in a make-believe world won't help. So, if we have to have apartheid we might as well insist on our own rights under it.

To suggest that our people should accept the situation and make the best of it. History is unpredictable. Perhaps one day things will change dramatically. The African wants to rediscover his personality and identity. He wishes to develop all his faculties — mental, physical, aesthetic. We wonder whether he can achieve this in the midst of White people. Competition will always be in their favour.

Don't get us wrong. We are not preaching racialism, because we despise and loathe racists. What we are preaching is *realism* and common sense.

Having set the scene, we want to enumerate a few grievances:

We deplore as well as condemn the *baasskap* and *miessieskap* of the White clergy and religion over their African counterparts. You will destroy our morale, personality and professional efficiency by the raw deal you constantly give us.

We deplore your perpetuation of the false image of the African priest as a 'glorified altar-boy' who happens to share in the White priesthood. With tears in our eyes, we deplore the marooning and exiling of some African priests without any redress. Even in a court of law, the accused is entitled to a fair, unbiased defence.

We humbly invite our Bishops to know their African parishes better. A fleeting snap purple appearance on confirmation days leaves much to be desired.

We respectfully request the hierarchy to open up new avenues for our priests, such as specialised apostolate, serving on the so-called national commissions, playing a meaningful role in the administration of dioceses and so on.

We ask the Hierarchy to expedite Africanisation. For instance why can't Soweto have its own Black Bishop? Why should our townships be dominated by the White clergy and African priests be dumped in the bush, in non-viable parishes?

No Cognizance of Human Rights

Open letter to Prime Minister Vorster of South Africa
from the Church Boards of the Evangelical Lutheran
Ovambokavango Church and the Evangelical Lutheran
Church in S.W. Africa (Rhenish Mission Church), signed
by the Chairmen of both Boards, respectively Bishop
Dr. Leonard Auala and Moderator Pastor Paulus Gowaseb,
in Windhoek (Namibia) on 30 June 1971.

His Honour,

After the decision of the World Court at the Hague was made known on 21st June, 1971 several leaders and officials of our Lutheran Churches were individually approached by representatives of the authorities with a view to making known their views. This indicates to us that public institutions are interested in hearing the opinions of the Churches in this connection. Therefore we would like to make use of the opportunity of informing your Honour of the opinion of the Church Boards of the Evangelical Lutheran Church in SWA and the Evangelical Lutheran Ovambokavango Church which represents the majority of the indigenous population of South West Africa.

We believe that South Africa in its attempts to develop South West Africa has failed to take cognizance of Human Rights as declared by UNO in the year 1948 with respect to the non-white population. Allow us to put forward the following examples in this connection:

(1) The government maintains that by the race policy it implements in our country, it promotes and preserves the life and freedom of the population. But in fact the non-white population is continuously being slighted and intimidated in their daily lives. Our people are not free and by the way they are treated they do not feel safe.

In this regard we wish to refer to Section 3 of Human Rights.

(2) We cannot do otherwise than regard South West Africa, with all its racial groups, as a unit. By the Group Areas Legislation the people are denied the right of free movement and accommodation within the borders of the country. This cannot be reconciled with Section 13 of the Human Rights.

(3) People are not free to express or publish their thoughts or opinions openly. Many experience humiliating espionage and intimidation which has as its goal that a public and accepted opinion must be expressed, but not one held at heart and of which they are convinced. How can Sections 18 and 19 of the Human Rights be realized under such circumstances?

(4) The implementation of the policy of the government makes it impossible for the political parties of the indigenous people to work together in a really responsible and democratic manner to build the future of the whole of South West Africa. We believe that it is important in this connection that the use of voting rights should also be allowed to the non-white population (Sections 20 and 21 of the Human Rights).

(5) Through the application of Job Reservation the right to a free choice of profession is hindered and this causes low remuneration and unemployment. There can be no doubt that the contract system breaks up a healthy family life because the prohibition of a person from living where he works, hinders the cohabitation of families. This conflicts with Sections 23 and 25 of the Human Rights.

The Church Boards' urgent wish is that in terms of the declarations of the World Court and in cooperation with UNO of which South Africa is a member, your government will seek a peaceful solution to the problems of our land and will see to it that Human Rights be put into operation and that South West Africa may become a self sufficient and independent State.

> With high Esteem,
> Bishop Dr. L. Auala
>   Chairman of the Church Board of
>   the Ev. Luth. Ovambokavango Church
> Moderator Pastor P. Gowaseb
>   Chairman of the Church Board of
>   the Ev. Luth. Church in S.W.A.
>   (Rhenish Mission Church)

Windhoek, 30th June 1971.

The False Impression of Peace
L. Auala and P. Gowaseb

*Letter from the Church Boards of the Evangelical
Ovambokavango Church and the Evangelical Lutheran
Church in S.W. Africa (Rhenish Mission Church) to the
Congregations and members of both Churches, signed
by the Chairmen of both Boards, respectively Dr.
Leonard Auala and Paulus Gowaseb, in Windhoek
(Namibia) on 30 June 1971.*

Dear Brothers and Sisters in Jesus Christ,

We greet you with the words of Jesus: 'Peace be with you' (John 20:19). On the 30th June, 1971 we gathered together as the Church Boards of our two Lutheran Churches because we felt that we must direct words of leadership and guidance to our congregations in this hour of need.

We are concerned about the future of this country and about the future of the various peoples who live here. We not only feel this concern today but because of the judgement of the World Court given on the 21st June, 1971, we can no longer remain silent. We feel that if we, as the Church, remain silent any longer, we will become liable for the life and future of our country and its people.

The judgement of the World Court was the answer to the prayers of many of our people, because this judgement involves the hope of freedom and recognition of personal worth. We believe that our people would not have betaken themselves to other bodies and also not to the UNO if the Government of South Africa had not withheld from them the basic rights of man.

The mandate which was given to South Africa included the obligation to create conditions of peace and freedom and to guarantee such conditions for all the inhabitants of South West Africa.

True peace does not allow people to hate each other. But we observe that our people are caught up with fear and that the hate between people is increasing, especially between white and non-white. In our opinion this fatal development is caused and upheld by the policy of apartheid. We believe that a false impression arises when it is stated that peace reigns in our country. The peace is maintained by forceful measures.

To the freedom of the people belongs also the freedom of the spread of the gospel. We are concerned that Christians of various population groups are hindered by numerous laws and regulations from freely gathering together for the word of God.

As a result of the application of the Group Areas Laws the activities of the Church are severely restricted and the unity of the various races of the Church curtailed. Individual Ministers of the Gospel and Christians are filled with fear and distrusted. They are also sometimes hindered in their evangelizing by the refusal of permits.

The true development of the inhabitants of South West Africa on a

Christian basis ought to lead to unity and fraternity between the races. We are convinced that this must be the lasting goal for further and future development. The Government, by the application of the Homelands Policy, constitutes to the creation and continuation forever of the divisions between the races. It is stated that this policy is intended to lead the races to self-government and independence. But our small race groups cannot really be aided by separation. They will be isolated and denied the chance to take a proper part in the development of the country.

We want to also inform the members of our congregations that we are determined to inform the Government of this state of affairs and of our convictions of what changes must occur. We appeal to you to maintain the peace and with a peaceful disposition to continue seeking our brothers in all racial groups. We want to advise you also to build bridges and not to break down contact.

Dear Congregations, we as your Church Boards do not intend sowing seeds of animosity, discord and strife. Our purpose is to stand for the truth and for a better future for our people and races, even when it involves suffering for us.

May the Lord be with you in His Mercy and give you guidance through His Spirit. Let us continue praying for all authorities (I Tim. 2:1-2), so that they may be prepared to alter the grievous circumstances and to take cognizance of the true interests of this country and its people.

> On behalf of the two Church Boards
> signed: Dr. Leonard Auala
> Chairman of the Church Board of the
> Ev. Luth. Ovambokavango Church
> signed: Paulus Gowaseb
> Chairman of the Church Board of the
> Ev. Luth. Church in S.W.A.
> (Rhenish Mission Church)

Windhoek, 30th June 1971.